The

WESTCLIFF-ON-SEA
MOTOR SERVICES LIMITED A

An Outline History

by

Alan Osborne

J.R. Young

Farley Publications

A.G. Osborne © 2011

Published by Farley Publications

7 Farley Drive, Seven Kings, ILFORD, Essex IG3 8LT

ISBN 978-0-9568158-0-4

Further copies of this book may be obtained at the price of £25.00 (plus £2.50 towards postage) whilst stocks last from the publisher, address above. Cheques should be made payable to 'Farley Publications'.

Alternatively contact   Dr. A. G. Osborne by e-mail; dimequin@bushinternet.com

Dr. Alan Osborne

An academic career in chemistry has been combined with a lifelong interest in buses focussed especially on south Essex and London but with forays to the wilder parts of the British Isles especially the Scottish Islands and even more remote northern locations. Publications on City Coach, Coastal Red, Eastern National Regents, buses in Greenland etc reflect this. He founded the Eastern National Enthusiasts Group and for many years was central to its success as Founder, Chairman, and later Secretary until it metamorphosed, in line with bus industry changes, into the Essex Bus Enthusiasts Group. The senior author, he has carried out extensive research on Westcliff during which time it became clear that this could usefully provide the basis for a book to fill the gap on coverage of this company. The result is before you.

Dr. Jim Young

An academic career in geography has been combined with a lifelong interest in buses though in this case through seasonal involvement with the industry. This started appropriately enough with conducting Eastern National buses at Brentwood and Southend in the sixties. This evolved into driving for ENOC, a variety of south Essex operators and then for Guernseybus seasonally every year until its demise. The former experience provides some input into the present volume but most of his bus-related enthusiast activities and publications have focussed on the Channel Islands. He founded the Channel Island Bus Society in 1985 and continues to run it. His work for this book has been the inital layout, computer design and editing, with additional text contributions, but not the final format and design.

> This book is dedicated to the memory of both authors' parents

Front cover illustration: *The most well known survivor of Westcliff-on-Sea Motor Services is the beautifully restored ECW bodied Bristol K5G of 1939 vintage, seen here arriving at the 1993 Southend Bus Rally.   AGO*

Fig.0.1 Title page: *Westcliff-on-Sea started as an operator of motor char-a-bancs. In this 1920s summer scene HJ3717, a normal control 'all weather' Daimler CK complete with white-wall tyres, waits outside the Pier Hotel, Southend.   EBEG*

Fig.0.2 Page 3 (opposite): *This view of Victoria Circus in the early thirties shows WMS in its short lived Daimler double-decker phase. HJ8677 is a Daimler CF6 with a Dodson lowbridge body of rather dated appearance that had been new in March 1929.   Behind it stands a most unusual bus, HJ7670 an ADC 802, better known as a 'London Six', one of only twenty ever built. Another photo of this bus can be found at Fig.6.11. Trolleybus overhead wiring and some period fashions add to the character of this scene.   PJSA*

Contents

Frontispiece   Fig.0.3 *AEC Regent HX2980 was new in 1931 with a Short 52-seat body. After being demonstrated to Burnley Corporation it was bought by WMS in April 1932 as this pre-delivery view shows. The company was clearly impressed since they then standardised on the Regent petrol-engined chassis. Park Royal, and later Weymann were chosen to body these chassis, complete with roof number boxes which became a WMS characteristic. For the later history of this bus see Chapter Eleven.   JCC*

Preface and Acknowledgements

It is over half a century since Westcliff buses last ran in service and nearly a century since they first started. I am old enough to have a few personal memories of their operations though these are somewhat limited and seen through the filter of early childhood. I well recall their red and cream buses mixed with the rather striking blue and cream of Southend Corporation and the refined green and cream of Eastern National. Our family usually arrived at Southend for a day trip on a distinctive brown and cream City Coach which seemed to have too many wheels, or so a small boy thought.

At the time I did not know the complexities that would lead three of these four liveries to become one, nor that the final colour would also become intertwined in a scheme that over fifty years later would cause me considerable head-scratching to sort out in order to write Chapter Four of this volume!

I also remember, a year or two later when our City Leyland made its steady way up Victoria Avenue into central Southend, that there was something different about the mix of buses in Southend. I had already noticed that the sky was clearer, not due to more sun but less wires, and there were no trolley-buses about. My next observation was that there were less, indeed hardly any, red and cream buses around, which was a mild disappointment. Once we had alighted at Tylers Avenue this was soon overcome by making two left turns into the High Street and a bee-line for the nearest Rossi's Ice-Cream Parlour. Then we headed for the delights of Peter Pan's Playground and Never-Never Land and the exciting thrills on offer to the 'wrong' side of the pier at the Kursaal before making for our favourite beach location at Uncle Tom's Cabin in Shoebury. You will have gathered from this that I was still at an age where my ideas of research did not envisage a career pushing back the frontiers of chemistry only to retire and do the same for Westcliff Motor Services. But maybe this was where the seed of this book was sown.

During a lifetime of interest in buses that was for many years focussed on the Eastern National Enthusiasts Group, later the Essex Bus Enthusiasts Group, I have attempted to fill various gaps in the information available about local bus companies. This has taken the form of *Fact Files* published by EBEG where piecemeal information published in ENEG newsletters was drawn together and enhanced with appropriate photographs to form twenty-eight page booklets, for example *Fact File 1: City Coach Company*. It was always my intention to include Westcliff-on-Sea Motor Services in this series. The task became more difficult as my researches progressed and the phrase 'quart into a pint pot' comes to mind. With the publication by EBEG of '*Blackwells of Earls Colne*' and the successful sales that resulted, a new opportunity presented itself – to produce a full-sized book that could do justice to

the fascinating story of Westcliff. This after all is the only Tilling company that has so far not warranted a full-sized book.

However, I am mindful that for many years three local authors have had 'work in progress' on WMS, a complete vehicle history and a comprehensive account of route developments. The present volume is not intended to duplicate their efforts: the reader will need to await these publications for this level of detail. There are of course several publications extant which deal with aspects of the Westcliff story, or of those companies or operations that were closely related to it. The present author together with Peter Snell has contributed to the '*In Focus*' volumes on WMS but these are of course photo albums with text limited to captions.

There are two key publications which should form part of any south-east Essex bus historian's library. '*The Years Between 1909-1969*' (Crawley et al.) provides an invaluable account of the growth and operations of the Eastern National Omnibus Company. It includes the definitive summary of the many small operators that existed within the area that ENOC grew to dominate. Many were competitors, to a greater or lesser extent, to WMS as it grew. Reference has been made to this source to supplement the present author's researches. The final reference deals with what was at various stages the major irritant to, then a significant factor in WMS growth, and then again a competitor before finally being absorbed into WMS. One entrepreneurial family's name crops up throughout the present volume. Their central position to the emergence and shape of PSV operations (and even to suburban growth) in south-east Essex cannot be underestimated and is described in the present work where it forms a part of the WMS story. Fortunately their activities have been meticulously researched and fully detailed in '*The Bridge Family and its Buses*'. The reader is referred to this for an entertaining and more complete discussion than is appropriate in our book.

The authors' aim in the present volume is to provide a depiction of WMS as it appeared just before its post-war peak in 1951. Having said that, to explain how the company arrived at its dominant position in south-east Essex an outline history of the development of the company, its operations and vehicles necessarily forms the bulk of the book. We have also taken the opportunity offered by the size and format of an A4 sized book on full art paper to include wide ranging photo coverage of WMS vehicles, operations and publications to allow the reader to become fully immersed in the company's aura. The result is now before you. We hope you agree with us that it has been worth all the labour expended. But before you sit back to enjoy our efforts we feel that some comment on the photos, always a central part of any transport book, may help you appreciate the selection made and the difficulties in making it.

Photographs

There were relatively few people who took photos of Westcliff and the associated company's buses, or photos which included WMS buses as part of a larger scene. Virtually all photographers would have been restricted by technology and cost to black and white images. Camera technology meant that good light and/or still subjects produced the clearest photos. All this is by way of saying that our choice of photos to illustrate this volume is largely limited to the same collections that have been available to other authors in the field of transport history who have written on WMS.

With these points in mind careful thought has been given to what to include and how to include it. We have attempted to illustrate the key points of each topic covered. Sometimes this has been better achieved by reproducing ephemera, timetables, publicity and contemporary publications. The majority of illustrations are however photos and many of the key, or best views have already appeared in Westcliff-related publications. However, our book is aimed at a wider audience and benefits from higher quality reproduction, both of which justify the inclusion of some of these photos. With photos of key importance to the story but of poor quality we have tried to reproduce them at the column-width size where their imperfections are less obvious but the story is enhanced by their presence. For all other photos the rule has generally been that their size has been determined by their quality and the interest of the scene.

In this volume in order to convey the atmosphere of the WMS operations throughout its operating area a conscious decision has been made to include a high proportion of the available illustrations in *Chapter Five (Bus & Coach Services at June 1951)*. This has of necessity meant a reduced photographic coverage in other chapters. So in order for you to find a view of your favourite vehicle we have included cross references throughout to figure numbers for this purpose *(see page 224)*.

This is an appropriate point at which to thank all the photographers whose labours have enhanced the volume, as well as the collectors who have made photos available for our use. Each photo is acknowledged where the source is known. As many photos come from a limited number of sources initials are used in the text and these are identified here. The major source is the late Peter Snell's collection, donated to the EBEG and known as the 'Peter Snell Archive' in recognition. This includes many individual photographers' works which are also indicated where known. We apologise to those photographers whose work is shown but not identified and thank all photographers for their work. All photos not acknowledged are from the author's collection.

ABC	A.B.Cross
ADP	A.D.Packer
AGO	Alan Osborne
AGOC	Alan Osborne collection
AMW	A.M.Wright
BAC	Brian Ashley collection
CC	C.Carter
DAJ	D.A.Jones
DSG	D.S.Giles
EBEG	Essex Bus Enthusiasts Group
ECW/SJB	S.J.Butler ECW collection
ENEG	Eastern National Enthusiasts Group
ERO	Reproduced by courtesy of Essex Record Office
FC	Frank Church
FWI	F.W.Ivey
HC	H.Cowell
JB	John Boylett
JCC	John Carman collection
JFH	J.F.Higham
JFP	J.F.Parke
JRY	J.R.Young
JRYC	J.R.Young collection
JS	John Shearman
LTPS	London Trolleybus Preservation Society
LWR	L.W.Rowe
MLWC	Martin Weyell collection
OS	Omnibus Society
PJSA	Peter Snell Archive
RFM	R.F.Mack
RM	Roy Marshall
SLP	S.L.Poole
STP	Surfleet Transport Photographs
VCJ	Vic Jones
WJH	W.J.Haynes
WRL	W.R.Legg

We have gone to some lengths to ensure that the photo selection, and quality and size of reproduction in combination with the text and research on which it is based will make this book a valuable and lasting record of WMS operations for some years to come and one that will enhance your library. Now it is time to sit back and enjoy our labours!

Abbreviations Used

The registered name of the operator has been '(The) Westcliff-on-Sea Motor Char-a-banc Company Ltd.,' and later '(The) Westcliff-on-Sea Motor Services Ltd.' The word 'the' appears in many instances mostly of a legal nature, but not in others. Moreover the fleet-name or fleet designation employed at different periods has been both 'Westcliff' and 'Westcliff-on-Sea'. Locally the company was always known simply as 'Westcliff'.

There is thus the potential for certain styles of name to be implied when they may be inappropriate. For the sake of brevity and to avoid any misunderstandings 'WMS' is used throughout the text to refer to the company whatever its legal title at the time. However, on the rare occasions when an especial attachment is implied then the appropriate designation as shown above has been used in full rather than 'WMS'. Other companies are also abbreviated to initials after the initial reference.

Acknowledgements

Our thanks go to the many people who have given generously of their time and knowledge, lent photos and clarified points without all of which this would have been a lesser book. In particular we would like to thank Brian Ashley, John Carman, Peter Clark, Richard Delahoy, the late Derek Giles, David Harman, Bob Palmer, Chris Stewart, John Taylor, Martin Weyell and Owen Woodliffe. Our thanks also go to the staff of the Essex Record Office at Chelmsford and of the Redbridge and Southend-on-Sea Libraries for their assistance and especially to David Pracey of the Vestry House Museum, Walthamstow.

For meticulously proof reading the final text we are indebted to Bob Palmer. Thanks also to Jim Whiting of Capital Transport who has given his valuable expertise to ensure the final book has been acceptable to the printers, and thus to you, good reader.

Finally for the preliminary design and layout of the book together with his editor's eagle eye I am indebted to Jim Young. Initially this was to be his only remit, but Jim's enthusiasm for the project has led to major restructuring of the book and considerable expansion to give its present form. Without his valuable expertise and editorial badgering this volume might well not have come to fruition in the present form. In recognition of his substantial contribution his name appears with mine on the cover as joint author.

Fig.0.4 (upper) WMS chose both Daimlers and, as seen here, Dennis single-deckers in its early years. JN955 is a Dennis EV dating from 1931 which was later used by the City Coach Company. *PJSA*

Fig.0.5 (lower) The pre-war ECW bodied Bristol K5Gs were long lasting and we are fortunate to have this colour view of JN9542 of 1937 at the end of its days as ENOC 1254 in service at Clacton. *EBEG*

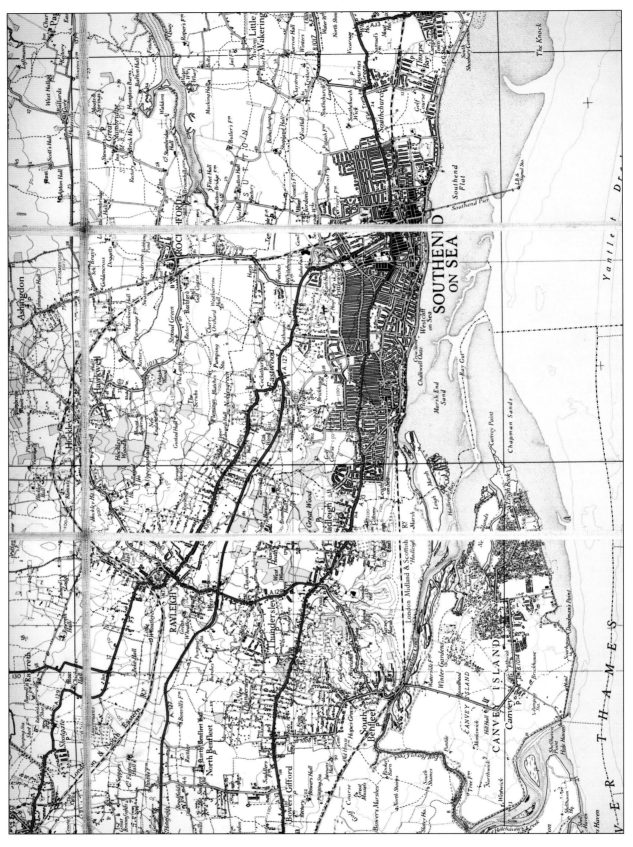

Fig.1.1 *The Ordnance Survey Fifth Edition 1:63,360 sheet 108 (Chelmsford & Southend) dated 1936 shows most of the WMS operating area at a time when considerable expansion of housing and bus services was taking place. It is reproduced such that one inch represents approximately one and one third miles. Useful comparison may be made with the WMS timetable maps of services reproduced in Chapter Two.*

Chapter One
Part 1: Introduction

Westcliff-on-Sea Motor Services Ltd., (hereafter abbreviated to WMS) was the major provider of bus services in the greater Southend-on-Sea area until 1955. It started as a motor char-a-banc company operating a range of excursions and extended tours in the 1920s. This side of the operation became highly successful and respected. Indeed the name 'Westcliff' survived the company and was used by Eastern National (ENOC) to market coach tours based in Southend until as late as 1961.

Southend Corporation Transport (SCT) provided electric transport within the borough in the form of trams and later trolleybuses, but initially did not venture into the field of motor buses. WMS and Borough Services both pioneered local services within Southend and longer distance routes in the neighbourhood (e.g. to Paglesham) and even inter-urban services to Grays, Rayleigh etc. During the early years after the First World War many other entrepreneurs tried their hand at 'running a bus'. Some failed, some succeeded and grew and most were taken over by the larger concerns Borough and WMS.

Initially the licensing of omnibuses was in the hands of the Southend Watch Committee which operated under the Town Police Clauses Act. Southend-on-Sea Borough Council was naturally anxious to protect its own (electric) operations and the Watch Committee also tended to favour well established operators like WMS with whom rapport had been established, perhaps on the golf-course or at the local Lodge.

The Road Traffic Act (RTA) of 1930 set up Regional Traffic Commissioners with powers to licence bus services. All applications were published in *Notices & Proceedings* and traffic courts sat to hear applications, representations and objections and then to make decisions and grant, or withhold, licences. Companies that had previous to the Act operated such services were termed 'established operators'. In Southend-on-Sea these were WMS, Borough, ENOC and some smaller concerns such as Shoeburyness Motor Services also fell into this category. Much to the Corporation's surprise they did not fall into this grouping as they had not run motor-bus services for many years and thus had no claim to any operating territory. This was a stroke of great good fortune for WMS and it brought about an extensive series of discussions with the object of co-ordinating all bus, tram and trolley services in the area, a process that was to stretch over nearly two decades before a satisfactory resolution was achieved. *Chapter Four* deals with this complex but vitally important aspect in the history of WMS.

The Geographical and Historical Context

In order to fully appreciate the development of WMS and why it progressed in the way it did it is necessary to have an understanding both of the nature of the area in which the company evolved as well as the economic and social, as well as legislative environment of the times. Reference has already been made to licensing arrangements and their change consequent on the RTA of 1930 so no more will be said here of that aspect.

Fig.1.2 *The seafront, pier, and associated attractions were the very essence of Southend-on-Sea. This EHM bus was owned by the Bridge family who were to play a significant part in the WMS story.* JRYC

WMS is of course named after the western side of the south end of Prittlewell. Southend is exactly that, a seaside development of the southern end of the established village and parish of Prittlewell, where much later WMS were to build their impressive new garage and workshops. The earliest significant development took place in the 1790s when a plan to develop the area as a watering place resulted in the construction of the Royal Terrace and Hotel, though little else. In 1803, a brief visit by Princess Caroline gave the always fashionable cache of regal approval (a fashion WMS were later to follow for a different type of Regal!). Unfortunately the suffix 'Regis' was not gained by the incipient resort. She stayed in the Royal Terrace which later was to gain greater fame in the world of the transport historian by becoming the point from which the first tours, excursions and bus services of WMS would start.

At this time South End was part of a total (Prittlewell) parish population of about 2000. It began its growth as a resort but was hampered by a lack of suitable accommodation and, along with everywhere else in the country, good transport links. There were two turnpike roads to London, one via Rayleigh and the other via Hadleigh which were much improved at the end of the eighteenth century allowing a coach service (of the horse-drawn Mail variety) to be started. In this, if we use a little imagination we may see the origins of both the City Coach and WMS services to London. However, this slow, expensive and uncomfortable link was rendered almost obsolete when in 1846 a 1¼ mile long pier was constructed. This was not built primarily as a pleasure pier but as a means of access to paddle-steamers, the new revolutionary (literally) means of transport, its long length being necessary to give a deep enough berth at low tide. This link to London increased Southend's accessibility considerably but it was to be a short lived advantage. Already steam technology was being applied to land transport with dramatic effect. When the Great Eastern Railway reached Brentwood it reduced the need to travel by stage coach all the way to London. But as with virtually every other seaside resort's development, it was the arrival of the railway in the borough, in this case the London, Tilbury & Southend Railway, which in 1854 kick-started the first period of major growth for Southend (as it had been very unimaginatively christened). The 'on-Sea' was added to enhance the resort as it now was. This was a considerable misnomer since Southend was actually on the Thames Estuary with plenty of London-derived mud but no local sand.

The original LT&SR ran via Tilbury, their later direct line via Laindon (1888) and subsequently the competing Great Eastern branch extension from Shenfield (1889) gave the critical boost to Southend to ensure its growth into a sizeable town. The railways also provided some local transport links by way of their stations close to Southend and the LT&SR in particular encouraged early growth along its west-east route with Leigh, Westcliff, Southend, and later in its extension to Shoeburyness (1884) soon attracting estate developers.

The railway link to London was crucial in Southend's growth both as a day-tripper destination, and a holiday resort. The LT&SR in particular promoted cheap season tickets together with a fast and efficient service. There soon started a process that continues to this day for all such resorts, that of day visitors gaining a liking for the place and later choosing to settle permanently either in retirement, re-location to a new local job or for those in the middle-classes with professional jobs as commuters back to their jobs in the City. These pressures gave rise

to a rash of speculative housing development, a veritable boom period in the 1870s and 1880s led by developers who had 'cut their teeth' on similar late Victorian and early Edwardian ventures in outer east London/Essex borders. In particular Sidney Ramuz became the 'king' of Southend developers offering affordable houses on easy terms, in the days before mortgages. All this gave rise to a population 'explosion'. The new residents of course needed to get around their new home town, now spreading outwards from the core through Westcliff towards Leigh and along the Southchurch Road, and through Prittlewell. The establishment of Southend as a self-governing Municipal Borough by Charter in 1892 acknowledged its rising population and importance, from about 5000 in the 1871 Census to 12,500 in 1891 and gave the opportunity for the new council

Fig.1.3 *'The Technical Institute, Southend', a commercial postcard nicely captures the atmosphere of the Edwardian period. Bicycles, long dresses and hats for the ladies, a horse-drawn carriage and of course the electric trams, which were the Corporation's pride and joy, grace the scene.* *JRYC*

to introduce tram services. The first electric trams were perhaps not surprisingly those installed on the pier (1890) but soon the public were to experience the benefits of electric traction through the streets.

In 1901 lines were opened to Leigh (via London Road), Southchurch (via Southchurch Road) with a branch to the sea, and to Prittlewell (circular). By 1913 extensions had been made in the east to Thorpe Hall and Bournes Green associated with road ('Boulevard') building but the more populous western side of the town did not benefit, fortuitously for the yet unborn WMS. In 1914 Southend was granted County Borough status having absorbed Leigh U.D.C. and its 10,000 residents in 1913. By 1914 the new C.B. contained no less than 80,000 people. The building boom had paid off but was temporarily halted by the outbreak of war as were further tram developments.

Trams of course rely on a relatively high demand and density of population to be viable. Before the war SCT had experimented with motor-buses to fill some spatial gaps but these were unsuccessful. This left the 'private sector' to literally fill the gaps. WMS was, as noted below, one of these and in retrospect the one we see as becoming most successful. Alongside another key bus operator Borough Services they pioneered a network of services to link most parts of the borough to the central shopping core which had developed between the two railway stations and the pier, reflecting the greatest pedestrian flows. However, WMS (and others) saw opportunities outside the municipal area and started services to market towns such as Rayleigh and Rochford (though already served by GER trains) and to smaller and previously isolated villages such as Paglesham.

At this point is it appropriate to look at a map of south-east Essex and remind ourselves just how 'out-on-a-limb' Southend is. It really is 'on the road (two to be precise the A127 and A13) to nowhere'. Shoeburyness had been established as a school of gunnery even before the LTS arrived, though it was the key factor in encouraging that railway to head east beyond Southend. It grew and Foulness Island was established as a military site so employment was created and a consequent need for bus links. However, in general this area of remote marshland between the River Crouch and the Thames Estuary remained largely undeveloped and offered few opportunities for bus operators.

WMS was, of course named after Westcliff, the more prestigious development that had grown up around the LT&SR station just a mile to the west of Southend High Street. The company's operations were to benefit from both the rapid growth of Southend and the fact that the greatest growth was in this direction. At the time of WMS foundation and initial growth, Southend was still a 'boom town' with developers offering both building plots as well as finished houses to east Londoners keen to leave the unhealthy conditions of the East End for a better life – and then commute back on the train.

In addition there were sales of plots of land in the countryside between Upminster and Southend, jointly sponsored by the LT&SR and land developers often involving marquees with free alcoholic drink to encourage the purchase process. From Laindon through Wickford, Benfleet and all over Canvey Island what became known as 'plotland' developed, though perhaps that is an inappropriate term as more often than not they did not develop. Initially these plots were often just weekend retreats on which a tent was all that was needed for a break from London and a bit of fresh air. In 1936 my parents purchased a plot in Wickford upon which our extended family erected a wooden bungalow complete with verandah. So began the Osborne family

connection with the City Coach Company travelling to and from our weekend retreat. In many cases these self-built bungalows became what had, perhaps, been intended, permanent homes, nowhere more so than in Canvey. This digression away from the all important topic of buses explains why there were far more opportunities for established and potential bus operators in what appeared on the 1900 Ordnance Survey map as just a fairly sparsely settled and unpromising rural area than might otherwise have been expected. Reference to the 1935 O.S. Fifth Edition map *(see Fig.1.1)* is most valuable for the WMS story as this map was surveyed in the early 1930s.

Fig.1.4 *The Leigh House Estate was typical of the many speculative developments around Southend in the 1920s and 1930s. In their early days they needed only small buses. It was exactly this need that got H. R. Bridge started in the bus business with major implications for WMS. Here are two of his Edwards Hall Motors buses at Leigh Broadway West. JRYC*

Before the 1914-18 war the Southend urban area was quite compact reflecting walking, cycling and using the trams as the ways of getting around. The return of peace saw urban expansion re-commence, made possible by WMS and the myriad of small unregulated bus operators which fed back to stimulate the development of more services into the thirties halted only by the outbreak of war in 1939. The thirties in southern England was a period of growth, rather than depression, with much suburban housing development associated with the rapid growth of light 'footloose' industry. For Southend the best known example was the E. K. Cole works best known for making 'Ekco' Bakelite radios, the quintessential thirties boom industry. There were however, still plenty of 'gaps on the map' compared with the present almost solid sprawl of Southend from Benfleet to Shoebury and it was these fields that were to provide the biggest stimulus to bus service provision as these too were built over.

This steady growth in population could have resulted in a continuous suburban sprawl from London to

Shoeburyness. However, the 1938 Green Belt Act for London and later the Town and Country Planning Act introduced by the 1945 Labour government prevented this by introducing strict development planning controls. The complementary legislation needed to allow for London's growth but to specifically focus it on key locations was the New Towns Act. This was another key factor in the south-east Essex population growth that would be a later part of the WMS story.

Fig.1.5 *Another commercial postcard from just a few years later continues the view seaward from Fig.1.2 to show the cliffs, including the future site of Never-Never Land in the trees, the Esplanade and Peter Pan's Playground with no less than four WMS saloons working the sea-front service 6A.* JRYC

The original plan for a south Essex New Town was for it to be located near Chipping Ongar. Strong protests in that unspoilt area combined with a vigorous

campaign by the MP for Billericay to have the New Town located in his constituency caused the government to re-locate the New Town to Basildon. This at first sight strange action by Sir Bernard Braine was as a direct result of the unplanned, and more particularly un-serviced rural low-density sprawl of plotlands, described at the time as an area of rural slums. The New Town designation of Basildon provided central government resources to deal with these problems, and had the timing not been coincident with other legislation from the same government to nationalise public transport, might have given WMS considerable opportunities for bus service development (see *Chapter Four*).

As it was, the Transport Act effectively caused the demise of WMS. But the pre-war growth that forms the major part of the background to our story could not have occurred without the provision of local bus services in those days when very few people owned cars. The likes of the dynamically-named bus operator 'Old Tom' of Laindon and of course the Canvey small operators were typical of the early growth, but it was those companies with sufficient financial resources, friends in the right places and of course entrepreneurial expertise that stayed the course and grew. WMS was an example par-excellence for our area. As the story that follows shows the able WMS directors guided their company from one of humble jobmasters to the thriving concern that Tilling was keen to buy, and ultimately BTC equally keen to take over in the heady days for the bus world of the early 1950s.

Fig.1.6 *'Leigh Broadway West, Coronation decorations May 1937' is the caption to this view from the ERO collection. Our interest lies in the almost new WMS Bristol JO5G/ECW which appears to be JN6885, just a year old, working service B.* ERO

Part 2: Background
The Other Operators: Thomas Tilling, Eastern National, City Coach and Southend Corporation Transport

This book attempts to demonstrate how WMS grew, in the face of severe competition, to become the dominant bus operator in south-east Essex. They were eventually ousted by the machinations consequent on the Transport Act of 1948 which resulted in ENOC taking over their legacy. To fully understand the complex story the other players must also be considered since they shaped the business environment and thus the pattern of services and operations that WMS was able to carve out. These players ranged from small to very large indeed. In the discussion that follows the smaller players such as Shoeburyness MS, Rayleigh MS and the like are discussed as they impinged on WMS. This is also the case with the most important player, Mr. H. R. Bridge with his various companies. Readers wishing to know more can do no better than refer to *The Years Between*, and *The Bridge Family (see Bibliography)*.

There were then four major players each of which is a well known name and has already had substantial amounts written about them. It is not appropriate here to expect the reader to consult these references *(see Bibliography)* as a part of 'required reading' to fully understand the WMS story told in the present book. For this reason an outline history of each company is provided as far as it is relevant to WMS.

Thomas Tilling Ltd.

Thomas Tilling was born on 3 February 1825 at Gutter Edge Farm, Hendon. He began business as a dairyman in 1845. His jobmaster business started on 12 May 1847 when a grey mare and carriage were purchased from Glover of Walworth, bus activities were started later in the year in partnership with Glover. The first horse bus worked in Tilling's name was 'The Times' running between Peckham and Oxford Circus in 1850.

The enterprise then rapidly expanded. After Thomas died on 8 January 1893, the business was continued by his two sons Richard and Edward. It was incorporated as Thomas Tilling Ltd. on 12 May 1897. By the end of the century 220 horse buses and 5000 horses were owned. The first motor bus, a Milnes Daimler, entered service on 30 September 1904 on the Peckham – Oxford Circus route, the last horse bus finally being withdrawn on 4 August 1914.

In 1913 through an Agreement with the London General Omnibus Co. Ltd. the Tilling bus fleet in London was limited to 150 vehicles, hence further operations needed to be developed elsewhere. In 1915 licences were obtained from Hove Council and the following year the Brighton, Hove & Preston United Omnibus Co. was purchased which established this Sussex coastal conurbation as Tilling territory.

After Richard Tilling became Chairman of Thomas Tilling Ltd. he set about buying an interest in many bus operating companies. The interests of Tillings and the British Electric Traction Company (an early pioneer of electric tramways) became so closely intermingled that both Companies decided to redistribute their interests. In 1928, Mr. Sidney Garcke became Chairman of their newly formed joint undertaking, the Tilling and British Automobile Traction Company.

Financial Structure of Thomas Tilling Ltd. Group (1942)

Company	Total capital	Capital in direct or indirect Tilling ownership		Railway capital		Outside capital
		owner	amount	owner	amount	
NOTC	£1,250,000	T. Tilling	£1,176,720	n/a	nil	£73,280
ENOC	£900,000	NOTC	£450,000	LNER	£225,000	nil
				LMS	£225,000	
SNOC	£542,000	NOTC	£271,000	SR	£271,000	nil
WNOC	£2,000,000	NOTC	£1,000,000	GWR	£1,000,000	nil
WMS	£250,000	T. Tilling	£227,076	n/a	nil	£22,974

Following on from the four mainline railways acquisition of certain bus company shares in 1929, Thomas Tilling Ltd., through the good offices of its subsidiary Tilling Motor Services, purchased a controlling interest in the National Omnibus & Transport Co. Ltd. (NOTC) in February 1931. One year later the formidable John Frederick Heaton joined the Tilling board. The Tilling bus interests in London passed to the London Transport Passenger Board in July 1933.

Fig.1.7 *Over the years WMS bought a number of buses from former Tilling company Brighton, Hove & District. These included AEC Regents and Dennis Lances, illustrated elsewhere. The only Bristol ever acquired was GO5G AAP829 formerly BH&D 6329. Unfortunately, no view is available of it in WMS service. It is seen here in Brighton in as delivered form. PJSA*

Tillings obtained a majority shareholding in WMS at the end of 1934, but it should be remembered that since WMS was a private Company there was no railway interest involved *(see table above).*

An important break in the partnership occurred in 1942 when Tilling Motor Services and B. E. T. Omnibus Services were formed to take over the interests of the respective partners in the Tilling and British Automobile Traction Company. The final Tilling Group Headquarters was at Crewe House, Curzon Street, London W.1. The curtain finally came down with the passing of the Transport Act, 1947 which set up the British Transport Commission to oversee a nationalised transport industry. At the Tilling Board meeting on 2 September 1948 it was announced that Thomas Tilling Ltd. had decided to sell out voluntarily to the B.T.C. for nearly £25 million.

The coaching division was formed into a separate Company known as Tillings Transport (B.T.C.) Ltd, based at Kings Cross, which later passed to ENOC.

Eastern National Omnibus Company Ltd.

The National Steam Car Co. Ltd. was registered on 19 June 1909 to take over the existing business of Clarkson Ltd. builders of steam-propelled vehicles at its works in Chelmsford.

Operations commenced in the London area on 2 November 1909 with steam buses running between Shepherds Bush and Westminster. In July 1913 provincial services started when National acquired the omnibus services radiating from Chelmsford which the Great Eastern Railway had inaugurated as long ago as 8 September 1905. Services initially ran to Great Waltham, Danbury and Writtle, soon afterwards extensions to Braintree, Maldon, Colchester and Halstead were introduced.

An Agreement was reached in 1919 with the Underground Group who controlled the London General Omnibus Co. Ltd. (LGOC) under which National were to withdraw their services in central London. These duly ceased on 19 November 1919. In exchange National would then operate services on behalf of LGOC in the area to the north of London. This was termed the 'Watford & North London area' where services were numbered with an 'N' prefix. In addition LGOC gave up their garage at Bedford to National who

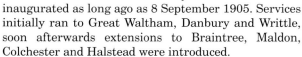

in turn gave up their garages at Nunhead and Putney Bridge to the General.

The name of the National Steam Car Company was changed to the National Omnibus and Transport Co. Ltd., and was formally registered on 13 February 1920. Expansion in the early 1920s was rapid, with Essex area bases being established in Colchester, Bishops Stortford and Grays. Services were also opened up in the west of England. The former LGOC operations in Bedford were also expanded with new services introduced in Stony Stratford, Hitchin and Luton.

The Railway (Road Transport) Act of 1928 became law on 3 August. This gave the railways wide powers to acquire and run road transport. Rather than compete with the bus operators the railways sought instead to seek partnerships. Since the National territory covered an area served by all the four major railways it was decided to convert the NOTC into a holding Company to control the new Companies who would cover the areas served by the railways, a 50:50 division of ownership being agreed. The extensive Great Western Railway bus services were soon transferred to the Western National Omnibus Co. Ltd. registered on

1 January 1929. The other new 'geographical' companies, viz the Southern, Eastern and Midland National Omnibus Cos. Ltd. were registered soon afterwards on 28 February. In addition Northern National was also registered as a non-trading Company to protect the name. Because of difficulty with the intermingling of the L.M.S. and L.N.E.R. railways in the Bedfordshire area, it was decided to combine the two eastern operations, the area becoming the Midland area of Eastern National, with the Head Office in New Writtle Street, Chelmsford. The agreement between the Eastern National Omnibus Co. Ltd. (ENOC) and the LNER and LMS railways was signed on 6 November 1929.

ENOC soon consolidated their position in the Clacton area by the purchase of the Silver Queen Motor Omnibus Co. Ltd. and the Enterprise Omnibus Co. Ltd. The Watford & North London area passed to the London General Country Services Ltd in 1932. Borough Services Ltd. of Southend was acquired in 1933 and was continued as a subsidiary company since it was a party to a joint operating agreement with WMS and Southend Corporation. Its services were eventually transferred to ENOC in 1940 when the company was placed in voluntary liquidation.

After the war control of ENOC passed to the British Transport Commission when the Tilling Group sold their bus operating interests to the Government. Control of Hicks Bros. of Braintree passed to ENOC on 1 January 1950 following their sale to the BTC. In 1952 a re-organisation of services took place in the Grays area to restore cross-town routes which had been severed in 1933 following the establishment of the London Passenger Transport area.

At this time the ENOC operating area covered most of Essex but did not enter the south eastern part of the county this being the province of WMS. The only ENOC services penetrating their area were 4 (Chelmsford – Pitsea), 11 (Chelmsford – Southend),

19/A (Clacton – Southend) and the former Borough Services 70 (Grays – Southend).

The British Transport Commission later set about consolidating bus operating territories. A significant re-organisation took place in 1952 when the Midland area of ENOC passed to the United Counties Omnibus Co. Ltd. of Northampton on 1 May, in compensation ENOC assumed control of WMS on 18 May.

Fig.1.8 ENOC continued a number of WMS services virtually unaltered. South Fambridge (The Anchor) was the erstwhile WMS service 11 terminus, re-numbered 13A in 1955 to avoid a clash with the established ENOC Chelmsford-Southend service. This now Saturday only operation was withdrawn on 13 December 1966. Bristol MW5G/ECW 1346 (206YVX) of 1961 is seen at South Fambridge in summer 1966. AGO

Following the subsequent acquisitions of Campbells of Pitsea in 1956 and Moores of Kelvedon in 1963 ENOC attained a virtual monopoly as the provider of bus services throughout the county of Essex.

City Coach Company Ltd.

The City Motor Omnibus Co. Ltd. was registered on 13 January 1923. London operations commenced on 10 March the fleet livery being brown and cream. Eventually City settled down to run route 536 between Highgate and Beckenham shared with Birch Bros. and United.

City purchased an interest in New Empress Saloons on 25 October 1928 and by December was running regular coaches between Kentish Town and Southend. In 1930 a joint timetable was introduced with the Wood Green to Southend service of WMS. Following the formation of the London Passenger Transport Board on 1 July 1933 City operations were compulsorily purchased by the LPTB on 7 November 1934. This provided revenue that could be invested elsewhere.

The WMS share of the Southend service was taken over from 12 January 1935 together with 13 Dennis E-type coaches. With their London operations

terminated the City Motor Omnibus Co. Ltd. was dissolved and on 16 March 1936 the name of the New Empress Saloons was changed to the City Coach Company. Expansion in the Brentwood area then followed with the takeover of a number of small undertakings including Old Tom Motor Services of Laindon and the Regent Bus Service, their service being passed to the LPTB becoming route 339A.

Between 1935 and 1937 a fleet of 36 six-wheel Leyland Tigers was assembled to work the trunk Southend service running at 15 minute intervals to their new, dedicated coach station and garage at Wood Green. During the war the service was split into three sections, Wood Green – Brentwood, Brentwood – Wickford and Wickford – Southend. Due to the failure to come to an agreement with Southend Corporation and WMS concerning the co-ordination of transport services in the Southend area, which would have extended as far as Wickford, City issued a writ against the proposal with the result that the said Agreement was never implemented. Profit for the year ended 5 July 1948 was £70,208.

The City Coach Company Head Office was at Ongar Road, Brentwood adjacent to their main garage and workshops. On 17 February 1952 City sold their business to the British Transport Commission who placed it under WMS control. The bus services initially ran un-numbered, then on 4 January 1953 the trunk service was numbered 251 whilst the local services became 252 – 261. The former City garages at Wood Green and Southend (Tylers Avenue) and the rebuilt Brentwood premises continued to be used by WMS. The City fleet at takeover had grown to over 100 vehicles comprising Bedford, Commer, Seddon and Leyland single-deckers supplemented by Daimler and Leyland double-deckers.

Initially there was little change but when control of WMS passed to Eastern National on 18 May 1952 vehicles emerged from the paint shops in green and cream with 'Westcliff-on-Sea' fleet-names though City fleet-numbers continued to be used. Two batches of vehicles ordered by City were delivered directly to WMS with Southend C.B.C. FJN registrations.

Even years later many older people, including my late parents, still referred to the 251 as the 'City' route.

Fig.1.9   City L1 (XV7551) a Leyland Lion picks up in Green Lanes amid a north London tramscape en-route from Kentish Town to Southend. This service was run by New Empress saloons in which City had a controlling interest. The name was changed to the City Coach Company on 16 March 1936.   ABC

Just one vehicle from the City fleet, Leyland PD1/1 LEV917, still survives in the UK preserved as an open topper in Eastern National livery *(see Chapter Ten).*

For more information on the City Coach Company, please refer to *Fact File Number 1.*

Fig.1.10   This beautiful colour photograph of City LD5 (NVX302), a stylish Roberts bodied Leyland PD1A of 1949, catches it at the Castle Hotel stop, Wickford. The bus has now completed forty-one minutes of its journey from Southend but still has nearly two hours to go before arriving at Wood Green. The buses overall appearance is much enhanced by the white lining out and application of white to the roof and between decks. For the senior author who used this service, and even this bus on occasions, to travel with his parents to their plotland 'holiday bungalow' at Wickford, this photo evokes many pleasant memories.   FC

Southend Corporation Transport

These notes provide some background on the electric operations of Southend Corporation Transport (SCT) insofar as they effect the various phases of the establishment of the Southend Co-ordination Scheme *(see Chapter Four)*. For a detailed history of SCT the reader is directed to the excellent book by Richard Delahoy *(see Bibliography)*.

Work on the tram system commenced in February 1900, with single track and passing loops to a gauge of 3' 6". The system opened on 19 July 1901 with a fleet of 14 cars. The routes all radiated from the High Street running to Leigh, Southchurch, the Beach and Prittlewell. The trams were extended through to Thorpe Bay Corner on 12 February 1912.

Fig.1.11 *JVW561 a Duple utility bodied Daimler had a varied local life. New to Benfleet & District in 1944 it passed to WMS and then ENOC, as 1198. It was bought by SCT in 1955 and was unique in being the only bus they acquired that had been bought new by the Bridge family. SCT converted 246 to an open-topper and it survived in this role until 1970. PJSA*

Following the opening of Southchurch and Thorpe Hall Boulevards a circular tram route was introduced which was also exploited for tours. The doubling of the track on the Southchurch and Leigh routes was finally completed in 1920. With the trams well established the need for bus services along these main corridors was not necessary. The Prittlewell route, however, was less successful, the section from the Blue Boar along North Road being closed from 1 January 1921. The rest of the short Prittlewell route remained single track and was supplemented by trolleybuses. This tram service was withdrawn after 18 December 1928. It was not until 1 May 1930 that the Leigh and Southchurch routes were linked to give a cross town facility. During the 1930s new trolleybus routes were started notably along Fairfax Drive and Hamstel Road. Following a dramatic drop in traffic due to the wartime conditions and depopulation, closure of the tramway came on 8 April 1942.

Further extensions to the trolleybus system were made in response to the proposed tramway closure. Trolleybuses were extended along the seafront from the Kursaal to Thorpe Bay from 4 June 1939. Later an extension from the terminal

at Chalkwell Park to Victoria Circus created a circular route. The final alteration was the linking of the eastern and western circulars in November 1951, to form a continuous 'figure 8' operation bearing the route numbers 28A/B and 63A/B. However, only one section, the western circular, remained open until 1954 and this was closed on 28 October. Thus the electrical implications for the proposed Co-ordination Scheme disappeared.

SCT first experimented with motor buses as early as 1914. The buses were only seen as feeders to the tram service which could not operate up Pier Hill because it was too steep. Uncertainties about reliability led to a mixture of vehicle makes being purchased. Three Tilling-Stevens petrol-electric, three petrol Straker-Squires and one Edison battery bus all fitted with Brush 22-seat bodies (HJ 28-34) were bought. The service started on 25 June 1914 running from the Kursaal to Westborough Road (Eastwood Lane) via Pier Hill. A further peak hour route to Prittlewell Station was soon withdrawn due to poor patronage. Wartime conditions and other problems caused the bus operation to cease on 18 March 1916.

Afterwards for many years the SCT concentrated on electrical traction only. Consequently, it was not until November 1929, after internal combustion engine technology had considerably improved, that a new bus route was proposed. However, by the time that the plans had been finally approved by the various committees and all of the residents' objections had been heard, the Road Traffic Act of 1930 had come into place. Since WMS was considered by the Traffic Commissioner as the established operator the SCT application for a road service licence was refused. As the Corporation was desirous to operate motor buses the door was opened for discussions to start between WMS and SCT. These would eventually lead to the co-ordination of road transport services in the Southend area.

Fig.1.12 *209 (JN9529), previously 159, was an AEC Regent with lowbridge English Electric body new in 1937 which lasted until 1958. Route 25 was the first to be jointly worked with WMS, from 1 October 1947. AGOC*

Fig.2.1 *We start this chapter with a superb pre-delivery view of two of the Southend-on-Sea & District Motor Omnibus Co. Ltd. Dennis double-deckers outside the Dennis Motor Car Agency offices in Albert Gate, Kensington. The rear vehicle, fleet-number 2, carries registration P14A1. This was an early form of trade plate the letter P signifying Surrey County Council whilst the designation A1 was allocated to Dennis Bros. Ltd. of Guildford.   PJSA*

Chapter Two
Foundations and the Development of Bus Services

This historical summary of WMS and other Southend-on-Sea company bus services is presented in chronological order and largely relates only the major alterations. It is not intended to be fully comprehensive. Year divisions have been inserted to facilitate cross references. For further illustrations of WMS vehicles at work on bus services throughout the Southend area, please see *Chapter Five (Bus and Coach Services)*.

Pre 1910

There had been some irregular horse omnibus services in the Southend area since the 1870s provided by local jobmasters Peter Trigg and Sydney Smith. These ceased when the Southend Corporation trams started on 19 July 1901 on routes to Leigh, Southchurch, Prittlewell and to the Beach *(for further details see Chapter One)*. The first regular motor bus services started in April 1906 when the Southend-on-Sea and District Motor Omnibus Company ran routes to Hadleigh, Rochford and to Wakering via Shoebury. This venture used three Dennis double-deckers two of which were registered F 1807/8. These carried Essex County Council issued registrations since this service started some eight years before Southend-on-Sea County Borough Council was formed. Unfortunately operations were not a success and the services were withdrawn by the year end.

Fig.2.2 *A Holmes & Smith Thornycroft char-a-banc F5654 is seen at the narrow entrance to their Royal Yard. Operations were moved just around the corner to Pier Hill in 1913. JRYC*

1914

Southend Corporation commenced bus operation on 25 June 1914 with a fleet of seven vehicles registered HJ 28-34. Unfortunately the operation was not a financial success and was abandoned by 18 March 1916. For further details see *Chapter One*.

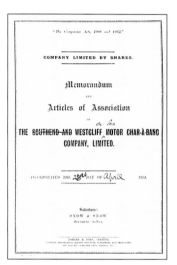

The foundations of WMS can be traced back to the merger of two rival local char-a-banc businesses. The older business dated back to about 1908 when Charles and George Holmes combined with the aforementioned Sydney Smith to provide a livery stable and carriage hiring business before introducing motor char-a-bancs from about 1911 which traded as 'The Royal Red Cars'. They were based at the Royal Yard near the Royal Hotel in High Street, Southend. The other founding partner was the Southend-on-Sea Charabanc Company of Henry Brown Jnr. and George Spencer which had been founded on 4 April 1913 and traded as 'The Royal Blue Cars Co. Ltd.' *(see Fig.3.11)*. Competition between the 'Reds' and the 'Blues' had soon become very keen and it was no surprise that a merger was sought. The two undertakings were initially to be combined with the somewhat cumbersome title of 'The Southend and Westcliff Motor Char-a-banc Co. Ltd.'

Why the name 'Westcliff' should have been chosen is not recorded, however, such a geographical choice would appear to be most appropriate since Westcliff (often mis-spelled 'Westcliffe') was considered a most prestigious suburb at this time and was also home to Managing Director Charles Holmes *(see Fig.9.12)*. Moreover, a distinction from the Southend Tramways would have been immediately evident. However, on all of the documentation placed before the Companies Registration Office the name was rationalised as 'The Westcliff-on-Sea Motor Char-a-banc Co Ltd' (WSMC) which was duly registered on 23 April 1914. The Southend-on-Sea Char-a-banc Company was quickly wound up a couple of months later. The new company traded as 'The Royal Red Cars' and was based at Pier Hill. Its activities at the time were the running of tours and excursions (see Chapter Three), bus services not being started until the finish of the 1914-1918 war.

1915

The western terminal of the SCT tram service was at Leigh. Leigh UDC officially became part of Southend on 9 November 1913 shortly before Southend-on-Sea became a County Borough. In September 1915 the Thundersley, Hadleigh and District Motors (THD) of Oak Garage, Hadleigh were granted licences for two motor buses to ply between Hadleigh and Leigh. Soon their red buses were established as the major operator on this route. Certain journeys were extended on a circular route from Hadleigh to Thundersley. THD was later to play a major part in the WMS story.

1918/1919

Soon after the war ended buses started running on Canvey Island to meet the ferry and thus allow connection with the trains at Benfleet Station. During 1919 the local vehicle proprietors got together and formed the Canvey Island Motor Association using a motley collection of conveyances. Also in 1919 THD took over the business of Henry Sefton and then converted into a public company.

1920

On 12 March 1920 representatives of the National Omnibus & Transport Co. Ltd. (NOTC, see Chapter One) attended a meeting of the Light Railways Committee (SLRC) in Southend regarding proposals for the establishment of daily motor bus services between Chelmsford and Southend and between Brentwood and Southend and also services to connect the borough with outlying districts such as Rochford, Hadleigh, Rayleigh, Eastwood and Shoeburyness. This was shortly followed by a letter from WSMC offering to establish similar services. At this time Southend Corporation Transport (SCT) had no plans to re-start bus services following their abortive effort a few years earlier, this despite there being considerable public demand.

At a subsequent meeting of the SLRC on 28 May it was agreed, subject to approval by the Highways & Works Committee, that WSMC be given permission to ply for hire until 31 December 1920 at hourly intervals on routes to the five outlying districts mentioned above and also on a local service within the borough, using vehicles fitted with pneumatic tyres. The local route started on 19 July 1920 as service 1 running every 15 minutes from Pier Hill (Royal Hotel) to Westcliff (Plough Hotel) via Clifftown Road, with a through fare of 3d, in 1d stages. One of the vehicles used at the outset was HJ580. On 30 July the Chelmsford – Southend applications by NOTC and WSMC were

then considered by the SLRC which requested further details before making a final decision.

1921

This year saw further WSMC bus services in operation using some Daimler and Dennis double-deckers running to Rayleigh via Hadleigh (service 2), a circular route to Shoebury (3/3A), to Rochford (4) and to Rayleigh via Eastwood (5).

WESTCLIFF-ON-SEA MOTOR CHARABANC CO., LTD.

1467—SOUTHEND ; Leigh* (15); Hadleigh (25); Thundersley (40); RAYLEIGH (47).
LEAVE Southend (Victoria Corner): Weekdays A.M. 9.0 & hourly till P.M. 10.0. Sun. A.M. 10.0 & hourly till P.M. 9.0.
RAYLEIGH ; Thundersley (7); Hadleigh (22); Leigh (34); SOUTHEND (49).
LEAVE Rayleigh : Weekdays A.M. 7.45, 10.0 & hourly till P.M. 10.0. Sun. A.M. 9.0 & hourly till P.M. 9.0. [F. 1/-] (2).
* For other Buses between Leigh & Thundersley see 1472. For other Buses between Southend & Rayleigh (via Eastwood) see 1471.

1468—SOUTHEND ; Bournes Gr. (8); Wakering (21); Shoebury (30); Bournes Gr. (43); SOUTHEND (51).
LEAVE Southend (Victoria Corner): Weekdays A.M. 9.0 & hourly till P.M. 10.0. Sun. A.M. 10.0 & hourly till P.M. 10.0. [F.] (3).

Fig.2.3 The Westcliff-on-Sea Motor Char-a-banc listing of bus services as shown in the June 1921 'Travel By Road' guide. At this time the service to Rayleigh via Hadleigh was numbered 2 and the through fare was 1/- (5 p).

To provide the link between Southend and Chelmsford, NOTC was eventually favoured over WSMC. The National timetable dated 3 June 1921 included new service 12 running via Galleywood, Stock, Billericay, Wickford and Rayleigh. It is interesting to note that the Southend terminal point was referred to as 'Cobweb Corner' colloquially named because of the profusion of tramway overhead installed at Victoria Circus.

Service No. 12.

Chelmsford, Billericay, Rayleigh, Wickford and Southend-on-Sea.

Week-days and Sundays.

	a.m.	a.m.	p.m.	p.m.
Chelmsford Station ...dep.	8.45	10.15	2.15	4.0
Galleywood, The Eagle arr.	9.0	10.30	2.30	4.15
Stock, The Bear .... „	9.15	10.45	2.45	4.30
Billericay, The Chequers „	9.30	11.0	3.0	4.45
Wickford, The Castle .... „	10.0	11.30	3.30	5.15
Rayleigh .... „	10.20	11.50	3.50	5.35
Southend, Cobweb Corner „	10.50	12.20	4.20	6.5
Southend, Cobweb Corner dep	11.0	12.30	4.30	6.30
Rayleigh ....arr.	11.30	1.0	5.0	7.0
Wickford, The Castle „	11.50	1.20	5.20	7.20
Billericay, The Chequers „	12.20	1.50	5.50	7.50
Stock, The Bear „	12.35	2.5	6.5	8.5
Galleywood, Eagle „	12.50	2.20	6.20	8.20
Chelmsford Station „	1.5	2.35	6.35	8.35

Major Albert Pearse (see Fig.2.6) entered the motor bus business in 1921 with two services from Benfleet Station to the Thundersley area essentially for railway passengers.

1922

WSMC had by now established a range of popular five- and twelve-day extended tours. In view of this the company name was changed to the more modern sounding Westcliff-on-Sea Motor Services Ltd (WMS) on 28 January 1922.

Fig.2.4   *In contrast to the previous photo this is an in-service view of Southend-on-Sea & District Motor Omnibus Co. Ltd. Dennis double-decker number 2, with driver and conductor on parade. The vehicle now carries Essex registration number F1808.   PJSA*

Fig.2.5   *Seen on service 2 to Pitsea is HJ1879, an early WMS Daimler CK double-decker with Strachan & Brown body-work. This service competed with Pearse's Motor Services as far as Tarpots Corner.   AGOC*

Fig.2.6 *Major Pearse stands by one of his buses at South Benfleet War Memorial terminal.   JRYC*

Major Pearse extended his sphere of operation with a service from Benfleet Station to Southend. WMS responded by introducing a new service 2 between Southend and Pitsea. Other new WMS services were the 6 to Ashingdon, the 8 to Paglesham (very short-lived), and another service 8 to Benfleet.

One of the features associated with the early WMS service network was the frequent re-numbering of services in order to maintain a block of consecutive numbers. Thus pioneering service 1 became 5 and finally 6. The long standing Southend – Hadleigh – Rayleigh service started as 2 and then became 1 a number which remains in use for this route at the time of writing. Likewise, the other main line London Road service to South Benfleet was initially numbered 8 for a few months

Fig.2.7 *Daimler saloon HJ1313 was purchased by WSMC in 1920 to operate their new bus services alongside existing B type double-deckers. Shortly afterwards the company became the WMS. At a later date following a serious accident this most unfortunately registered bus was re-registered HJ9628. AGOC*

in 1922 before becoming service 3. The only early service to retain its number throughout was the 2, which ran to Pitsea and Vange and later on to Grays. Frequent service re-numberings fortunately ceased thereafter.

In 1922 National introduced a second route running between Chelmsford and Southend (service 11) which went by way of Great Baddow, Rettendon, Battlesbridge, Rawreth and Rayleigh. The timetable dated 17 July 1922 showed two return journeys with a running time of 1 hour and 40 minutes. It is interesting to note that this was by then the fourth service to which NOTC had allocated the number 11. However, it then proved to be very long lived indeed since at the time of writing service 11A, now run by Regal Busways, still links Southend and Chelmsford though only on Sundays. The journey follows essentially the same route and takes about 1 hour and 15 minutes.

DUPLICATE FOR THE FILE.

No. *135399*

Certificate of Change of Name.

I hereby Certify, That the

Westcliff-on-Sea Motor Char-a-banc Company, Limited having, with the sanction of a **Special Resolution** of the said Company, and with the approval of the BOARD OF TRADE, changed its name, is now called the

Westcliff-on-Sea Motor Services Limited

and I have entered such new name on the Register accordingly.

Given under my hand at London, this *Twentyeighth* day of *January* One Thousand Nine Hundred and *Twenty-two.*

Registrar of Joint Stock Companies.

Certificate received by *H Brown Secretary*

Date *2/2/22.*

1923

The fairly extensive parish of Eastwood lay between Southend-on-Sea and Rayleigh and was essentially an agricultural community within the Rural District of Rochford at this time. As Southend grew in size and importance the potential of the area for residential development became clear to one Henry Ritchie Bridge, a successful builder based in Leigh. He now turned his sights towards Eastwood where he purchased Upper and Lower Edwards Hall estate comprising farmland and farmhouses. Bridge commenced building houses on this land creating Eastwood Rise, Tudor Road and Bosworth Road. The Bridge family themselves then took up residence in Upper Edwards Hall.

Bus service provision in the area, however, lagged behind the house building. Eastwood Parish Council thus approached WMS in 1923 for an improved service but this met with a negative response. As was often the case the developer, in this case Bridge, then decided to provide a service himself, a decision which WMS was later to have cause to regret. The Bridges approached George Weston to acquire the licence for his service which ran between Eastwood and Leigh Church a few times each weekday. On 11 December 1923 the Leigh licence was granted and Edwards Hall Motors Ltd. was registered, named after the family home. The business was generally known as the 'Blue Buses' the company name being abbreviated to EHM Ltd. on the tickets. Their first new service was from Eastwood to Southend via Woodcutters Arms and Leigh Elm Hotel.

On 8 June 1923 WMS ventured onto Canvey Island and started service 12 from Benfleet to Leigh Beck in competition with the local Canvey operators.

No. 12 Service.		BENFLEET and LEIGH BECK.		
Leave Leigh Beck—			**Leave Benfleet—**	
A.M.	6 40	P.M.	3 0	A.M.	7 10	P.M.	3 30
	7 40		3 30		8 20		4 0
	8 20		4 0		9 0		4 35
	9 0		4 45		9 30		5 30
	9 30		5 20		10 0		5 55
	10 0		6 0		10 35		6 40
	10 30		6 30		11 0		7 0
	11 0		7 0		11 30		7 25
	11 30		7 30		12 0		8 0
	12 0		7 55	P.M.	12 30		8 25
P.M.	12 30		8 25		1 15		9 10
	1 15		9 0		2 5		9 40
	1 40		9 35		2 30		10 10
	2 30		10 40		3 0		11 15
		All Buses will wait for Trains when possible.		

1924

Early in 1924 WMS introduced circular service 13 (Southend – Leigh – Eastwood – Prittlewell – Southend) to compete against the new EHM service from Eastwood via Leigh and Prittlewell. This heralded the start of a bus war between the Edwards Hall 'Blues' and the Westcliff 'Reds'.

For the summer season a new venture was started by WMS in the form of service 6A, promoted as 'The Grand Marine Drive'. It ran from the Kursaal along the sea-front past the Pier all the way to Chalkwell Shelter then turning inland to terminate at Chalkwell Park. The service was provided by specially purchased 'toast-rack' open-sided Berliet single-deckers.

1925

In the meantime, the Bridge family's taste for bus services was growing and they turned their attention to opening up new routes going west from a terminus at Leigh Church. This was because their attempts to run east were frustrated by Southend Council Watch Committee refusing EHM licences as SCWC were most reluctant to allow additional departures from the now overcrowded Victoria Circus.

However, this move west brought the EHM Blue Buses into direct competition with the 'Hadleigh Red' buses and Major Pearse. The Blue Bus services from Leigh, which were all un-numbered went to Hadleigh and thence onwards to Rayleigh and Benfleet thus competing with THD. THD quickly responded by starting a competing Leigh – Eastwood route which followed the Blue Bus service to the Woodcutters Arms where it branched off to Gowers Corner, later known as Coombes Corner after Inspector W. Coombes of WMS who lived in the house at the road junction!

As noted the main stumbling block to securing new bus licences in the Southend area was the overcrowding at Victoria Circus. Thus if an alternative off-street terminal could be found then the Bridges could establish a firm foothold. This they did by coming to an agreement with the LMS Railway to use the forecourt of the LMS Station (now Southend Central). This was a prime town centre location half-way down the High Street from the LNER Victoria Station (WMS terminated at Victoria Circus) to the sea. With this problem solved EHM Blue Bus Services to Rayleigh and Wickford via Leigh or Eastwood and Hullbridge were soon established.

1925 witnessed the end of the WMS foray on to Canvey Island due to the severe competition from the locally based island operators. The August 1923 time-table noted that the WMS buses on Canvey would wait for trains when possible. However, after a train had arrived at Benfleet Station intending passengers would have needed to walk down to the landing stage then either board a rowing boat across the creek or use the stepping stones at low tide. So just how long the buses actually waited would have been open to speculation.

On 16 October 1925 Southend Corporation commenced their first trolleybus operation on the Prittlewell route. Over a period of time trolleybuses were to feature very strongly in SCT operations, electric traction clearly being preferred over the internal combustion engine *(see also Chapter One)*.

1926

Competition between the WMS 'reds' and the EHM 'blues' showed no signs of abatement. WMS upped the stakes by starting service 16 which exactly duplicated the EHM route to Rayleigh via Leigh and Eastwood. Unfortunately this did not have the desired effect. Instead EHM responded by introducing their own sea-front service to directly compete with WMS on that company's prime territory. Towards the end of the year after an extended battle over licences Major Pearse finally succeeded to increase his service from Benfleet to Southend to run at hourly intervals from 7 December.

1927

Early in 1927 the Southend Council Watch Committee issued twelve new licences to EHM for a variety of routes. With the thought of further possible expansion, coupled with their valuable town terminal point EHM was now in a very strong position. It was perhaps not surprising that WMS now invited EHM to discuss the future of bus services. On 25 March 1927 terms were agreed such that Edwards Hall Motors would become a wholly owned subsidiary of WMS. Both businesses would continue to operate side by side but now in co-operation though their two bus fleets would remain distinct. The name Edwards Hall Motors was henceforth included on the cover of the WMS timetables. The completion date was fixed for 2 May. H. R. Bridge and his eldest son H. A. Bridge gained seats on the WMS board, their appointments being passed on 2 December and confirmed on 5 January 1928. H. R. Bridge's second son Stanley took up a position at the WMS workshops in Fairfax Drive, whilst the third son Norman became an Inspector. The Head Office of EHM was re-located to the WMS offices at Pier Hill. In September 1927 a rationalisation of the competing services took place producing significant operating economies. The wisdom of the two concerns coming together was soon justified since just as one chapter of competition closed another was about to open.

A chain of events had started earlier in the year when Arthur Rogers and H. 'Bert' Smith began applying for licences for services in the area. These were always refused. However, through sheer persistence they eventually settled on a service which did not impinge on other operators territories. This ran from Southend to Eastwood via Boston Avenue and Fairfax Drive and was licensed on 31 October 1927. The service was started using a pair of Gilford vehicles in a brown livery with the fleet-name 'The Borough Services'. From this innocuous start great things were to follow. Using surplus Blue Bus vehicles resulting from the merger and service rationalisation, WMS started some new services. One was to Eastwood to compete against the newly established Borough and two other local services to the Hamstel Road area both starting from the LMS Station.

Another other chain of events was started on 27 May 1927 when A. H. Young pioneered a new express service from Palmers Green and Wood Green to Southend, terminating at the Borough Garage on Old London Road (no connection with Borough Services). A company known as New Empress Saloons Ltd was registered on 3 July 1928 to continue this pioneering enterprise using the latest Dennis saloons painted in a purple/maroon livery. The new saloon coach service, which picked up and set down en-route, ran from Kentish Town to Southend (Kursaal) via Romford, Brentwood, Wickford, Rayleigh and Eastwood at regular hourly intervals. Here was another case where great things were to follow.

In June WMS modified their Thursday only service 15 between Southend and Brentwood (which initially operated via Herongate). It became daily routed via Laindon and Billericay with a two hourly frequency. This Brentwood connection was later to assume considerable significance.

1928

During 1928 Major Pearse made further licence applications but these were refused by the Southend Watch Committee. Canvey UDC also refused him permission to extend his service from Benfleet onto the island and thereby connect Canvey with the rest of the world. Major Pearse had by this time established a sub-depot on Canvey but even this local presence was of no advantage (see Fig.2.14). The only alternative therefore was to expand westwards where there was little control of bus licences and so he started services from Benfleet to Stanford-le-Hope via Pitsea and to Wickford via Nevendon.

On 28 February 1928 a company known as Service Saloons Ltd. was registered to complete against New Empress Saloons. They used green ADC coaches on a route between Southend and Brentwood with occasional journeys extended to Kings Cross.

WMS decided that it must compete with these new coach services since their operations threatened its Southend – Wickford service (acquired from EHM Blue Buses) and also its summer express coach services (see Chapter Three) from various points in North London to Southend. Accordingly on 18 June 1928 a new service of Royal Red Pullman Saloons (initially un-numbered, but later service 16) was started running hourly from Southend (Victoria Circus) to London (Wood Green, High Road). Half of the vehicles for the service were garaged at the premises of WMS's wholly owned subsidiary Ardley Bros. of Tottenham. The Wood Green starting point was later changed to Jolly Butchers Hill.

In the summer of 1928 WMS received notice to vacate its Pier Hill premises where the Head Office and coach booking and departure station were located. This property was shared with and rented from Holmes and Smith the leasehold owners whose car hire business was also based there. This action precipitated a long period of disharmony amongst the WMS directors. Next door to the coach station stood the Temperance Billiards Hall and H. R. Bridge set about securing these premises as replacement. It had originally opened as a cinema in 1909 closing in 1920 when it was converted into its later guise. On acquisition it was reconstructed into a new coach station which continued in use well into ENOC days before finally closing after the 1966 season (see Chapter Nine).

Borough also expanded during the year on 23 September securing a licence to extend through to Grays thus providing that town with a new link to Southend initially running six times a day.

Fig.2.8 HJ3812 was one of a pair of Berliet open-sided toast-rack vehicles which were used on sea-front service 6A. Note the destination boards on the side listing places of interest along the route.   ENEG

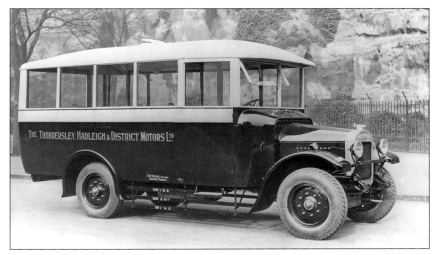

Fig.2.9 This superb photo is a pre-delivery view of EV587 a Thornycroft A12 saloon for The Thundersley, Hadleigh & District Motors Ltd. dating from about 1925.   RM

Fig.2.10 Typical of the small buses used on Canvey Island in the twenties was this 14-seater Ford, PU3365, seen at Leigh Beck. Mr. Knight stands by his smart bus 'Bright Knight' the fleet-name of which is almost larger than the bus.   PJSA

Fig.2.11 HJ6882 was one of the Vulcan saloons operated by Edwards Hall Motors. It dated from 1927 after WMS had gained control. The then still very rural Hamstel Road terminus is the location for the photo. PJSA

Fig.2.12 Seen on their Eastwood service is HJ7334, one of a pair of Gilford LL166 saloons introduced by Borough Services Ltd in 1927. AGOC

Fig.2.13 Loading at Romford Market Place on Royal Red Pullman Saloon service 16 to Southend is HJ8034, a Dennis E saloon. The logo carried is the new-style simplified 'Westcliff' fleet-name. JFH

Fig.2.14 This advertisement for Pearse's Garage and Motor Works appeared in 'Captivating Canvey' a local guide published in 1927. As is shown, by this time a sub-office had been established on Canvey Island.

A	Southend LMS – Eastwood (competing with Borough)
B/C	Southend LMS – Hamstel Lane, the new local services mentioned earlier (see 1927)
D	Southend LMS – Rayleigh – Hullbridge
E/F/G	Services from Leigh Church
H	Southend Pier – Leigh Pall Mall, shortly afterward combined with WMS service 19

1929

New Years Day 1929 saw the introduction of a co-ordinated (but not joint) timetable between City and WMS on the Wood Green service. In March Service Saloons took delivery of a new Gilford coach, acknowledged for its speed, and extended its Brentwood service through to Seven Kings. However, halfway through their second year of existence Service Saloons was beginning to experience financial problems and their vehicles were repossessed by the finance company. Operations ceased. WMS stepped in to pick up the licences and on 2 August extended service 15 to Seven Kings *(see Fig.2.15)*

To compete with Borough further extensions of the Pitsea services were introduced during the spring of 1929. Service 2 (via Corringham) was extended to Grays and 2A (via Homesteads) to East Ham via Rainham, Dagenham and Barking.

On 26 August Rayleigh Motor Services Ltd. was registered to continue the business of New Imperial Motors. Their sphere of operations was a route from Hullbridge to Southend via Rayleigh and Rochford. The company also initiated a new service from Colchester to Southend via Danbury or Latchingdon and Maldon, which proved successful because of poor rail facilities and lack of through buses. This development caused ENOC to extend their service 19 from Maldon to Southend.

An important development was the conversion of Borough Services into a limited company on 26 February and also the formation of Pearse's Motor Service Ltd. with Major Pearse then in a partnership. A new service was started by Pearse between Benfleet

Shortly afterwards on 25 October 1928 a controlling interest in New Empress Saloons was purchased by the City Motor Omnibus Co. Ltd. *(for details see City Fact File 1)*. The City brown and cream livery and distinctive logo was applied to the fleet but with the New Empress name retained and displayed over the front destination box.

Finally late in the year THD withdrew their Leigh – Eastwood service that had competed with the EHM Blue Buses and also ceased operations west of Hadleigh to instead concentrate on their frequent Leigh local service. Whether this action resulted from the WMS/EHM Blue Bus consolidation is not known with certainty.

At the close of 1928 route letters were allocated to the former EHM Blue Bus services presumably to distinguish them from the numbered WMS services that appeared in the joint timetable. The letters introduced were:

Blue Bus Ser. E.   LEIGH, HADLEIGH, DAWES HEATH & WOODMANS ARMS.

No. 1	NS	NS	A.M.	A.M.	A.M.	P.M.		P.M.	P M	P M
LEIGH CHURCH ....d	740	840	9 40	1040	1140			1240	140	240
Hadleigh	752	852	9 52	1052	1152	12 5		1252	152	252
Dawes Heath......	757	857	9 57	1057	1157	1215		1257	157	257
WOODMANS ARMS ....a	8 0	9 0	10 0	11 0				1 0	20	3 0

No. 2	P M	P M	P M	P M	P M	P M	P.M.	P.M.
LEIGH CHURCH ....d	340	440	540	640	740	840	9 40	1040
Hadleigh	352	452	552	652	752	852	9 52	1052
Dawes Heath......	357	457	557	657	757	857	9 57	1057
WOODMANS ARMS ....a	4 0	5 0	6 0	7 0	8 0	9 0	10 0	11 0

No. 1	NS	NS	A M	A.M.	A.M.	A.M.	P.M.	P.M.	P M
WOODMANS ARMS....d	7 5	8 5	9 5	10 5	11 5			1 5	2 5
Dawes Heath........	710	810	910	1010	1110	1157	1215	1 10	210
Hadleigh	720	820	920	1020	1120	12 5	1220	1 20	220
LEIGH CHURCH........a	732	832	932	1032	1132		1232	1 32	232

No. 2	P M	P M	P M	P M	P M	R M	P M	P.M.
WOODMANS ARMS....d	3 5	4 5	5 5	6 5	7 5	8 5	9 5	10 5
Dawes Heath........	310	410	510	610	710	810	910	1010
Hadleigh	320	420	520	620	720	820	920	1020
LEIGH CHURCH........a	332	432	532	632	732	832	932	1032

NS Not Suns.

Westcliff-on-Sea Motor Services, Ltd.

Service 15—Southend-on-Sea to Brentwood.

On and after FRIDAY, AUGUST 2nd, 1929

the above Service will be extended to

Romford and Seven Kings

TIMES OF DEPARTURE AS FOLLOWS:

SOUTHEND—BRENTWOOD—SEVEN KINGS.

Leave.								
Southend ...	7.35	9.35	12.5	1.5	2.5	4.5	6.5	8.5
Brentwood ...	9.5	11.5	1.35	2.5	3.35	5.35	7.35	9.35
Romford ...	9.25	11.25	1.55	2.25	2.55	5.55	7.55	9.55
Seven Kings...	9.40	11.40	—	2.40	—	—	8.10	10.10

SEVEN KINGS—BRENTWOOD—SOUTHEND.

Leave.								
Seven Kings...	9.45	11.45	—	2.45	—	—	8.15	10.15
Romford ...	10.0	12.0	2.0	3.0	4.0	6.0	8.30	10.30
Brentwood ...	10.20	12.20	2.20	3.20	4.20	6.20	8.50	10.50
Southend ...	11.50	1.50	3.50	4.50	5.50	7.50	10.20	12.20

For the benefit of local residents a Special Cheap **2/6** Return will be issued on all Buses up till 1.5. Other fares are as shown on the Fare Tables.

Phone: Marine 6288

By Order, H. M. LOMAX, Secretary, Pier Hill Garage, Southend-on-Sea.

5m/8/29. *L. Washburn, Printer, 25 & 27 Queens Road, Southend-on-Sea.*

Fig.2.15 This leaflet is of particular significance to the author who resides just a couple of hundred yards from the former Seven Kings terminal.

and Brentwood via Vange and Billericay running on Sundays only to cater for visiting days at the County Mental Hospital at Warley.

Finally a new coach operator Multiways Ltd. of Station Road, Westcliff-on-Sea was registered which was to feature in the WMS story later on.

Pearce's Service.					BRENTWOOD & BENFLEET.				
	S		T	S		S		T	S
BRENTWOOD	2 0	......	......	4 10	**BENFLEET**	1250	......	......	......
Shenfield	2 20	......	......	4 30	Tarpots	1240	......	......	......
Billericay	2 30	......	3 45	4 40	Barge Inn	1248	......	3 0	3 0
Fortune of War.	2 40	......	3 55	4 50	Fortune of War.	1 15	......	3 30	3 30
Barge Inn	3 0	......	4 15	5 10	Billericay	1 25	......	3 40	3 40
Tarpots	......	......	4 28	5 23	Shenfield	1 45	......	......	3 50
BENFLEET	......	......	4 35	5 30	**BRENTWOOD**	1 55	......	......	4 10

(S Suns. only. T Thurs. only.)

1930

This year saw many last minute service introductions, expansions and acquisitions by a variety of operators to beat the requirements of the impending government legislation in the form of the 1930 Road Traffic Act. For further details see *Chapter One*.

In March the first new operator appeared. This was Shoeburyness Motor Services Ltd. with a route from Shoeburyness to Southend in opposition to WMS. An

attractive light blue livery was used. The required licences were secured on appeal with backing from Shoebury Council because they considered the WMS service to be inadequate.

This was followed on 3 April by the appearance of Rochford & District Motor Services Ltd. running from Southend (Tylers Avenue) to Rochford and Creeksea *(see Chapter Seven)*.

In June Borough took control of Rayleigh Motor Services Ltd. Their long service to Colchester was taken over by Borough but the other two Rayleigh services were continued as before using the Rayleigh name.

Fom 23 June WMS diverted service 15 to operate via Rayleigh and Wickford and further extended it from Seven Kings to Stratford Broadway and at the same time increased the frequency to hourly. The route was then marketed as another Royal Red Pullman Saloon Service. From 8 November service 15 was withdrawn and the journeys diverted to Wood Green over service 16. One journey per hour was diverted via Ramsden Bellhouse. At the same time City increased their New Empress Saloons service to two journeys per hour thus giving a combined 15 minutes co-ordinated (not joint) service. Thus from Southend after leaving their new terminal in Tylers Avenue, New Empress called at Victoria Circus at 00 and 15 minutes past the hour bound for Wood Green and Kentish Town. WMS service 16 started from Victoria Circus departing at 30 (via Ramsden Bellhouse) and 45 minutes past the hour for Wood Green. Thus each operator worked two consecutive journeys.

As a replacement for the 15, an hourly service was introduced between Southend and Billericay via Pitsea and Laindon. This had also been put on for a short time the previous year. Somewhat confusingly this Billericay service was numbered 2A, despite this designation already being in use.

With several regular services now operating into the London area, a series of leaflets featuring these Royal Red Pullman Saloons was introduced listing all the facilities available. These included the routes to Wood Green, East Ham and Stratford. Some leaflets also gave details of the express services running into central London. Examples are reproduced in a special section towards the end of *Chapter Five (see Figs.5.78 and 5.79)*.

A review of operations by WMS/EHM indicated that Blue Bus route D was largely redundant so it was withdrawn whilst route G at Leigh was converted into a circular service to Eastwood (Jones Corner) running outward via Woodcutters Arms and Bellhouse Lane returning via Kent Elm Corner and Coombes Corner.

With all this independent activity taking place Southend Corporation Transport eventually decided in November 1929 to introduce motor bus services to supplement their trams and trolleybuses. In October 1930 after some deliberation as to whether single- or double-deckers were required, an order was placed for seven AEC Regals and applications were made for the licences for their proposed new services. Unfortunately the Corporation failed to appreciate the full signifi- cance of the forthcoming new Road Traffic Act of 1930. This was to recognise the growing collection of other organisations as the 'established operators' of bus services in the local vicinity and not SCT, which must have been a severe blow to civic pride. For further details see *Chapter Four*.

The limited company that Major Pearse had formed with his new partners had not proved to be successful and consequently was dissolved. He was then operating once again on his own account as Pearse's Motor Services.

This is an appropriate point to record some activities further up river. From 1 April 1926 Canvey had been elevated to the status of an Urban District and the new Council had set to work to control the local bus operations which were still giving problems. On 25 November 1930 the local Association was re-named Canvey Auxiliary Motors. Further significant Canvey events were soon to follow.

1931

For many years the motley collection of buses on Canvey Island needed to splash their way through a muddy ford from Benfleet. At high tide a primitive ferry would transport passengers across and they would then board their bus on the island. All this changed on 21 May 1931 when the long awaited Colvin Bridge (named after the Lord Lieutenant of Essex) was opened. On 29 October 1931 a new company 'The Canvey & District Motor Transport Co. Ltd.' was registered formed of fifteen of the sixteen partners of the former Canvey Auxiliary Motors combine. This was necessary since the Traffic Commissioners, unlike the local Urban District Council, were not prepared to licence the individual owners. However, one operator D. E. Williams Jnr. preferred to remain separate.

Around April 1931 some changes were made to WMS service 2 (Grays via Corringham) and 2A (East Ham via Homesteads). The latter service was re-numbered 2B with the number 2A then being allocated to the service from Southend to Billericay via Pitsea, Vange and Laindon. Reference to the 1932 WMS route map *Fig.2.24* illustrates the country services operating in the western sector at this time.

Meanwhile, the seven AEC Regals ordered by SCT were delivered in 1931 as 150-6 (JN820-6). However, as licences had not been forthcoming there was no route

Fig.2.16 *The crew of Borough Services 15 (HJ9578) pose, driver complete with jackboots, outside Southend Victoria Station before returning to Grays. Their impressive steed is a Gilford 163DOT with a Beadle L26/24R body. This was the only 163DOT ever built and had been exhibited on the Gilford stand at the 1929 Commercial Motor Show in Borough Services livery. It had a very short life and was withdrawn in 1930 after an accident.   PJSA*

Fig.2.17 *The acquisition of Shoeburyness Motor Services brought EV1925, a Duple bodied Dennis HV new in 1931 into the WMS fleet. In this pre-take-over view the waistband display of the points served on the Shoebury-Southend route is prominent.*   JFH

Fig.2.18 *The Colvin Bridge was opened in 1931. Prior to this date a motley collection of small buses ran across the island. When the link to the English 'mainland' was in place the service was extended to turn at South Benfleet (Canvey Bridge). Soon afterwards high capacity double-deckers were introduced to cope with the increased loadings. Here is a magnificent Karrier competing in majesty with the sailing craft on Benfleet Creek.   PJSA*

for them to operate and so they were placed in store pending further licence applications.

Another operator experiencing problems with the Traffic Commissioners was Pearse's Motor Services. Major Pearse regarded the whole licensing process with considerable disdain and at first would have nothing to do with it. He eventually conceded and applied for licences. Unfortunately the Brentwood service did not qualify for a licence and the Thundersley run was also refused due to past irregular operation. He did succeed in getting a licence for an hourly service on the trunk

route from Benfleet to Southend which was increased to half-hourly on appeal.

Late in 1931 WMS secured control of Rochford and District and immediately transferred WMS service 11 to Fambridge to its new subsidiary.

In November the WMS Chairman Henry Brown and Managing Director George Spencer, the co-founders of the original 'Royal Red' Cars retired from the WMS board. There then followed a period of considerable disunity.

1932

Changes to the London Road bus services were introduced in June. Borough Services increased their service to Grays to run every 30 minutes whilst WMS diverted service 2A at Laindon to run through to Romford via Upminster and Hornchurch.

The financial position of Pearse's Motor Services at this time had become very weak, with most of the vehicles in an unfit state. Major Pearse had been in negotiation with WMS for assistance but he then had a chance meeting with H. R. Bridge. Although Henry initially indicated that he was 'finished with buses' they then negotiated a takeover deal of the Major's rather cash strapped business.

Relationships on the WMS board deteriorated during 1932 resulting in Henry Ritchie Bridge resigning his seat on 15 June. The Bridge family now wanted their capital from WMS to complete the deal with Major Pearse. Unfortunately due to all the recent competition

Fig.2.19 *In 1933 Mr. H. R. Bridge bought a trio of brand new Tilling Stevens double-deckers with 52-seat Park Royal bodies. These were JN2681-3, numbered 1 – 3 in his new Benfleet & District fleet and were bought to operate between South Benfleet and Southend. The route number chosen, as displayed by the buses was 3, the same as the WMS service. This posed view catches them before their entry into service.   PJSA*

the financial position of WMS had deteriorated over the past couple of years which meant that cash was short. The Bridges decided to accept in part payment the business of Ardley Bros. of Tottenham on 17 July 1932 (*see Chapter Three*).

Shortly afterwards H. R. Bridge met up again with Major Pearse. One of the more bizarre transactions that led to the acquisition of a bus company followed. Bridge offered a flock of sheep and four hundred acres of marshland at Pitsea for Pearse's business and the offer was accepted. It is not recorded whether the Major was more successful with sheep than he had been with buses. On 29 October H.R. Bridge formed the Benfleet & District Motor Services Ltd. to continue the operations. This action caused H. A. Bridge to resign from the WMS board on 21 November due to a conflict of interests and he then joined his father at Benfleet & District.

About this time WMS opened new premises at Victoria Arcade, Victoria Circus. Included were a travel and ticket office at street level and a staff canteen on the first floor. A Busman's Social Club was also established.

SCT motor buses eventually made their re-appearance on 5 July 1932 on a service from the Sea Front (Prittlewell Square) to Southchurch Park (Shaftesbury Avenue) via Heygate Avenue and York Road using the batch of AEC Regals that had been in store. Following a suggestion by the Traffic Commissioners negotiations were started between WMS, SCT and Borough Services to agree a scheme of co-ordination. It was agreed that the County Borough be divided into two zones, east and west the former becoming SCT preserve with 'the Companies' keeping to the west. SCT then bought

certain company services to establish their territory. The operating agreement was finally concluded on 22 December 1932. For further details see *Chapter Four*.

1933

The new territorial agreement came into effect from 1 January 1933. SCT acquired WMS service 14 Southend – Sutton Cemetery (the infrequent extension to Shopland Corner being abandoned) and also former EHM/Blue Bus local routes A, B & C (*see 1928 listing*). SCT also acquired the Southend – Westcliff portion of the Borough circular service to Eastwood.

Also on 1 January 1933 the Wickford service of Benfleet & District was reduced to a Monday only market day service. Their sage green and cream double-deckers continued to run half-hourly between Benfleet and Southend co-ordinated with WMS to provide a 15 minute service. However, there was no inter-availability of return tickets. A fine new garage was built at Victoria House Corner, London Road, Hadleigh to house the fleet (*see Chapter Nine*). The Benfleet & District operations were developing into a very profitable operation with many duplicate vehicles being needed this reflecting the growth of population in the area as houses replaced the fields. Following the Bridges departure from the WMS board from 14 March the Blue Buses business was wound up though the remaining letter designated services (E, F & G) continued unchanged. This was followed by the absorption and winding up of Rochford & District in May 1933.

On 5 May 1933 the Eastern National Omnibus Co. Ltd. (ENOC, see Chapter One) secured control of The Borough Services Ltd. and also their subsidiary Rayleigh Motor Services Ltd. These acquisitions were to have far reaching consequences. ENOC thus established their first base in Southend by taking over the small Borough garage at 49/51, London Road just a few yards away from the WMS premises at 33, London Road. The former Rayleigh MS Colchester to Southend service was incorporated into ENOC services 19/A. The other Borough routes which were within the WMS area were retained by Borough which became an ENOC subsidiary. This was necessary since ENOC was only allowed to work into Southend along the Eastwood Road. The Southend to Grays service was then numbered 70 and the local service between Leigh and Eastwood became 71 this being co-ordinated with WMS service G. Borough had also operated an express service from Enfield to Southend which they retained (see Chapter Three).

The other Rayleigh Motor Services routes between Rayleigh and Southend were transferred to WMS. This secured Tilling Group (see Chapter One) representation on the WMS board. Within two years, Tilling were able to purchase sufficient shares from the smaller WMS shareholders to eventually give Tilling effective control.

On Canvey Island, the main line route was extended about a third of a mile eastward from High Street/ Seaview Road along the newly made-up road to terminate at Leigh Beck Farm. At this time the Bridge family started to acquire the holdings of the individual shareholders of Canvey Motor Transport in order to gain eventual control.

Over at Leigh, Thundersley, Hadleigh & District started a new route to the Highlands Estate. Then on 28 December 1933 WMS obtained control of the business. The former THD services were given letter designations A and D, the letter A being re-used following the transfer of the earlier service A to SCT. WMS registered another company of the same name (THD) to administer the property (Oak Garage, London Road, Hadleigh) which WMS continued to use until 1951 (see Chapter Nine).

1934

New Years Day saw the opening of the new railway station at Belton Way, Leigh a quarter of a mile on the London side of the old station. A bus terminal was provided at the station entrance which meant that the previous scrambles by competing operators to board passengers emerging from the old station pathway by Leigh Church became a thing of the past.

WMS acquired the business of Eric Hart t/a Shoeburyness Motor Services from 3 January. WMS then formed a new subsidiary company, Shoeburyness Motor Services Ltd. to continue the operations. The SMS main route was incorporated into WMS service 5 whilst the summer service to Shoebury Common (Beach) became service 5B.

Events were also moving along on Canvey Island where the Bridge family had by the beginning of 1934 acquired about half of the share capital of the Canvey & District Motor Transport Co. Ltd. Then on 30 April they bought out the Williams Bus Service whose timings were incorporated into the C&DMT timetable. Construction of a new modern garage in Point Road, Leigh Beck was started (see Chapter Nine) and before the year end the last remaining shareholders in C&DMT were persuaded to sell their holdings to the Bridges.

In July WMS and Borough started a new joint service, formed from WMS service B and Borough 72 which ran from the new Leigh Station to Westcliff (Somerset Crescent) to serve new housing development. Each operator supplied one vehicle operating every 40 minutes to provide a combined 20 minute frequency.

During 1934 the WMS interests in North and East London underwent a dramatic change due to the formation of the London Passenger Transport Board. On 18 July service 2B was curtailed at Grays the onward section to East Ham being compulsorily purchased by the LPTB as this section ran in their newly established

Fig.2.21 (opposite) An interesting set of photographs has been deposited at the Essex Record Office showing AEC Regent JN5457 involved in an accident in Pall Mall, Leigh in 1936. No less a personage than Harold Macmillan appears to be studying the small black (or red?) plate with the legend F 09 in white characters on the waistband. This is thought to be either a running number or possibly a garage parking area indication. The letter F could stand for Fairfax Drive. Post-war vehicles do not appear to have been so equipped. Fig.2.26 shows a vehicle on service 8 carrying number 32. *ERO*

Fig.2.20 *JN2767 is a Park Royal bodied AEC Regent new in 1933, seen here in pristine condition when just a few months old at Grays. Its original owner, Borough Services Ltd. had become an ENOC subsidiary on 5 May 1933 when the vehicle was numbered 3444. Borough continued to run their service 70 between Grays and Southend jointly with WMS service 2, until the subsidiary was wound up in 1940, the service then being continued by ENOC.   JFH*

Fig.2.22 The original frontage to the WMS London Road garage in Southend was at 33/35. When the garage was expanded, a new entrance was opened at 17/21, London Road with the exit now at 33/35. In this view 1939 Bristol K5G/ECW BHJ533, by then 1273 in ENOC ownership, is exiting at 33/5. The Jackamans furniture store which featured on many bus advertising panels is seen next door separating the two garage frontages.   AGOC

Fig.2.23   Typical of the WMS vehicles delivered under Tilling control was JN7499, a Bristol JO5G with ECW bodywork. Note the ornate upper-case style 'WESTCLIFF' fleet-name. ECW/BAC

area. Negotiations were started with City Motor Omnibus Co. Ltd. for the sale of the Southend – Wood Green Pullman service 16.

By September the WMS Head Office had been transferred from Pier Hill to the Victoria Arcade at 18/20, Victoria Avenue. By December the Tilling Group *(see Chapter One)* had acquired sufficient shares to take control of WMS. WMS was kept as a separate unit in Essex since there was no railway financial interest involved as was the case with its neighbour ENOC.

1935

Early in the year the WMS share in the Wood Green to Southend service was sold to the City Motor Omnibus Co. Ltd. who then became the sole operators on the route from 12 January. Under Tilling control a start was

made to wind up the WMS subsidiary companies. The assets of Shoeburyness Motor Services and Thundersley, Hadleigh & District were taken over by WMS on 31 July 1935 followed by those of Rayleigh Motor Services on 6 May 1936. The licences were transferred shortly afterwards and the companies duly wound up.

On 2 July 1935 for the first time a representative of the Tilling Group was present at a Southend Borough Council Transport Committee meeting to discuss transport services in the borough. This was the start of a process which took nearly twenty years before achieving the desired result – effective co-ordination of bus services in the borough. *Chapter Four* covers these negotiations in full thus only brief progress summaries are noted here at the beginning of each year under the heading *SJS (Southend Joint Services)*.

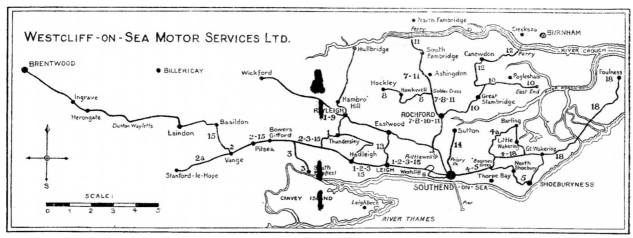

1927

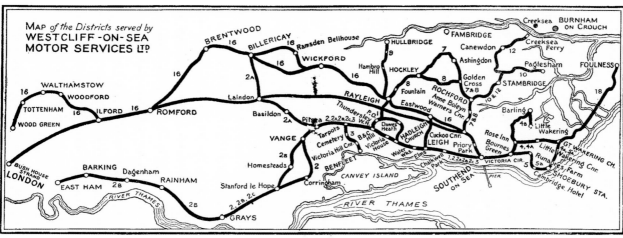

1932

Fig.2.24 *WMS bus route maps for 1927* **(top)** *and 1932* **(centre)** *illustrate service developments to the west. In 1927 service 2A only reached as far as Stanford-le-Hope whilst Brentwood was only served on Thursdays by the 15. Contrast this with the 1932 map which shows Pullman service 16 to Wood Green as well as the express service to London (Bush House) via the Arterial Road. Service 2A is shown running to Billericay. Although the 2C to Grays is shown, this number never appeared in the timetable. The later WMS bus maps for 1934* **(lower)**, *1938* **(overleaf upper)**, *and 1939* **(overleaf lower)** *show the growth of the network. Developments to the Romford service 2A should be noted.*

1934

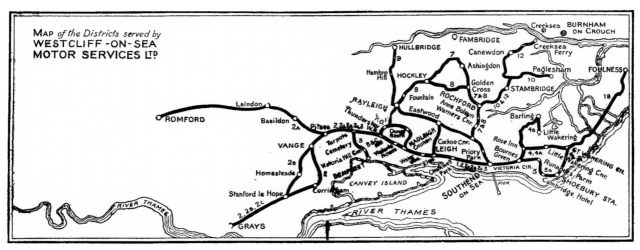

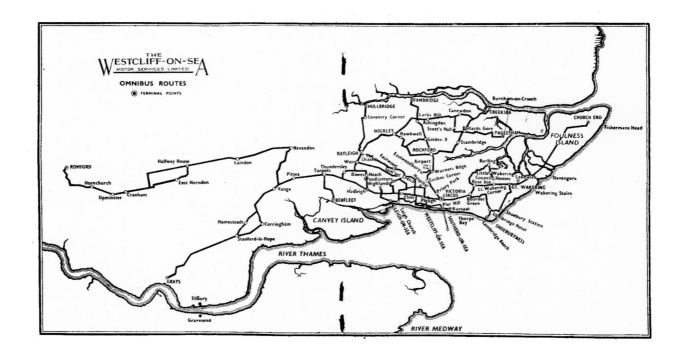

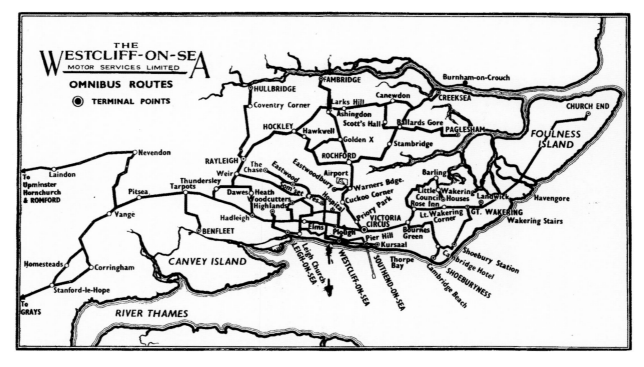

Timetable maps for 1938 (upper) and 1939 (lower)

1936

SJS   Discussions in progress

AEC Regent JN5457 was involved in an accident in Leigh in 1936 and the event was recorded in an interesting set of photographs which was later deposited at the Essex Record Office. This has revealed an intriguing vehicle identification system which still remains a mystery *(see Fig.2.21).*

1937

SJS   Merger between SCT and Tillings rejected. No further proposals.

Certain revised services were introduced from 31 March 1937. There was a combined timetable for services 7 and 8 resulting from the transfer of the licences of Rayleigh Motor Services to WMS. New service 6B (Westcliff – Prittlewell – Rayleigh) was introduced. Service 9 journeys between Rayleigh and Hullbridge were transferred to service E, and a new service 9 (Southend – Eastwoodbury, Avro Road) started.

The Head Office was moved again on 2 September 1937 from Victoria Arcade to 17/21, London Road following an extension and expansion of the old WMS garage at 33/35, London Road *(see Chapter Nine)*.

1938

Former THD service D (Hadleigh – Leigh) was merged with services A & F from 5 October.

An interesting element of the monthly financial returns recorded is a payment for a 'Steamer Emergency Service' *(see page 222)*. This took place in the event of a paddle-steamer failure at Southend Pier when coaches would transport stranded passengers to London (Aldgate).

Fig.2.25 *The very first new AEC Regent purchased by WMS was JN2796 delivered in 1933. It had Park Royal body complete with roof number box and running plate (?) holder beneath the front nearside window. The most attractive livery carried has three areas of cream and the fleet-name carried was the underlined capital letter version. The photo was taken outside the newly opened Leigh Station and the bus is working service A, acquired from Thundersley, Hadleigh & District, later to be re-numbered to 20A. EBEG*

1939

SJS *Traffic Commissioners consider 1932 Agreement not in public interest.*

Under Tilling control the WMS portfolio of bus services had stabilised. For lists of services operated during this period please refer to *Chapter Seven*, including that from the timetable dated 24 May 1939, just before the outbreak of hostilities destroyed the established pattern (*see Chapter Seven: Tenth Series*).

After war was declared Southend was designated an 'evacuation area'. Many people moved out voluntarily fearful of bombing raids on nearby military establishments (Foulness and Shoeburyness) and others left because jobs linked to tourism disappeared. As a consequence many services needed to be either withdrawn (e.g. 5B, 6A and 19) or curtailed. WMS thus had a surplus of buses which were loaned elsewhere (*see Chapter Five*). The SCT trams also suffered a marked decline in traffic.

1940

SJS *The 1932 Agreement was terminated.*

In 1940 WMS acquired the licences of Multiways Ltd. which included several coastal express services details of which are included in *Chapter Three*. The 1932 east-west territorial agreement was terminated from 5 July 1940. The need for Borough Services Ltd. to continue as a separate ENOC subsidiary ended. From 30 October 1940 their two local Leigh services (71/2) were continued by WMS alone whilst service 70 to Grays was transferred to ENOC running out of the Borough garage at 49, London Road. Shortly afterwards on 2 August Borough Services Ltd. was voluntarily liquidated.

An indication of the fall in passenger numbers during the war may be judged from the following WMS figures:

Year	1937	1940	1947
Revenue (£000)	181	139.5	340
Mileage (000's)	4325	2950	4525
Passengers (m)	17.1	11.85	25.8

1941

SJS *After an air raid on Plymouth, the Ministry of War Transport encouraged adjacent operators to pool resources.*

1942

SJS *Southend Standard newspaper gave significant coverage to the co-ordination progress.*

On 19 August 1942 the remaining lettered services, some of which dated back to the days of Edwards Hall Motors were given service numbers as follows :

A/F	20A/F
E	22
B	21
G	23
C	24

> SAVE PETROL
> SAVE RUBBER
> ● PASSENGERS CAN HELP BY USING
> ONLY *RECOGNISED* 'BUS STOPS

The Southend Corporation tramway system finally closed on 8 April 1942 and was replaced by cross-town municipal buses from Southchurch to Leigh.

The Ministry of War Transport directed that all late evening and Sunday morning journeys would cease to operate from 16 November. Services 5B, 6A, 19 and 24 were completely suspended for the duration of the war.

Fig.2.26 *This is one of a series of views showing AEC Regent/Weymann JN3715 close to a bomb crater in Rochford Road near to the junction with Oaken Grange Drive whilst on service 8 on 1 November 1940. In one of the close-up views of the nearside running number 32 is displayed (see also Fig.4.6).* ERO

1943

SJS   Negotiations were completed, the Joint Committee formed and area and pooling agreements made. It was agreed that ENOC and WMS were to lease the trolley equipment.

1944

SJS   Other operators were consulted.

1945

SJS   Other operators raise objections.

1946

SJS   An Agreement was signed, starting date fixed, extended powers applied for, public meeting held, and objections and writ issued by the City Coach Company. Further discussions followed.

The first meeting of the Southend Joint Transport Committee (SJTC) which included representatives from both WMS and SCT took place on 21 March 1946. This committee continued to function and was able to consider joint working arrangements that did not impinge upon the 'other operators' in the area that were not part of the proposed Agreement.

1947

SJS   The whole co-ordination scheme was placed in abeyance

On 10 February the Excursions and Tours licences of Canvey Motor Transport were passed to Supreme Coaches which left the Benfleet/Canvey companies solely as bus operators.

On 1 July the sea front services re-commenced. Service 6A was re-numbered 19A and a combined timetable for the 19/19A introduced. Albeit a rather limited affair the first joint service, arranged by the SJTC started on 1 October when the municipal Leigh to Thorpe Bay services were linked with WMS service 20A as joint services 25A/25B. WMS was very much the junior partner.

The passing of the Transport Act, 1947 set up the British Transport Commission to oversee a nationalised transport industry.

1948

A defining event occurred this year. WMS came under state ownership when Thomas Tilling Ltd. sold out voluntarily to the British Transport Commission (*see also Chapter One*).

Fig.2.27 *Tilling-Stevens/Park Royal JN2681 working service 3 to Benfleet loads up outside the competitor's headquarters at Victoria Arcade in this early 1930s view. Note 'BENFLEET for Canvey Island' on the destination blind indicating the need for passengers to walk from the War Memorial terminus of this route and across the level crossing to the terminal point for the Canvey & District at the creek.   VCJ*

Fig.2.28 *14 (KEV534) a 1945 Brush utility bodied Daimler CWA6 is seen with a full load of passengers at Victoria Circus. In the background a SCT trolleybus loads for Westcliff where it will pass Hamlet Court Road, advertised on the Daimler as containing 'the centre of fashion', which in the 1950s was true of this then prestigious shopping street. No.14 was taken into WMS stock (along with the Company) then passing with WMS to ENOC in 1955 finally being withdrawn in 1956.   VCJ*

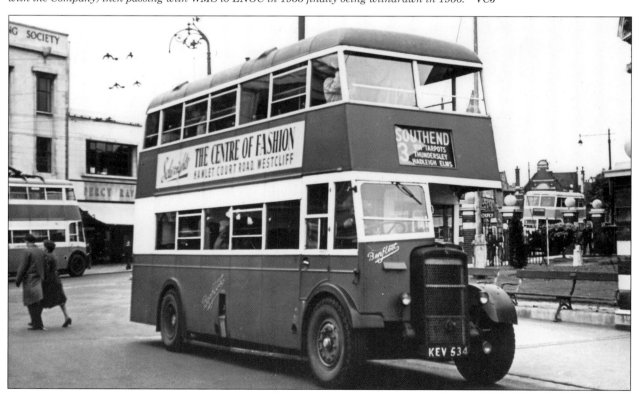

Fig.2.29 *The predecessors of WMS routes 26 and 26A, the 1 and 1A and indeed the Canvey operators earliest un-numbered services merit a book to themselves even given the discussion in 'The Bridge Family and its Buses'. This monster is one of a number of similar six-wheelers that replaced the motley collection of 14-20 seaters when the Road Traffic Act came into force, even in off-shore Canvey! HF5341 is a Karrier WL6 with 66-seat Hall Lewis body new to Wallasey Corporation Motors as their number 16 and whose destination display arrangement it retains. It is seen at Canvey sea-front on service 1A. PJSA*

Fig.2.30 *As the registration number indicates, AEC Regent HF7435 had also been new to Wallasey Corporation Motors, in this case in 1931 twenty years before this photograph was taken. C&D bought it in 1938. Re-bodied by Northern Coachbuilders in 1944, it survived long enough with WMS to be taken into the ENOC fleet and numbered 1156. This example is seen at the South Benfleet (Canvey Bridge) terminus. VCJ*

Fig.2.31   *The number 26 is the key to this photo. This remarkable survivor, an open-staircase Dodson bodied TD1 GN184 is loading on what would become service 26. But most remarkable is its history. GN184 was new to the Westminster Omnibus Co. Ltd. of London N.7 as their WR16. As a 'pirate' operator, one of the routes worked was the **26D** from Ilford to Chigwell Row, points which have special significance for both authors though for different reasons. GN184 passed to London Transport in July 1934 becoming TD95. Withdrawn in 1939, C&D bought it as their No.**26** though it lasted only until 1943. In this wartime view (note masked headlamps) it is seen at the ferry terminus in snow and the temperature may be judged by the driver's greatcoat and the misted spheres of condensed breath on the upstairs windows. No doubt an east wind is pressing home the point straight up the open staircase to the discomfort of both crew and passengers alike on this bleak day.   PJSA*

Fig.2.32   *Two classic Canvey & District buses wait at Benfleet terminus. Both buses date from 1933. No. 3 (JN2683) is a Tilling-Stevens with Park Royal body (see Fig.2.19 for a view of it new) and No.7 (WN4761) an AEC Regent. This started life with South Wales Transport, later gaining a replacement utlility NCB body in 1944/5. Both buses passed to WMS and remarkably the Regent survived until 1954 though was not taken over by ENOC.   DWKJ*

1949

A scheme of co-ordination between ENOC and Luton Corporation Transport came into effect on 2 January with the formation of Luton & District Transport.

Southend Corporation started to use route numbers from 1949, these commencing at 51 so as to avoid clashes with WMS and ENOC. Another joint working agreement involving the Southend – Shoeburyness corridor (WMS service 5, SCT service 5A) was introduced from 7 December.

1950

SJS   The Joint Committee continued to meet.

In 1950, Henry Ritchie Bridge felt it was now time to take retirement and preliminary discussion took place with WMS regarding the sale of his business.

1951

SJS   Discussions recommenced.

In 1951 the Bridge Benfleet and Canvey operations were sold to the British Transport Commission who immediately placed them with WMS. Thus from 2 March 1951 service 3 became every 15 minutes incorporating the Benfleet timings, whilst the Monday only market day service to Wickford became service 27. The

Fig.2.33 *Laindon, Station Approach is the location of this view showing former City G3 (HVW214) on service 260 to Ongar via Brentwood, very much a step down from its former 'main road' work. The vehicle is one of the five famous Leyland Gnu TEC2 with Duple full front coachwork dating from 1939 that City owned. As can be seen City fleet-numbers were retained into the WMS era.   FC*

Fig.2.34 *This appears to be an official photo taken at the Bata Shoe factory in East Tilbury. The line-up of vehicles would seem to have been especially rostered replacing the antique selection that WMS usually employed on this contract work. The buses are a Bristol K5G/ECW CJN324 and three utility Daimler CWA6s (FOP459, KHK863 and KEV535) and their destinations are (left to right) South Benfleet, Corringham and Pitsea (the terminus of service 80).   PJSA*

main line operation on Canvey became service 26 with the additional summer only service becoming 26A.

In 1933 the London Passenger Transport Board had been formed to operate all bus services within the newly formed London Passenger Transport Area. Unfortunately the area boundary passed right through the centre of Grays. All services to the east had been retained by ENOC but those to the west passed to London Transport. Cross-town links were therefore completely lost. After the formation of the BTC it was decided to restore through services across the centre of Grays, so the ENOC local services and the Argent Street garage passed to London Transport, this all taking place on 30 September 1951. Although the longer distance services were not affected some associated changes became necessary. Thus ENOC service 80 (Pitsea – Bata Shoe Factory) and 84 (Grays – Benfleet) were transferred to WMS. The former retained its number whilst the latter was incorporated into service 2B.

1952

SJS   The abandonment of trolleybuses approved

There had been several significant developments involving ENOC since the war. On 2 January 1949 a co-ordination scheme had been brought into effect in Luton which had considerably benefited both operators. Then exactly one year later on 1 January 1950 Hicks Bros. sold their business to the British Transport Commission which placed it under ENOC control. This was followed by the sale of the City Coach Company *(see Chapter One)* to the BTC on 17 February 1952 with WMS initially assuming responsibility for the operation. It will be recalled that City had issued a writ against the 1946 Co-ordination Agreement so now with BTC ownership one of the major obstacles to the scheme was overcome.

As part of a scheme to rationalise the areas served by the ex-Tilling companies it was decided that the Midland section of ENOC *(see Chapter One)* should be transferred to United Counties effective from 1 May 1952. As compensation for the loss of half its area, control of WMS passed to ENOC as from 18 May. It is interesting to compare the respective sizes of the two fleets when they were re-numbered. ENOC contributed 239 vehicles against WMS's 277. Furthermore in 1953 WMS carried 50.4 million passengers compared to the ENOC figure of only 41.5 million this reflecting the latter operators more rural area. Thus WMS was in no way the minor partner in the merger.

On 1 June 1952 the very last WMS timetable appeared, but with a new cover design *(see Chapter Seven)*. It still showed 17/21, London Road, Southend as the Head Office and included the acquired City services (which lacked numbers). The 1 June 1952 ENOC timetable included the Hicks Bros. of Braintree services which were prefixed by the letter 'H' (H10 – H52) although these numbers were not displayed on the vehicles.

1953

SJS   The Southend Committee was renamed, a reduced co-ordination area agreed, and a final plan approved by Mayor of Southend's casting vote. The Agreement was thus sealed.

The first issue of the combined ENOC/WMS timetable showing New Writtle Street, Chelmsford as the Head Office for both companies appeared on 4 January 1953. The WMS services were prefixed with a 'W' (W1 – W27 & W80) whilst the former City services had by then been allocated ENOC service numbers 251 – 261. The Hicks Bros. services had also been numbered into a new ENOC series by the addition of 300 to their original numbers (310-352). The Hicks and WMS services were also shown on the new style folded ENOC map affixed to the inside rear cover *(see Fig.2.37)*.

Although ENOC had assumed control of WMS in May 1952 in the summer 1953 issue of the *ABC Coach & Bus Guide* the two operators were still afforded separate entries by the publishers. The WMS bus and coach services were listed and a specially drawn map of the network was included. As far as the author is aware this is the only WMS map ever published that includes the former City Coach Company network. However, closer inspection reveals a couple of interesting errors *(see Fig.2.35)*. It can be seen that Canvey is not shown as an island and also that services 3 and 26 are linked at South Benfleet which was not the case passengers still being required to cross the level crossing on foot.

WMS inaugurated their first service to the new and rapidly expanding Basildon New Town on 23 August 1953 when the former service number 84 was revived to operate between Grays and Basildon (Whitmore Way) via Pitsea *(see Fig.2.39)*.

1954

SJS   New Agreement dated 1 January 1954, Appointed Day agreed, apportionment of services agreed, linking of services postponed.

Two further town services were started by WMS on 14 February these being W44 (Pitsea – Basildon, Whitmore Way, Quendon Road) and 262 (Bishops Hall Estate – Brentwood – Three Arch Estate). The final new bus services introduced by WMS were the 13 (Southend – Hullbridge) and 14 (Southend – Romford via Arterial Road) which both commenced on 31 May *(see Fig.2.39)*.

By this time, vehicles were being repainted into the standard ENOC green and cream livery but with City, Hicks or 'Westcliff-on-Sea' fleetnames and their own series fleet-numbers (where applicable). It was now time to amalgamate the three fleets into a single system with a unifying ENOC fleet re-numbering taking place on 18 July 1954.

Shortly afterwards the last stumbling block to the introduction of the long awaited Co-ordination Scheme was removed on 28 October 1954 when the Southend Corporation trolleybus system closed.

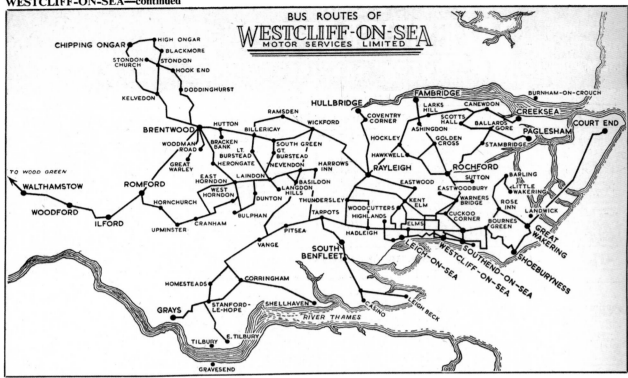

Fig.2.35 *The summer 1953 ABC Coach & Bus Guide included as usual a separate entry for WMS. Uniquely the 1953 map showed, in addition to WMS services, the City Coach Company route network that had just been acquired. This was the only map in any WMS publicity to do so. Notice that Canvey has been mistakenly incorporated into the mainland and a through bus link shown.*

Fig.2.36 *In this view taken on 2 August 1951, Bristol K5G/ECW DHJ609 is seen on service W5. Although the 'W' designation appeared in the combined EN/WMS timetables it was not shown thus on the vehicles where latterly the WMS service number was enclosed within a square.   VCJ*

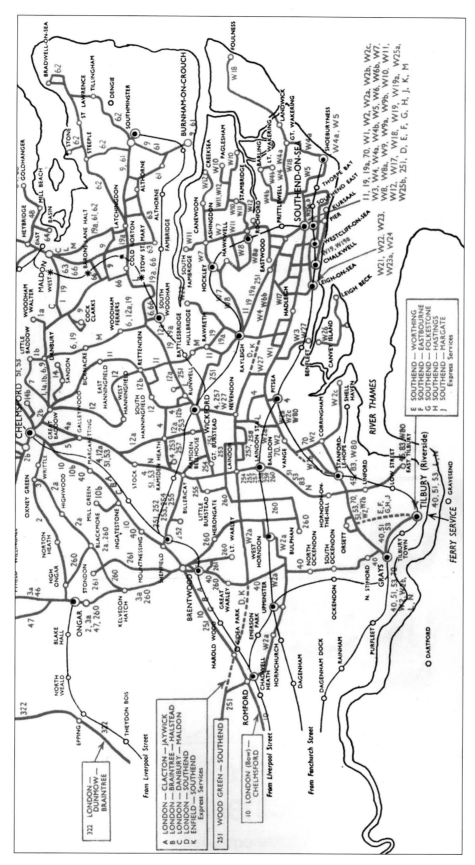

Fig.2.37 *This is the route map from the ENOC 4 January 1953 timetable. WMS services are prefixed by 'W' and former City Coach Company services are numbered 251-261. Also shown is former Hicks Bros. of Braintree service 322.*

1955

The newly established Southend & District Joint Services area covered about 96 square miles, being bounded by the River Crouch, Rettendon (Turnpike Corner), Benfleet (Tarpots Corner) and Canvey Island. The area covered was smaller than that originally proposed in 1946 presumably so as not to include any of the new Basildon New Town area, for further details *see Chapter Four*. The scheme came into effect on Sunday 2 January 1955 the day after the assets of WMS were transferred to ENOC. Under the terms of the arrangement 63% of the mileage was to be operated by ENOC and 37% by Southend Corporation. The only bus operation within the area which was not part of the co-ordination agreement was the Pitsea Station – Hadleigh Church commuter route 6 operated by Campbells of Pitsea.

It must be remembered that the Co-ordination Scheme at its outset involved WMS, ENOC and SCT and hence all three operators' names appeared on the cover of the first S&D timetable booklet. This was the case since the road service licences were at this time still in the name of WMS. Individual applications to transfer the myriad of licences from WMS to ENOC were submitted on 12 January 1955 the majority being granted in *Notices & Proceedings* issue no. 641 some months later (*see also Fig.2.39*).

There were two clashes of service numbers in Southend between long distance ENOC service 11 (Chelmsford – Southend) and WMS 11 (Southend – South Fambridge) and between ENOC 19/A (Clacton – Southend) and WMS 19/A (Kursaal – Leigh, summer only) and supplementary service 19A (Westborough Road – Chalkwell Station). With the introduction of the second Southend & District Joint Services timetable dated 28 May W11 was re-numbered 13A (*see Fig.1.8*) whilst the sea-front services were re-cast as 67/67A & 68/68A and the local Chalkwell service became 65.

A start was then made on the re-numbering of all the ENOC services into a single series based on their geographical location. This had become necessary because of the general haphazard development of new services over the years and also because the WMS services that extended beyond the area boundary duplicated ENOC service numbers elsewhere in Essex. The services affected were:-

2/2B	Southend – Grays
2A	Southend – Romford
2C	Southend – Shellhaven
14	Southend – Romford
27	Benfleet – Wickford
44	Pitsea – Basildon
80	Pitsea – East Tilbury
84	Basildon – Grays

Once underway the service re-numbering process was performed on a garage basis at approximately weekly intervals. Thus on 21 August 1955 under the Basildon scheme W44, W80 and W84 became ENOC 244, 245 and 248. The Chelmsford scheme (18 September) saw conflicting services 2 (Chelmsford – Ongar), 2A, 2B and 14 re-numbered 32, 32A, 42 and 54 respectively. At Colchester (2 October) ENOC 27 (Colchester – Wormingford) was re-numbered 82, whilst the former WMS number 84 was used for a new ENOC service between Colchester and Langham. In the Southend area (25 September) ENOC 70 (the old Borough service number) was re-numbered 2 (thus regaining the former WMS number), whilst service 27 continued with its original number the Colchester duplication soon to be removed.

Consequently the third Southend & District timetable published on 25 September listed ENOC and SCT only. The WMS bus operations had come to an end. However, over many years WMS had built up an extensive range of very popular tours and coastal express services which were held in considerable esteem by the public. It therefore came as no surprise that the 'Westcliff-on-Sea' name continued to be used to market these activities and as a Southend based fleet-name for a few more years.

Southend area bus timetables also appeared in the *Southend Standard Time & Tide Table Guide* which was published monthly. It is interesting to note that when the Co-ordination Area was originally proposed, since it was to have extended as far as Vange, the local bus services of Campbells of Pitsea were all included. These ceased to appear after 1946 when the scheme was placed in abeyance. Although Campbells service 6 (Pitsea Station – Hadleigh Church) did enter the revised 1954 Co-ordination Area its timetable was never included in either the Southend Joint Services or *Southend Standard* booklets. However, after ENOC acquired Campbells bus services on 19 February 1956 a timetable of the replacement ENOC service 235 then appeared in both publications.

The Bridge family continued to run Supreme Coaches (later Supreme Travel) and also Abridge (A. Bridge) Enterprises which continued to compete with ENOC in the local excursions market for many years.

1961

It was announced at the end of 1961 that the 'Westcliff-on-Sea' name would no longer be used in the forthcoming season. This coincided with the numbering of ENOC express services into a new 'X' series from Easter 1962 (*see Chapter Three*).

1962

A new underpass beneath the railway at Benfleet Station was opened on 29 January 1962 replacing the notorious level crossing which had precluded through operation of buses. After a short strike on Saturday 3 February through operation commenced and for the first time Canvey Island was connected by bus to the mainland and to the rest of the ENOC network (*see Fig.2.39*). Also from this date SCT vehicles worked on to the island.

The new through services (operating garages in parentheses) were:

3   Canvey (Leigh Beck) – Southend via Tarpots (CY, HH, SCT)
3A   Canvey (Leigh Beck) – Southend via Essex Way   (CY, HH, SCT)
26   Canvey (Point Road, EN Depot) – Basildon (CY)

1966

Pier Hill Coach Station, for many years the Head Office of WMS and the hub of the express coach services network, was last used during the 1966 season. It was sold in 1967 and the area has now been completely redeveloped *(see also Chapters Three and Nine)*. Please refer to *Chapters Five and Nine* for details of the fate of the WMS garages in the area.

1977

Most appropriately, the very last item to report is that the Westcliff-on-Sea Motor Services Ltd. (company number 135399) was finally dissolved on 4 November 1977. But this was not the end..........

1985 onwards

In November 1985 a new company (no. 01961457) was registered in the name of 'The Westcliff-on-Sea Motor Services Ltd.' to act as the 'vehicle' for the buyout of the Eastern National Omnibus Co. Ltd. by its management. This was as part of the privatisation process of the National Bus Company (successor to British Transport Commission and Transport Holding Company). The company name was changed in February 1987 to Eastern National Ltd. then in December 1995 to Essex Buses Ltd. and finally in January 2003 to First Essex Buses Ltd. the company that still operates over much of Essex and is thus the successor to the original WMS.

Fig.2.38a   *This photo also shows a 5, in this case worked by a bus doing its best to look like a the standard post-war ECW bodied Bristol shown in Fig.2.36. The chassis of JN4745 is fifteen years older than the K5G in Fig.2.36 though the body was only a few years old when this photo was taken outside Victoria Station. Note the ENOC Bristol KSW5G/ECW working the 11 to Chelmsford and the SCT trolleybus.   PJSA*

Fig.2.38b   *WMS vehicles continued to operate in Southend for many years though in green and cream livery and bearing ENOC fleet-names. This view shows CHJ255, a Bristol K6B with ECW bodywork in Southchurch Road working service 62 on 31 July 1960. This was an SCT route before the joint services agreement came into force, but now most appropriately a former WMS bus is running on it to Westcliff.   GM*

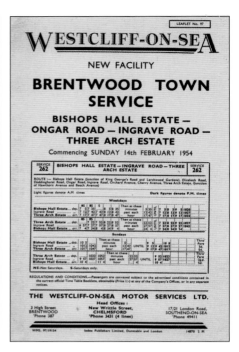

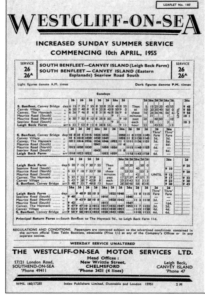

Fig.2.39 *A selection of service leaflets from later years.*

Service 84   This service was the first venture by WMS into Basildon New Town. Basildon took many years to construct and buses ran to new areas as the houses were finished and people moved in, sometimes along unfinished roads.

Service W44   This became the Basildon 'main line' service eventually being extended to the town centre on 4 May 1958.

Service 262   Brentwood was also expanding with new council estates and these gave rise to the need for a new town service. It linked the two estates via the town centre and was numbered on from the City series.

Service 13   The last new services to be introduced by WMS were on 31 May 1954, one year before the start of the Southend Coordination Scheme.

Services 26/A   This announces increases to the Sunday service. But just look at the date, 10 April 1955. By now WMS was fully owned by ENOC and the services run by ENOC, but they were still licensed to WMS, hence the leaflet heading.

Southend & District   The introduction of through services between Canvey and the English mainland were at last possible from 29 January 1962, to Southend by 3 and Basildon by 26.

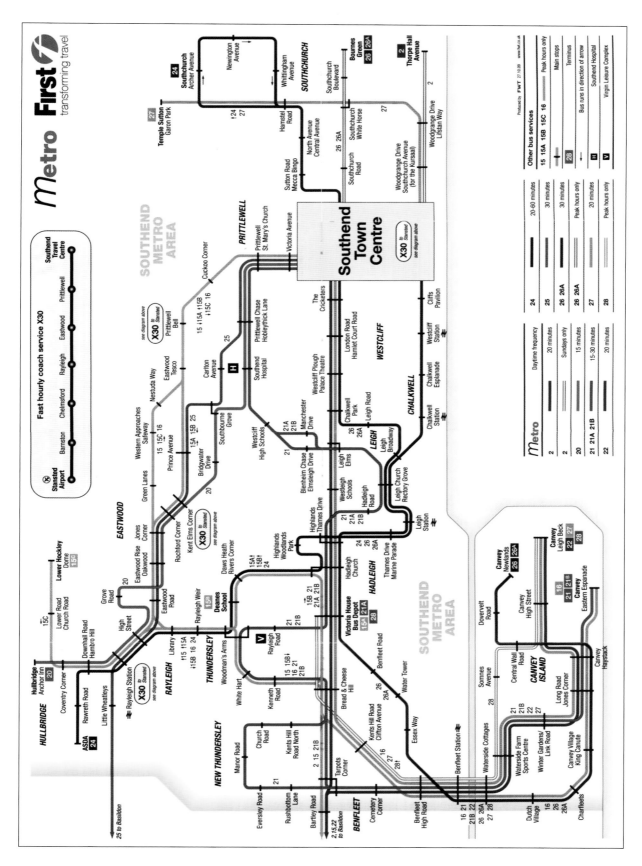

Fig.2.40 *The 2010 First Essex map of their Southend area services. Service 2 still runs along the London Road and Canvey is still served by the 26 and 27. The tube style diagrammatic layout is perhaps intended to make the high proportion of former Londoners who live in the area feel at home and more positive towards using bus services.*

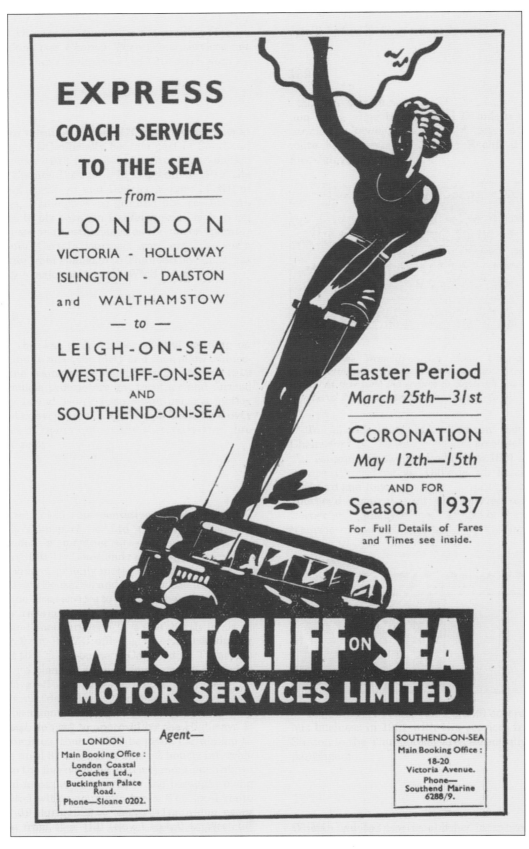

Fig.3.1 *This wonderful art-deco style artwork is not perhaps our first idea of WMS in the thirties, but it indicates a fashion conscious modern company, very aware of the importance of publicity. And, yes, the glamorous girl is water-skiing using a WMS coach as her surf-board!   AGOC*

Chapter Three
Coach Services and Tours

EXPRESS COACH SERVICES

This section covers those express coach services that have been operated by WMS where seats needed to be booked in advance.

The Westcliff-on-Sea Motor Char-a-banc Co. Ltd. started a daily service around 1921 of Royal Red Motor Coaches between Walthamstow (James Powell Livery Stable, Hoe Street) and Southend (Pier Hill) via Leytonstone, Wanstead and Forest Gate with somewhat expensive fares for the time set at 6/- (30p) single and 10/- (50p) return. Holmes & Smith used their old jobmaster connections to organise a chain of booking agencies and picking up points. They linked with Lambs Ltd. with branches at Walthamstow and Wood Green and also with Powells which served as their terminal point.

Westcliff-on-Sea Motor Char-a-banc Co., Ltd.,
PIER HILL, SOUTHEND-ON-SEA.   Phone 47 Southend.

A

Daily Service
OF THE

ROYAL RED MOTOR COACHES
WILL BE RUN BETWEEN

Walthamstow, Leytonstone, Wanstead & Forest Gate
AND
WESTCLIFF-ON-SEA and SOUTHEND-ON-SEA,

Leaving James Powell Livery Stable at Hoe Street Station at 8.30 a.m.; Leytonstone Station, 8.40 a.m.; Wanstead 8.50 a.m. and Forest Gate 9 a.m.

RETURNING FROM SOUTHEND-ON-SEA AT 6.30 P.M.

Chars-a-Banc may be booked for Private Parties, Race Meetings, and Tours of all descriptions. Terms on application.

Fares: Single, **6/-**   Return, **10/-**

Luggage can be sent by Carter Paterson & Co., who deliver in Southend and District.

L. Washburn, Printer. 25 & 27 Queens Rd., Southend-on-Sea.

In 1923 WMS took over the Southend Char-a-banc Company based at 330, London Road, Southend. This concern traded as the Cream Cars running between Leytonstone (Green Man Garage) and Westcliff-on-Sea (Queens Hotel). Later their departure point had been from their local premises at 744, High Road, Leytonstone

(opposite Bearman's Furnishing Department). There were picking up points at Wanstead, Manor Park and Ilford, the fares charged were 5/- (25p) single and 8/- (40p) return.

By the end of 1924 the WMS Walthamstow terminal had become Lambs Garage in Hoe Street. At this time their coach services had become very popular since the 'cockney paradise' of Southend-on-Sea was a great attraction. It thus became necessary to find some accommodation for the increasing number of vehicles needed to be kept in the area. So in 1924 the business of Ardley Bros. of Dowsett Road, Tottenham was acquired. Their address was sometimes given as Reform Row but the premises were the same. Although continuing to operate in the Ardley name, the Tottenham vehicles were painted in the rich scarlet livery of the WMS fleet. The garage premises also provided a base for WMS char-a-bancs operating the pioneering programme of five- and twelve-day all-inclusive tours from Southend and London.

The A127 Southend Arterial Road was opened by HRH Duke of Gloucester (then Prince Henry) on 25 March 1925. Coach operators were not slow to take advantage of this new direct road. WMS started a daily express service from Southend via the A127 to Bush House, Aldwych, London where facilities for passengers were handled by Globe Travel with whom WMS had an agency for its range of extended tours.

During 1927 WMS reorganised its East London booking agencies. An interest in Henderson Hire Services Ltd. of Walthamstow was acquired. Hendersons had been incorporated in August 1927, having taken over the car hire part of their neighbour, Lambs Ltd. with premises opposite Hoe Street Station, which was the terminal point of the Southend express service. This provided WMS with a valuable booking office in Selborne Road and also garage premises in nearby Hoe Street.

In April 1928 an express service of 'De Luxe All-Weather Safety Coaches' was started running from Wood Green (High Road), picking up at Harringay and Palmers Green and then driving through the country via Chingford, Chigwell Row, Romford and Laindon to set down in Leigh, Westcliff and Southend. There were two departures per day. The terminal point in the High Road at Wood Green was Lambs Ltd. The fares were now set at just half the earlier levels mentioned (see Fig.3.5a). This service was supplemented from 18 June 1928 by a hourly service of Pullman Saloon Coaches (see Fig.5.79), though this was eventually sold to the City Motor Omnibus Co. Ltd. For further details see Chapter Two.

A more direct twice-daily service of Pullman Saloon Coaches was inaugurated between London (Kings Cross) and Southend via Islington, Tottenham, Walthamstow, Romford, Wickford and Rayleigh on 25 June 1928. Although the publicity indicated that the service started from Kings Cross, the actual terminal point was at Bensons Travel Agency, Upper Street, Islington *(see 1929 Fig.3.5b)*. There were two return journeys per day, which was increased to three the following year.

An interesting development took place in May 1929 in far away Hampshire but which was nevertheless to have far reaching effects on the WMS story. Orange Luxury Coaches (Portsmouth) Ltd was incorporated with Sidney H. Carr as Chairman and directors Frank Monkman, Keith Davies and Sydney A. Smith. The last named person was also Chairman of the board of WMS. This explains why the registered office of the Portsmouth company (which dealt with coach bookings from Hampshire) was at Pier Hill, Southend. This liaison between WMS and Orange opened a new era of co-operation notably the sharing of the Orange Coach Station in Lordship Lane, Wood Green *(see Chapter Two)*.

By June 1929 (the precise start date is not known) another twice daily express service to central London was in operation running this time to Aldgate and Victoria, terminating at the London Coastal Coaches departure station at 1a, Lupus Street, Pimlico. The coaches travelled by way of Shoreditch, Stratford and Romford *(see opposite)*.

WMS were clearly sufficiently encouraged by the successful rapid expansion of their long distance coach services that in September 1929 they tried a somewhat surprising experiment. This was to start a long distance coach service to Cardiff using a fleet of six Tilling-Stevens with bodies featuring armchair seats and many other high quality fittings. The vehicles were based at

the Ardley Bros. premises in Tottenham and carried 'Welsh Pullman' as their fleet-name. Competition on this route proved to be particularly intense and the service ceased after only a short period. Future express services would be restricted to a much more local basis.

With the passing of the Road Traffic Act in 1930, express coach services and their picking up points were required to be licensed from 1 April 1931. Reference to a WMS leaflet published in August 1930 shows their express services running between Southend and London prior to licensing. The routes operating were to Victoria (Lupus Street) via Romford, Stratford and Aldgate; to Kings Cross (Bensons, Islington) and Bush House via Walthamstow and Dalston; to Walthamstow (Hendersons, Hoe Street), via Wanstead Flats, and to Wood Green (High Road) with onward connections to Enfield, Finchley and Barnet. The Bush House fares were 2/6 (12½p) single, 3/- (15p) day return and 4/6 (22½p) period return.

In 1931 the garage at Hoe Street, Walthamstow was purchased from Henderson Hire Services and then let to Messrs Holmes & Smith (Directors of WMS) at a rental of £550 per annum. WMS thus gave up their base in Walthamstow in favour of the above partnership. This was advertised in the *Walthamstow Guardian* for 27 March 1931 where it was announced that Holmes & Smith Ltd. had taken over the business of Henderson Hire Services Ltd. and would continue to trade from their premises opposite Hoe Street Station.

The travel agency part of the Henderson business passed to Walter Couch (Cream Coaches) based nearby at 86, St. Mary Road. It was also announced that an augmented private hire car service would be operated together with a fleet of the 'finest Sunshine Pullman Saloon Coaches in North London' from the Holmes & Smith garage at the rear of 188/210, Hoe Street.

In the 15 May 1931 *Walthamstow Guardian* a further

Fig 3.2 *Despite its poor quality this photograph is included because of the historical significance of the event recorded. The location of this view is Bush House, Aldwych, London and it is thought that this was the very first departure of the WMS express service to Cardiff, a service which lasted only a few weeks. Note the 'Welsh Pullman' fleet-names on HJ8588, a Tillings-Stevens with London Lorries body.   AGOC*

Fig. 3.3 *JN 841 was one of the six Dennis coaches introduced by Holmes & Smith's Black & White coaches in 1931. Note the fleet logo similar in style to the London Transport roundel. Their registered office was at Pier Hill, Southend.   JFH*

advertisement announced that Holmes & Smith Ltd. were to commence a programme of daily excursions and tours from Wednesday 20 May using the fleet-name 'Black & White Pullman Coaches (Holmes & Smith Ltd.)'. The destinations featured were Portsmouth & Southsea, Whitstable & Herne Bay and Margate, Broadstairs & Ramsgate (all for 7/6, 37½p, day return) and also Brighton (6/-, 30p). All services would depart from opposite Hoe Street station at 9.15 a.m. The initial fleet comprised six Dennis coaches. These were registered in Southend, the registered office being at

their premises at Pier Hill, Southend. The logo used was very similar to the London Transport roundel.

It is not known why this name had been chosen; it may possibly have originated from the livery of the hire cars. However, this new operation had no connection whatsoever with the established Leyton based Black & White Coaches. Thomas Henry Hoppe was trading as Classic Motor Coaches of Leyton from 1924 to 1930 when the partnership was dissolved. Hoppe then operated Black & White Coaches Ltd. which was re-named Black & White Coaches (Leyton) Ltd. in October 1932 presumably to avoid confusion with the newer concern.

Also in 1932 WMS amended their Victoria service to use the impressive new Victoria Coach Station in Buckingham Palace Road, which had opened on 10 March 1932. In Southend the coach services were now proving to be so popular that it became necessary to arrange additional loading facilities in Tylers Avenue to prevent the London passengers becoming mixed up with coach tour participants at Pier Hill.

Following the deteriorating relations on the WMS board (see Chapter Two) the Bridge family parted company with WMS and took over the business of Ardley Bros. of Tottenham on 17 July 1932. Since the presence of WMS vehicles and staff at Ardley's after acquisition by the Bridge family would have been somewhat uncomfortable for both parties a new base was urgently needed.

Mention has previously been made of the connection between Sydney Smith of WMS and Orange Luxury Coaches (Portsmouth) Ltd. To resolve the problem WMS therefore purchased a further interest in the Hampshire concern and then transferred all their London operations to the new Orange Luxury Coach Station at Wood Green which had recently opened in Lordship Lane on the site of a former wood yard. The Ardley Bros. operation was eventually acquired by the Ewer Group in 1952.

On 5 May 1933 ENOC secured control of The Borough Services Ltd. of 49, London Road, Southend. Borough held a licence for an excursion from Enfield Town to Southend which the new owners were successful in converting for the 1933 summer season as a July to September daily express service. It is most important to stress at this point that this was a completely different operation to the WMS express service that ran from Enfield Town to Southend via Bush Hill, Wood Green and Walthamstow (see Fig.3.4).

For the 1934 season (see Fig.3.5d) the WMS London express services then operating all departed from Tylers Avenue were given reference letters as follows:

A	VICTORIA (Coach Station) via Bethnal Green and Forest Gate
B	HOLLOWAY (Orange Coach Station) via Islington and Dalston
C	BARNET (High Street) via Finchley and Tottenham
D	ENFIELD (Cecil Road) via Wood Green and Walthamstow

After the Tilling Group had acquired control of WMS in December 1934 the economics and policies of the new owners together with the implications of the 1933 London Transport Act led to a great deal of tidying up of properties and commitments.

The changes under Tilling control soon started to occur apace. First, the WMS share in the Wood Green to Southend Pullman service ceased after 11 January 1935 leaving the City Motor Omnibus Co. Ltd as the sole operator (see Chapter One). In the 'roaring twenties' City had operated London route 536 in collaboration with Birch Bros, of Kentish Town. Birch had a similar sphere of operations to City. They operated a regular hourly express service (route BK) to Bedford and Kettering as well as a network of local bus services in Hertfordshire and Bedfordshire. As a consequence of the London Transport Act of 1933 Birch decided to concentrate on its bus and express services only. At a public sitting of the Metropolitan Traffic Area on 12 April 1935 Birch Bros. consequently withdrew their applications to renew their seven express licences to seaside resorts. An opportunity was then taken by the Traffic Commissioners to rationalise the pattern of picking up points for seaside express services from North London. Prior to the hearing, WMS had passed its two summer season Southend express services C (from Barnet) and D (from Enfield) to New Empress Saloons Ltd. (the coaching arm of the City Motor Omnibus Co. Ltd.). Without ever operating these two services New Empress then passed them on to Birch. Birch also did not operate them but included them in their portfolio. At the Metropolitan Traffic Area hearing Orange Luxury Coaches gained these two new services to Southend these becoming their first operations to the Essex resort.

Back in Walthamstow, in June 1936 there was another change to relate. The Holmes & Smith licences and the rental of the WMS owned Walthamstow garage were transferred into the name of Sydney Smith (Black & White Coaches Ltd.) at 55, Selborne Road. The name of Sydney Smith continued to be associated with Black & White Coaches until April 1952 when the Managing Director, Benjamin Alexander Davis, applied for the licences. The Company was later purchased by the Ewer Group in 1956. For the 1935 season there were two remaining WMS express services to Southend, each running twice daily during the summer period, viz:

A   LONDON (Victoria) – Walthamstow (Holmes & Smith, Selborne Road) – SOUTHEND (Tylers Avenue)

B   HOLLOWAY (Orange Coach Station) – Dalston – SOUTHEND (Tylers Ave)

The day return fares were 3/6d (17½p) Monday – Friday and 5/- (25p) Saturday, Sunday and August Bank Holiday Monday.

By 1937, both WMS services were once again terminating at Pier Hill, the fares being unaltered. For the 1938 season from 22 June these two remaining WMS London services were combined to run un-lettered from Victoria via Islington, Dalston and Walthamstow to Southend. This became the established pattern for many years. The 1939 fares stood at 3/- (15p) single, 3/6 (17½p) day return and 5/6 (27½p) period return, these levels being very similar to the prices charged in the late 1920s. Examples of publicity for the London services are shown in *Figs.3.1, 3.8 and 5.77*. When war was declared operation ceased for the duration.

Route A.—VICTORIA to
Leigh-on-Sea, Westcliff-on-Sea & **SOUTHEND-ON-SEA.**

VICTORIA (London Coastal Coach Station,
    Buckingham Palace Road) ... 9.30 a.m.
    (Main Booking Office)
BETHNAL GREEN (Devonshire St., Mile End Rd.) 10.0 a.m.
FOREST GATE (Sprouston Rd., nr. Princess Alice) 10.20 a.m.

Returning at the following Times—
SOUTHEND-ON-SEA (Tylers Av. Coach Station) 6.15 p.m.
WESTCLIFF-ON-SEA (Holmes & Smith,
    Plough Corner) ... ... 6.25 p.m.
LEIGH-ON-SEA (Public Library) ... ... 6.35 p.m.

FARES.

From the Friday before Whit-Saturday up to the second Friday in September inclusive except as stated in column 2.			On Saturdays, Sundays and Bank Holidays from Whit-Saturday to the second Sunday in Sept. inclusive.			From the Monday following the second Sunday in September to the Thursday before Whit-Saturday inclusive.		
Single	Day Return	Period Return	Single	Day Return	Period Return	Single	Day Return	Period Return
3/0	3/6	5/6	3/6	5/0	7/0	3/0	3/6	5/6

Route B.—HOLLOWAY to
Leigh-on Sea, Westcliff-on-Sea & **SOUTHEND-ON-SEA.**

			S.S. & B.H.
HOLLOWAY (Orange Coach Stn.) Parkhurst Road ...	a.m. 8.50	a.m. 10.20	p.m. 5.45
ISLINGTON (Benson Tourist Agency) The Green ... (Main Booking Office)	9.0	10.30	5.55
DALSTON (King Henry's Walk) ...	9.10	10.40	6.5

Returning at the following Times:—

	p.m.	p.m.	p.m.
SOUTHEND-ON-SEA (Tyler's Av. Coach Station) ...	6.30	8.0	3.0
WESTCLIFF-ON-SEA (Holmes and Smith, Plough Corner) ...	6.40	8.10	3.10
LEIGH-ON-SEA (Public Library) ...	6.50	8.20	3.20

S.S. & B.H.—Saturdays and Sundays and Bank Holidays Only.

FARES.

From the Friday before Whit-Saturday up to the second Friday in September inclusive except as stated in column 2.			On Saturdays, Sundays and Bank Holidays from Whit-Saturday to the second Sunday in Sept. inclusive.			From the Monday following the second Sunday in September to the Thursday before Whit-Saturday inclusive.		
Single	Day Return	Period Return	Single	Day Return	Period Return	Single	Day Return	Period Return
3/0	3/6	5/6	3/6	5/0	7/0	3/0	3/6	5/6

Route C.—BARNET to
Leigh-on-Sea, Westcliff-on-Sea & **SOUTHEND-ON-SEA.**

BARNET (Lee's Garage, High Street) ... (Main Booking Office)	8.30 a.m.
FINCHLEY (Tally Ho ! Corner) ...	8.50 a.m.
TOTTENHAM (Dowsett Road) ...	9.20 a.m.

Returning at the following Times—	S.S. & B.H.	
SOUTHEND-ON-SEA (Tylers Av. Coach Stn.)	7.0 p.m.	3.0 p.m.
WESTCLIFF-ON-SEA (Holmes & Smith, Plough Corner) ...	7.10 p.m.	3.10 p.m.
LEIGH-ON-SEA (Public Library) ...	7.20 p.m.	3.20 p.m.

S.S. & B.H.—Saturdays and Sundays and Bank Holidays Only.

FARES.

From the Friday before Whit-Saturday up to the second Friday in September inclusive except as stated in column 2.			On Saturdays, Sundays and Bank Holidays from Whit-Saturday to the second Sunday in Sept. inclusive.			From the Monday following the second Sunday in September to the Thursday before Whit-Saturday inclusive.		
Single	Day Return	Period Return	Single	Day Return	Period Return	Single	Day Return	Period Return
3/0	4/0	5/6	3/6	5/0	7/0	3/0	4/0	5/6

Route D.—ENFIELD to
Leigh-on-Sea, Westcliff-on-Sea & **SOUTHEND-ON-SEA.**

ENFIELD (Cecil Road)	8.30 a.m.
BUSH HILL (The Parade) ...	8.40 a.m.
WOOD GREEN (Coach Station Lordship Lane)	8.55 a.m.
WALTHAMSTOW (Holmes & Smith, Ltd., Selbourne Road)	9.20 a.m.

Returning at the following Times—		
SOUTHEND-ON-SEA (Tylers Av. Coach Stn.)	7.0 p.m.	3.0 p.m.
WESTCLIFF-ON-SEA (Holmes & Smith, Plough Corner) ...	7.10 p.m.	3.10 p.m.
LEIGH-ON-SEA (Public Library) ...	7.20 p.m.	3.20 p.m.

S.S. & B.H.—Saturdays and Sundays and Bank Holidays Only.

FARES.

From the Friday before Whit-Saturday up to the second Friday in September inclusive except as stated in column 2.			On Saturdays, Sundays and Bank Holidays from Whit-Saturday to the second Sunday in Sept. inclusive.			From the Monday following the second Sunday in September to the Thursday before Whit-Saturday inclusive.		
Single	Day Return	Period Return	Single	Day Return	Period Return	Single	Day Return	Period Return
3/0	3/6	5/6	3/6	5/0	7/0	3/0	3/6	5/6

Back in 1929 a new company 'Multiways' was registered at Station Road, Westcliff. It soon started an express service from Westcliff to Kings Cross via Islington and Dalston on Mondays to Fridays only throughout the year though this was withdrawn in 1933. Later a group of coastal express services radiating from Southend was started using coaches in a brown livery. Multiways operated from a number of different locations including Browns Garage at 35, London Road. WMS purchased some shares in Multiways in October 1939, then in April 1940 all operations were suspended due to the war conditions and the licences sold to WMS. The services, all seasonal, ran to Brighton & Worthing, Eastbourne, Folkestone and Hastings all using the Tilbury ferry, and also to Lowestoft & Great Yarmouth.

The WMS London service and the acquired coastal express routes re-commenced in summer 1946 *(see Fig.3.8)*. In 1952 a service to Canterbury & Margate was introduced.

Returning to Walthamstow for the final time we find WMS still maintained a presence there. After sustaining war damage the rental on the Hoe Street garage was reduced. Sydney Smith resigned from the WMS board on 31 December 1948 the Walthamstow premises were then disposed of thus ending the London E17 saga.

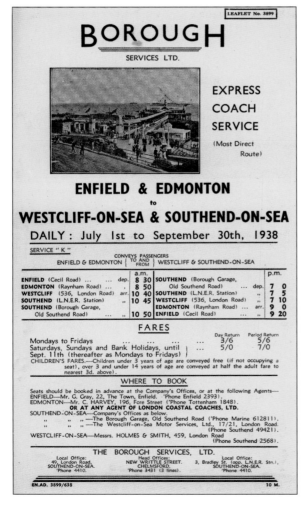

Fig.3.4 (left) *Since a 1933 Borough Services leaflet is not available, one for the 1938 season is reproduced. Their terminal was at the Borough garage in Old Southend Road, also used by City before the opening of Tylers Avenue. These premises were not owned by Borough, their base being at 49, London Road. The terminal of the service was later revised to Pier Hill. Holmes & Smith acted as booking agents for Borough, at Essex House (see Chapter Nine).*

*Fig.3.5 Early WMS publicity for express services. Note for each leaflet: **(a) upper left** – the scenic route described; **(b) upper right** – the Kings Cross terminal is actually at Islington; **(c) lower left** and **(d) lower right** leaflet covers for the North London express services, (see p.57 for 1934 timetables).*

59

Fig.3.6 *JN7501, a Bristol JO5G with ECW dual-purpose bodywork runs empty into Victoria Coach Station, London for its return journey to Southend-on-Sea.   RM*

Fig.3.7 *This superb Duple pre-delivery view of one of the two petrol-engined AEC Rangers (JN8584/5) emphasises the luxurious nature of the specification for these small extended tour coaches. As well as twenty-four generously spaced leather and moquette high-backed seats, there is a sun roof, glazed quarter-lights, and curtains fitted at the side windows.   JCC*

60

Fig.3.8   *Pre- and post-war publicity styles for WMS London express service leaflets 1938, 1939, 1946 and 1949.*   AGOC

After control of WMS passed to ENOC, from 4 January 1953 the express services were allocated route-letters mostly using vacancies created by the transfer of the Midland area to United Counties *(see Chapter One)*. Those serving Southend are shown in *Fig.3.9*:

D	X10	Southend	to	London
E	X20	Southend	to	Brighton & Worthing
F	X21	Southend	to	Eastbourne
G	X22	Southend	to	Folkestone
H	X23	Southend	to	Hastings
J	X24	Southend	to	Margate (new 1952 by WMS)
K	X11	Southend	to	Enfield (ex-Borough, operated by ENOC)
M	X25	Southend	to	Great Yarmouth

Fig.3.9 Express service re-numbering 1953 and 1962.

Fig.3.10 The very last express coach services leaflet to feature the 'Westcliff-on-Sea' name was dated Summer 1961.

All express services (except K) continued to be referred to as 'Westcliff Coach Services' until the end of the 1961 season. In the Eastern National timetable dated 26 November 1961 it was announced that new service identification numbers in a new 'X' series, would take effect from Easter 1962 *(see Fig.3.9)*. Many of these coastal services formed the nucleus of the

'Dartford Tunnel Coachways' which involved joint operations with East Kent, Maidstone & District and Southdown from May 1964.

It is worth recording that the X10 service between Southend and London was later developed from a pre-bookable coach service operating just a few times a day to a regular hourly operation with all tickets issued onboard the splendid Bristol FLF double-deck coaches operating the service.

Finally it has to be recorded that Pier Hill Coach Station, for many years the Head Office of WMS, ceased to be used after the 1966 season. In January 1967 the express services were modified to start either from Seaway E. N. terminal or from Southend, London Road. It is perhaps somewhat ironic to record that express service X24 still continued to terminate at Ramsgate, *Westcliff* Coach Station! Pier Hill Coach Station was sold in 1967. The area has now been completely redeveloped as the Royals Shopping Centre *(see Chapter Nine)*.

EXCURSIONS AND TOURS

It has previously been mentioned *(see Chapter Two)* that the Westcliff-on-Sea Motor Char-a-banc Co. Ltd. was formed by the amalgamation of two local operators known as the 'Royal Red Cars' (Holmes & Smith) and the 'Royal Blue Cars' (Brown & Spencer).

Fig.3.11 Photos of the very short-lived Royal Blue char-a-bancs of Brown & Spencer are rare but this view of what appears to be a church outing has survived. PJSA

Holmes & Smith started as jobmasters. They later converted their fleet of hearses from horses to motors. Motor char-a-bancs were introduced from 1911 fitted with solid tyres running on Petrofina, a mixture of paraffin and petrol. At this time many local country roads were unmade and motor vehicles were few so char-a-banc rides were quite an adventure and very popular. Outside the Royal Hotel the drivers in their long white frock coats would offer a selection of twenty- and thirty-mile local drives. A trip to Benfleet Woods and Nevendon would cost 2/6 (12½p) whilst a thirty-mile drive to Battlesbridge was priced at 3/6 (17½p). The drivers would have needed to seek the assistance of the passengers to raise the hood should it come on to rain.

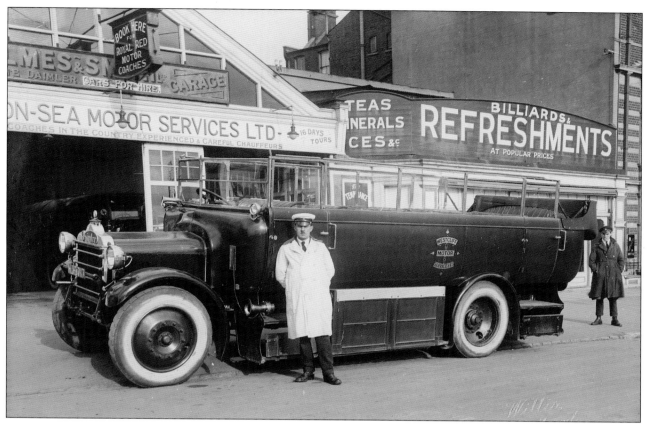

Fig.3.12 *A wonderful period view of WMS Daimler 'all-weather' saloon HJ3717 outside the first Pier Hill Coach Station. Note the driver wearing his summer dust coat, all part of the experience. These premises were shared with the car hire fleet of Holmes & Smith. The Temperance Billiards Hall next door later became the site of the second Pier Hill Coach Station (see Fig.3.23).*   ERO

Fig.3.13 *Passengers assemble for their group portrait outside the Gwydyr Hotel in Bettws-y-Coed on the North Wales extended tour, in front of their tour coach HJ 8038, a Daimler CF6.*   AGOC

Fig.3.14 *These early examples of WMS tours brochures date from 1929 (upper) and 1930 (lower). Note the use of the heraldic device on the 1930 brochure which was also carried on the side of the coaches as shown in Fig. 3.15.*

COMFORT ————————— SERVICE ————————— SAFETY

THE ABOVE ILLUSTRATION SHOWS THE TYPE OF COACH (CLOSED) USED FOR TOURS
AS DESCRIBED IN THIS GUIDE

THIS ILLUSTRATION SHOWS THE SAME TYPE OF COACH (OPEN) USED FOR TOURS
AS DESCRIBED IN THIS GUIDE

Fig.3.15 *WMS included illustrations of their latest coaches in their 1929 (upper, middle) and 1936 (lower) tours brochures.*

DATES FOR COACH TOURS
SEASON 1936.

DATE	Tour No.	No. Days	TOUR	FARE £ s. d.
June 8	2	6	North & South Devon ...	8 15 0
„ 8	4	6	North & Mid Wales ...	8 15 0
„ 13	1	8	Cornish Riviera ...	11 12 6
„ 15	3	6	English Lakes ...	9 2 6
„ 15	5	12	Cornwall, Devon, Wye Valley & North Wales	17 17 0
„ 22	2	6	North & South Devon ...	8 15 0
„ 22	4	6	North & Mid Wales ...	8 15 0
„ 22	6	12	Scotland (A) ...	18 10 0
„ 27	1	8	Cornish Riviera ...	11 12 6
„ 29	3	6	English Lakes ...	9 2 6
„ 29	5	12	Cornwall, Devon, Wye Valley & North Wales	17 17 0
July 6	2	6	North & South Devon ...	8 15 0
„ 6	4	6	North & Mid Wales ...	8 15 0
„ 6	6	12	Scotland (A) ...	18 10 0
„ 11	1	8	Cornish Riviera ...	11 12 6
„ 13	3	6	English Lakes ...	9 2 6
„ 13	5	12	Cornwall, Devon, Wye Valley & North Wales	17 17 0
„ 20	2	6	North & South Devon ...	8 15 0
„ 20	4	6	North & Mid Wales ...	8 15 0
„ 20	6	12	Scotland (A) ...	18 10 0
„ 25	1	8	Cornish Riviera ...	11 12 6
„ 27	3	6	English Lakes ...	9 2 6
„ 27	5	12	Cornwall, Devon, Wye Valley & North Wales	17 17 0
Aug. 3	2	6	North & South Devon ...	8 15 0
„ 3	4	6	North & Mid Wales ...	8 15 0
„ 3	6	12	Scotland (A) ...	18 10 0
„ 8	1	8	Cornish Riviera ...	11 12 6
„ 10	3	6	English Lakes ...	9 2 6
„ 10	5	12	Cornwall, Devon, Wye Valley & North Wales	17 17 0
„ 17	2	6	North & South Devon ...	8 15 0
„ 17	4	6	North & Mid Wales ...	8 15 0
„ 17	6	12	Scotland (A) ...	18 10 0
„ 22	1	8	Cornish Riviera ...	11 12 6
„ 24	3	6	English Lakes ...	9 2 6
„ 24	5	12	Cornwall, Devon, Wye Valley & North Wales	17 17 0
„ 31	2	6	North & South Devon ...	8 15 0
„ 31	4	6	North & Mid Wales ...	8 15 0
„ 31	6	12	Scotland (A) ...	18 10 0
Sept. 5	1	8	Cornish Riviera ...	11 12 6
„ 7	3	6	English Lakes ...	9 2 6
„ 7	5	12	Cornwall, Devon, Wye Valley & North Wales	17 17 0
„ 14	2	6	North & South Devon ...	8 15 0
„ 14	4	6	North & Mid Wales ...	8 15 0
„ 14	6	12	Scotland (A) ...	18 10 0
„ 19	1	8	Cornish Riviera ...	11 12 6
„ 21	3	6	English Lakes ...	9 2 6

BOOKING AGENTS

American Express Co. (Inc.), 6 Haymarket, London, S.W.1 ; 'Phone Gerrard 1203 ; Hotel Cecil, 'Phone Gerrard 60 ; Hotel Metropole, 'Phone Gerrard 8121 ; also 16 Bury Street, London, E.C., 'Phone Avenue 7610.

Ardley Bros., Reform Row, High Road, Tottenham, N.17 ; 'Phone Tottenham 2279.

Central London (London Transport) Station, Ltd., Crescent Place, Cartwright Gardens, W.C.1 ; 'Phone Museum 9631.

Dean & Dawson Ltd., 81 Piccadilly, London, W.1 ; 'Phone Grosvenor 2873/5.

C. C. Drake, Ltd., 12a Berkeley Street, Piccadilly, W.1 ; 'Phone Mayfair 3766.

Franco-Belgique Tours, 177 Regent Street, W.1 ; Phone Gerrard 5044.

Frank Tourist Co. (Inc.), Norway House, 21/4 Cockspur Street, S.W.1 ; 'Phone Regent 3138.

A. W. Gamage Ltd., Holborn, London, E.C.1 ; 'Phone Holborn 2700.

The Globe Travel Co., Ltd., Bush House, Strand, London, W.C.2 ; 'Phone Temple Bar 2167.

W. H. Hayward & Son, 4 Union Passage, Birmingham ; 'Phone Midland 6242.

J. D. Hewitt & Co., Ltd., 11 (Lower) Regent Street, S.W.1 ; 'Phone Regent 6626 (2 lines). Telegrams Etthewcom, Piccy, London.

Hendersons Hire Services, Ltd., Opposite Hoe Street Station, Walthamstow ; 'Phone Walthamstow 1111.

Highways Ltd., 281 Regent Street, Oxford Circus, W.1 ; 'Phone Mayfair 3314.

Leiths Service Depot, 243 Linthorpe Road, Middlesbrough ; 'Phone Middlesbrough 4010.

Lep Travel Bureau, 27 Piccadilly, W.1. (under Piccadilly Hotel), 77 Upper Thames Street, E.C.4 ; Telegrams Lepaerial, Piccy, London ; 'Phone Gerrard 4387 and 8560, Central 7383.

Sir Henry Lunn, Ltd., 5 Endsleigh Gardens, London, N.W. ; 'Phone Museum 3962.

Minn's Tours, 99 Buckingham Palace Road (facing Victoria Station), London, S.W.1 ; Telegrams Minztourz Sowest, London ; 'Phone Victoria 4951.

The Polytechnic Touring Association, Ltd., 309 Regent Street, London, W.1 ; Telegrams Polytechnic, Wesdo, London ; 'Phone Mayfair 6100.

Red Triangle Tours, 8 Great Russell Street, W.C.1 ; Phone Museum 4812/3.

Selfridge & Co., London W.1 (Travel Bureau) ; 'Phone Mayfair 1234.

World Acquaintance Travel (Inc.), 189 Regent Street, W.1 ; 'Phone Regent 7354.

Road Travel Bookings, Ltd., Bush House, Aldwych, W.C.2 ; 'Phone Central 9534/9.

2

Fig.3.16 *Pages from WMS coach tour brochures of the 1930s. (a) top: coach tours dates for 1936, a very extensive programme requiring a substantial number of coaches; (b) above: list of booking agents including well known London stores as well as names associated with WMS history; (c) right: route map of coastal tour.*

Fig.3.17 *JN8584, one of the unusual AEC Ranger coaches is at work on an extended tour. The unmistakable background places it at Dunster in Somerset. This is 'Tour F, 8 days Torquay, Ilfracombe and Districts' leaving Southend and London on Fridays (twelve departures, fare £15:15:0). It must be Monday when the coach travels from Ilfracombe (overnight) to Minehead (lunch), Dunster, Bampton, Tiverton, Exe Valley, Exeter (visit cathedral) and Torquay (staying three nights at Grand Hotel).   PJSA*

Fig.3.18 (above) *Here we see the classic combination of Bedford OB/Duple Vista C29F which was ideal for short tours and private hire work. DHJ22 is seen here on the latter activity.   RM*

WESTCLIFF MOTOR SERVICES, LIMITED.

Route Map—Nine Days Coastal Tour.

Fig.3.19 *The day tours were often run by the fleet of AEC Regals including AHJ 404 delivered in 1939 with Duple bodywork seen here relaxing by the fish market at Hastings with the East Cliff lift in the background. This vehicle was later exported to Malta, re-bodied by Schembri and ran for many years in its rebuilt form (see Chapter Nine). LWR*

Fig.3.20 *In later years ENOC coaches allocated to Southend carried 'Westcliff-on-Sea' fleet-names to continue the tradition of WMS extended tours. This example is provided by 481 (280 NHK) a 1959 Bristol MW6G with ECW C39F bodywork, allocated to Prittlewell (PL). AGOC*

The Royal Red fleet comprised four 30hp Thornycrofts, whilst three 28hp Dennis's made up the Royal Blue fleet. All the vehicles carried 24 passengers seated on cross-benches.

The prospectus for the new Westcliff-on-Sea Motor Char-a-banc Co. Ltd. offered 30,000 shares at £1 each. There was considerable oversubscription with many small shareholders. It was anticipated that the fleet would be expanded to 15 vehicles, however, operations had to be curtailed because of the outbreak of war, when the char-a-bancs were then engaged on military transport duties, including taking wounded soldiers from the local hospital units on outings.

When peace returned the char-a-banc fleet was expanded and further destinations added. Holmes & Smith also operated hire cars which were based at Pier Hill and a fleet of Humber Limousines garaged at Essex House, 459-61, London Road, Westcliff (see Chapter Nine).

By 1922 char-a-banc reliability had improved to such an extent that a programme of extended tours of between five and twelve days duration was started. A very high standard was enjoyed and enormous goodwill earned, not only on their home ground but also in London where several major travel agencies actively promoted the tours. Some of the coaches and char-a-bancs used on these tours were later based at the Ardley Bros. garage in Tottenham. Picking up points in both Southend-on-Sea and London were offered.

The directors reported in 1923 that the London trade had increased, and that negotiations were taking place with a leading tourist agency with a view to running motor coaches in Paris. They considered that it was due to the excellence of their vehicles that they had been approached for this purpose. It is not known whether this 'French Connection' actually ever happened.

In 1929 WMS obtained a contract to transport a group of Canadian farmers who were visiting the country and to transport them all over England. The coaches engaged on this work were the very first to pass through the gates of Buckingham Palace.

To advertise the operations, an impressive *Illustrated Tour Handbook and Official Guide* was published each year. The cover of the 1929 edition was particularly attractive and is accordingly reproduced in *Fig.3.14*. The 1930 edition of this guide was also distributed by the Globe Travel Company Ltd of Bush House, Strand, London from whence many motor coach tours started. The booklet amounted to 72 pages and described in detail the itineraries of the Royal Red Coaches extended tours. Ten tours were listed lasting between six and fourteen days (see *Fig.3.16*). Tour 'A' to the Wye Valley, Shakespeare Country and Peak District lasted for six days and cost £12. Tour 'E' reached as far as Lands End (£14), whilst tour 'G' featured North- and Mid-Wales (£15 15s.). The longest tour, lasting 14 days was tour 'J' to Scotland which ventured as far north as Inverness, costing 27 guineas (£28.35p). The range of booking agents was very impressive (see *Fig.3.16*) including several high profile London stores such as Gamages and Selfridges as well

as other organisations such as American Express. The tours could also be booked through several road travel specialists including Highways Ltd. and the aforementioned Globe Travel. Several WMS associated outlets were also featured including Ardley Bros. of Tottenham and Hendersons Hire Service in Walthamstow. The brochures also included illustrations of the coaches used (see *Fig.3.15*).

For the 1936 season three 20 seat Leyland Cubs were purchased for the luxury motor coach cruises to allow passengers the opportunity of 'Seeing Britain from Her Highways'. An illustration of one of these vehicles, taken from the *Official Handbook* has been included (see *Fig.3.15*).

The intensity of the coach tour programme can best be realised by reference to the 1936 coach cruise list as shown in *Fig.3.16*. A similar pattern of tours continued to be offered until the outbreak of hostilities. The next batch of vehicles used for tours were unusual Duple bodied AEC Ranger coaches with 24 luxurious seats. During the war many vehicles were kept available standing-by for use as ambulances as required by the ARP (Air Raid Precautions).

From 24 May 1939 timetable

Following the war the extensive range of day and afternoon tours was re-started all departing from Pier Hill Coach Station (see *Fig.3.21*). The programme for the summer of 1952 is reproduced in *Fig.3.22*. The afternoon tours featured a short hop to Langdon Hills for just 4/- (20p). Evening mystery tours were also run often ending up at a suitable pub. The whole day tours were usually operated by AEC Regal or Bristol LS coaches whilst the shorter excursions were handled by the Bedford OBs. A fine line up of glistening vehicles all with painted tour boards propped up against their radiators is a lasting memory of Pier Hill Coach Station (see *Figs.3.23 and 9.16*).

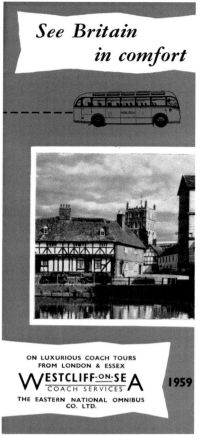

Fig.3.21 *Some examples of post-war WMS tours and excursions publicity. AGOC*

WHOLE DAY TOURS
from
PIER HILL COACH STATION
SOUTHEND-ON-SEA

	Fares †
	Adult / Child

					Adult	Child
ALDEBURGH	...	...	...	...	13/3	6/9
BOGNOR	...	...	...	...	17/–	8/6
BURY ST. EDMUNDS	...	...	...		10/9	5/6
CLARE	...	...	...	...	10/9	5/6
CANTERBURY	...	...	...	...	11/7	5/11
CAMBRIDGE	...	...	...	...	10/9	5/6
COLCHESTER	...	...	...	...	8/–	4/–
CHESSINGTON ZOO	...	...	...		10/9	5/6
CLACTON	...	...	...	...	10/9	5/6
CROMER	...	...	...	...	19/3	9/9
DOVER	...	...	...	...	14/1	7/2
DOVERCOURT	...	...	...	...	10/9	5/6
ELY	...	...	...	...	13/3	6/9
FELIXSTOWE	...	...	...	...	13/3	6/9
FRINTON	...	...	...	...	10/9	5/6
HAMPTON COURT	...	...	...		10/9	5/6
HARWICH	...	...	...	...	10/9	5/6
HERNE BAY	...	...	...	...	14/1	7/2
HUNSTANTON	...	...	...	...	18/3	9/3
LAVENHAM	...	...	...	...	10/–	5/–
MARGATE	...	...	...	...	14/1	7/2
NORWICH	...	...	...	...	13/3	6/9
OXFORD	...	...	...	...	16/–	8/–
REGENTS PARK ZOO	...	...	...		6/9	3/6
SOUTHWOLD	...	...	...	...	13/3	6/9
SANDRINGHAM	...	...	...	...	17/3	8/9
STRATFORD-ON-AVON	...	...	...		19/3	9/9
TUNBRIDGE WELLS	...	...	...		11/7	5/11
WINDSOR & VIRGINIA WATER	...		...		10/9	5/6
WALTON-ON-THE-NAZE	...		...		13/3	6/9
WHIPSNADE ZOO	...	...	...	...	13/3	6/9
WINCHESTER	...	...	...	...	16/9	8/6

† Includes passenger charge for Tilbury-Gravesend Ferry where applicable

For times and dates of departure see printed programme obtainable gratis upon application at any of the Company's Enquiry Offices.

172

AFTERNOON TOURS
from
PIER HILL COACH STATION
SOUTHEND-ON-SEA

BRADWELL	...	...	...	...	8/–
BURNHAM-ON-CROUCH	...	...	...		5/3
BADDOW, RODNEY & DANBURY	...		...		5/3
BEELEIGH ABBEY & MALDON	...		...		6/9
BRENTWOOD	...	...	...	...	6/3
BRAINTREE	...	...	...	...	8/–
CHELMSFORD	...	...	...	...	5/3
CIRCULAR TOUR	...	...	...		6/9
CASTLE HEDINGHAM	...	...	...		8/–
DANBURY	...	...	...	...	5/3
DUNTON BULPHAM	...	...	...		6/9
EASTON LODGE	...	...	...	...	6/9
FLATFORD MILLS	...	...	...		8/9
GALLEYWOOD	...	...	...	...	4/9
LANGDON HILLS	...	...	...	...	4/–
MILLBEACH	...	...	...	...	6/9
MALDON	...	...	...	...	5/3
RYE HOUSE	...	...	...	...	8/–
SAFFRON WALDEN	...	...	...		8/–
SOUTH WEALD	...	...	...	...	6/9
STONE	...	...	...	...	5/3
WITHAM	...	...	...	...	8/–
WEST MERSEA	...	...	...	...	8/–

For dates and times of departure see printed programme obtainable gratis upon application from the Company's Enquiry Offices.

173

Fig.3.22 *Day and afternoon coach tour programme for 1952 from the 6 June timetable booklet.*

Fig.3.24 *Another superb Duple publicity photograph, this time of an AEC Regal, AHJ405 allows us to consider the body styling and livery application on this 'top spec' touring coach. There is no doubt that the combination of the clean yet stylish lines of the Duple body complement   the refined slender lines of the AEC radiator to produce what was perhaps the epitome of excellence in pre-war motor coach design. Everything seems in proportion from the rake of the driving cab window, the quarter-light windows to the double paired side windows. Pehaps the flash seems a little 'weak', the lower beading not joining the front of the mudguard as with many designs. The WMS coach livery application of red to the area behind the flash rather than the flash itself accentuates the point.* JCC

Fig.3.23 (opposite) *To conclude this chapter what better way could there be than to enter a time-warp and go back to the glorious days of the early 1930s. Just feast your eyes on the magnificent scene, and then look more closely. This wonderful atmospheric view is of the new Pier Hill coach station (see Fig.9.16) constructed on the site of the Temperance Billiards Hall (Fig.3.12). There is so much to see. The drivers in their summer uniforms are encouraging prospective customers to book. Two Dennis F 'all-weather saloons' HJ9875/6, the former bound for London, wait ready. Numerous painted boards display travel opportunities, London, Brighton and Epsom races. A chalk board advertises an afternoon tour for Canewdon and Paglesham for 2/6 (12½p). Various services to east and north London are listed with the reminder to day trippers that their return coaches will depart from Tylers Avenue. All this is having the desired effect as indicated by the queue at the booking office. What a wonderful scene!* ERO

70

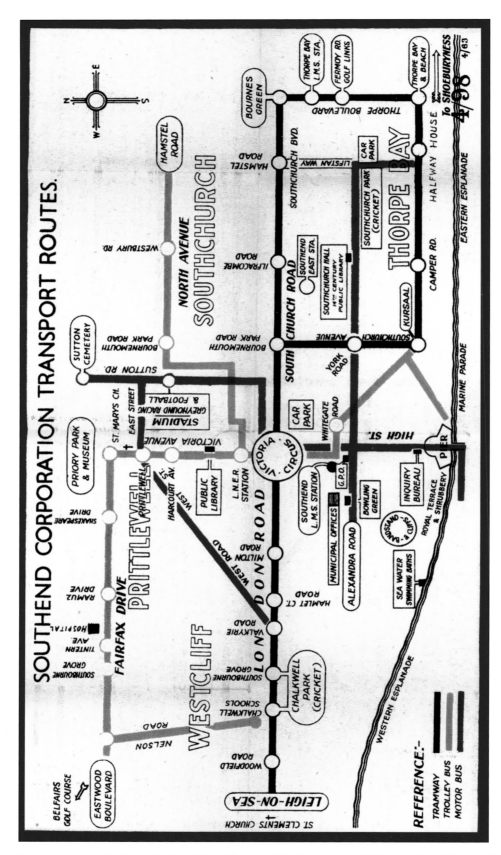

Fig.4.1 *This diagrammatic map is from the July 1936 SCT timetable. As post-war SCT timetables did not include a map this provides the best official visual representation of the network of Corporation tram, trolleybus and bus services existing prior to the co-ordination scheme.*

Chapter Four

Westcliff M.S. and the Co-ordination of Bus Services in Southend-on-Sea

Thirty-five years. How long? Thirty-five years is the remarkable length of time it took to achieve the co-ordination of bus services in Southend. Co-ordination may be considered as the efficient operation of public transport within urban areas providing optimum cross-town facilities for the public, full interchange of tickets and with maximum utilisation of vehicles and resources for operators. In this chapter the full and complex story, of potentially great significance to the development of WMS, is outlined. Cross references to related significant events are provided in *Chapter Two* under *'SJS notes'*.

In the late 1920s public transport in the Southend area was mainly in the hands of two dominant operators, Southend Corporation Transport (SCT), with trams and trolleybuses (but no motor buses) and Westcliff-on-Sea Motor Services (WMS) with bus operations both within and beyond the borough boundary. Eastern National Omnibus Company (ENOC) also ran into Southend from Chelmsford along the Eastwood Road.

new services. Progress within the bureaucracy of the Southend-on-Sea County Borough Council was somewhat more sedate. The responsibility for Corporation bus services lay with the Transport Committee (TRC). However, it would appear that the Aldermen and Councillors were not appreciative of the full implications of the impending Transport Act which required that all services, vehicles and staff needed to be registered by 9 February 1931.

Phase 1   The East/West Divide

At the Southend TRC meeting on 12 November 1929 an outline plan of a motor omnibus route extending from the borough western boundary in Leigh to Shaftesbury Avenue in Southchurch was proposed. The Routes Sub-committee indicated that this was to be 'the first instalment of the bus routes to be traversed by the Corporation buses'. Further details were given on 28

Fig.4.2 *SCT was all electric in the 1920s. This view in the High Street shows 1929 Garrett trolleybus 104 (HJ7363), a former demonstrator, heading for Priory Park. Going to, and advertising, the Kursaal is 111 an English Electric of 1930, its pristine white-wall tyres suggesting it is newly arrived and thus 1930 as the date of this photo. MLWC*

During this decade, several smaller independent operators had started local bus services. These included Edwards Hall Motors (under WMS control from 1927), Borough Services (started 1927), New Empress Saloons (1927, later becoming the City Coach Company), Pearse's Motor Services (1921, later to evolve into Benfleet/Canvey & District), Rayleigh Motor Services (1929), Rochford & District Motor Services (1930), Shoeburyness Motor Services (1930) and Thundersley, Hadleigh & District Motors (1915).

Just before the introduction of the 1930 Road Traffic Act many new operators had appeared and started

January 1930. The service would run every ten minutes and require six double-deckers. Tenders for the supply of vehicles were invited on 22 April and the costs passed by the Finance Committee on 9 September. On 14 October approval was granted for the purchase of seven AEC Regal saloons rather than the double-deckers originally proposed. The service would run from Walker Drive via Kings Road, Hamlet Court Road, Cliff Town Road, Tylers Avenue and York Road to Southchurch Park (Shaftesbury Avenue) serving the eastern and western sides of the borough. On 25 November the TRC rejected a proposal by WMS that they operate the service for a period of one year at a cost of 1/- (5p) per mile. This was a decision they would come to regret.

Between the inception of the idea and the endless committee meetings that were a part of municipal government, the wider world of bus legislation changed. In 1930 the Road Traffic Act was passed requiring any bus services started after 9 February 1931 to be licensed. Whereas private operators (including WMS) reacted speedily and established routes prior to the deadline, SCT did not. As an operator of only electric traction it was not an established motor-bus operator and could not introduce the route for which the Regals had been bought until it had made and succeeded with a licence application under the new legislation. Not surprisingly WMS, Borough and Major Pearse all objected. Although the seven Regals were approved as fit for service by the Traffic Commissioners in May 1931 a licence for the proposed service was refused since SCT was not an established bus operator in the area.

Fig.4.3 JN 823 was one of the seven AEC Regals ordered by SCT in 1930 for their bus routes revival. Licensing problems led to the 1932 Agreement and the east/west divide. 203 (originally no.153) was remarkably long lived and was still around in 1955 when the Southend & District Joint Services started, though by then much rebuilt by SCT. RFM

The TRC then decided to apply for separate routes in the eastern and western portions of the borough. On 10 November a licence for a new eastern route from Alexandra Road to Southchurch Park was applied for, running every 20 minutes needing three vehicles. This was followed on 24 November by a further application for a new western route to act as a feeder to the tram service from Sutherland Boulevard to Leigh. In February 1932 the Traffic Commissioners refused the western route as it competed with established WMS and THD services. The eastern service was allowed but with modification. The revised service started on 5 July. Following these licensing problems the Traffic Commissioner suggested that the parties meet to discuss local road service operations. A meeting was thus arranged for 22 March with representatives of SCT, WMS and Borough Services present to formulate a comprehensive scheme for road service co-ordination. A sub-committee was formed which presented a report on 12 July in which it was proposed that the borough be divided into two spheres of operation. The final Agreement was sealed on 22

December 1932 and the east/west territorial Agreement came into operation on 1 January 1933. Thus WMS service 14 (Southend – Sutton, extension to Shopland abandoned) and EHM service A (Southend – Prittlewell Chase) and services B & C (Southend – Hamstel Lane) and part of Borough Services Eastwood Circular route (Southend – Westcliff portion) passed to SCT.

This was clearly not a co-ordination scheme, rather the town was split into two distinct operating areas. The east zone became the SCT preserve with 'the Companies' keeping to the west. SCT was allowed to continue their existing tram route (which had become a through facility from 1 May 1930) and also their trolleybus route along Fairfax Drive, despite these both being in the western zone. The routes that 'passed' to SCT noted above were accompanied by the buses needed to operate them. The purchase price of these buses no doubt reflected the value to SCT of the revenue gained from the routes. SCT did not want the buses and promptly sold them back, nine buses to Edwards Hall/WMS for £750, and three to Borough for £250. ENOC was not a party to the scheme since their country services ran along the Eastwood Road and then entered the borough along the boundary between the two zones.

Phase 2   The Tilling Era

In May 1933 an event occurred which was to have far reaching effects on Southend bus services: ENOC acquired control of what was the most successful of all the local omnibus businesses in the Southend area, Borough Services Ltd. Furthermore, Borough had recently obtained a controlling interest in Rayleigh Motor Services Ltd. but continued to operate it as a separate entity. As the Borough garage was at 49, London Road just along from the WMS premises this now gave ENOC a presence right in the heart of the WMS domain.

Fig.4.4 Borough AEC Regent/Park Royal JN2310 asserts its right to work into Southend and to be part of the 1932 Agreement. It 'lays-over' outside Southend Victoria Station. PJSA

Borough ran two long distance services into Southend from Colchester via Maldon and from Grays via Vange. These had necessitated Borough being a party to the 1932 Agreement mentioned above (Phase 1). The Colchester service was immediately incorporated into

ENOC route 19. However, since the 1932 Agreement only permitted ENOC to approach Southend via the Eastwood Road, Borough was retained as a subsidiary company to enable their existing services to continue. These were soon re-numbered 70 (Southend – Grays) and 71 (Leigh – Eastwood).

Rayleigh Motor Services still ran from their home town into Southend on two routes both of which were in competition with WMS. With the take-over of Borough by ENOC the stage was set for this problem to be resolved. Although it would initially appear that this was but a small side issue it was to have considerably more significance in subsequent negotiations between ENOC, Tilling and WMS. A more thorough discussion will be found in Frank Simpson's *The Years Between* but an outline is given here as an essential part of the WMS story. Some re-shuffling of directors took place between the boards of ENOC, Rayleigh, Borough and WMS. Rayleigh MS was made a subsidiary of WMS rather than ENOC. At first sight this seems a surprising decision. It may be recalled that ENOC had wanted to acquire Borough primarily for the Colchester service. It appears that the associated RMS services were negotiable within a larger strategy. The new Rayleigh board had three directors, two nominated by ENOC (a Tilling company) and one from WMS. The transfer to WMS was a classic example of 'a spratt to catch a mackerel' such that this arrangement gave Tillings a small toe-hold into the WMS empire. Within two years, no doubt following informal director meetings at the RMS board, the Tilling representative had been able to persuade a sufficient number of the 400 WMS shareholders to sell their shares to Tilling to give it effective control of WMS by December 1934. The Tilling Group was at the time controlled by their dynamic Managing Director J. F. Heaton. In the light of recent events Tillings considered that the time was right to approach Southend Council with a view to re-modelling bus service provision in the borough. Although the process commenced in 1935 it was not to be until 2 January 1955 that the scheme finally went into operation. So at a special meeting of the Southend TRC on 7 May 1935 it was resolved to invite a director of Thomas Tilling Ltd. to discuss the matter. The meeting took place on 2 July in Southend with J. F. Heaton representing Tilling. At a further meeting on 12 December, additional financial information was requested by both sides, and the matter was raised again at the 5 May 1936 meeting.

The TRC thought it appropriate to seek expert advice. An approach was made to A. R. Fearnley, General Manager of Sheffield Corporation Transport to fulfil this role. It is worth noting here that the Sheffield Joint Omnibus Committee started on 1 January 1929. Moreover, the son of the appointee was Ronald

Fearnley previously General Manager of the Keighley undertaking from July 1925 to March 1929 and then General Manager at Southend from 1929 to 1933 before he moved to Coventry. The Tilling proposal effectively amounted to a merger of the SCT and WMS transport undertakings to operate as a single unit. It should be recalled that such a merger had already taken place with the formation of Keighley – West Yorkshire Services on 1 October 1932, though the financial situation which precipitated that combination was very different to that existing in Southend. A. R. Fearnley submitted his report to the TRC on 10 December 1936 and after due consideration the TRC concluded at their meeting on 5 January 1937 that although the Corporation should not transfer control, efforts should be made to reach a working agreement with WMS with a view to avoiding unnecessary competition. The motion not to merge was carried at the Southend Town Council meeting on 19 January. A special Council meeting was convened on 2 February with J. F. Heaton and A. R. Fearnley in attendance. After extended discussions it was resolved that SCT was not prepared to enter into a merger. J. F. Heaton indicated that Tilling was prepared to consider any proposals for a closer working arrangement, but none were forthcoming from SCT. Following a further communication from J. F. Heaton at the TRC meeting on 12 November the Town Clerk was instructed to reply that there was no useful purpose in re-opening the discussion, and there matters stood.

Phase 3 Termination of the 1932 Agreement

Serious thought had been given to the replacement of the SCT trams by either trolleybuses or motor buses as early as 1933. The Prittlewell tram route had closed in December 1928 and the next stage of the abandonment (the Boulevards) started on 7 July 1938. Later trolleybuses replaced the section between the Kursaal and Thorpe Bay. After war was declared on 3 September 1939 traffic slumped so dramatically that it would have then been appropriate to close the entire tramway. However, the provision of replacement cross-town buses would breach the 1932 Agreement which had established specific operating areas. Likewise the need for ENOC to maintain Borough Services as a subsidiary to operate services within the Southend area was an additional administrative strain which ENOC was keen to dispense with. Thus both parties had an incentive to modify the 1932 Agreement and raised the matter with the Traffic Commissioner.

At the TRC meeting on 4 July 1939 it was reported that the Traffic Commissioner considered that the 1932 Agreement was not operating in the public interest since cross-town facilities could not be introduced. After some consideration, on 8 January 1940 notices were received from WMS and Borough asking that the 1932 Agreement should be terminated with effect from 5 July 1940. The services operated by Borough would be taken over by WMS from 30 October. SCT raised no objection to this and thus some measure of rationalisation was achieved.

Fig.4.5 Once SCT had established (by purchase) the right to operate motor buses it required double-deckers. This pre-delivery view shows AHJ835 a Weymann bodied AEC Regent of 1938. RM

Phase 4   Wartime and the First Co-ordination Agreement

The next event relevant to the history of the Co-ordination scheme took place in distant Plymouth. In March 1941 there was a heavy air raid on the dockyard at Devonport. The city centre was devastated and both the Western National Omnibus Company (WNOC) garage at Laira Bridge and the Plymouth Corporation Transport (PCT) garage at Milehouse suffered direct hits. There then followed multiple applications by both WNOC and PCT for service revisions with subsequent counter objections from either side. The Regional Transport Commissioner requested an urgent meeting to reach a working agreement. The conference took place on 5 December following which a Joint Committee was set up which then reported to the City Council. On 7 September 1942 the Council approved the report from the new Joint Committee and Plymouth Joint Services became effective on 1 October 1942.

Fig.4.6 Southend also suffered bombing. An AEC Regent/ Weymann JN3715 working an 8 was confronted by a bomb crater near Oaken Grange Drive in November 1940. It was another severe air raid on Plymouth in March 1941 which was to spearhead the resumption of discussions on the co-ordination of bus services in Southend.   ERO

Meanwhile, back in Southend a motion was proposed by Cllr. Mackintosh at the TRC meeting on 31 October 1941 that negotiations be resumed with Thomas Tilling but it was not adopted. At the full Town Council meeting of 10 November a new motion was proposed to ascertain the possibilities of a merger or co-operation of interests between SCT and WMS to improve travel facilities in the borough, reduce local expenditure and help the war effort by elimination of unnecessary waste of manpower, electricity, fuel etc. However civic pride won the day and the motion was defeated. Following this rejection on 5 December the TRC noted that WMS had lodged an objection to the replacement bus services to be introduced by SCT following the abandonment of the tramways. This set back the achievements of 5 July 1940 to the Corporation's disadvantage.

In December 1941 a circular letter was sent out to Regional Traffic Commissioners by the Ministry of War Transport (MoWT) in which it was suggested that the Commissioners use their powers to bring about co-ordinated working between services of adjacent operators. The events of 5 December 1941 vividly contrasted the progress at Plymouth, where a joint working conference was taking place, and Southend where objections to tramway replacement bus services were lodged.

Following an enquiry by the Traffic Commissioners the WMS objections were overruled and the SCT application for revised tramway replacement bus services was granted. This was unusual in that in other towns tramways were retained during the war to save on imported fuel for motor-bus replacements. It seems probable that this decision reflected MoWT directives to reduce waste in this time of national emergency specifically relating to the under-used nature of SCT's trams in the now de-populated town. The Regional Traffic Commissioner proposed to host a meeting to review services operated over the common section of route between Victoria Circus and Chalkwell Schools and significantly this was later extended to cover the whole area. Mr. H. Muscroft (previously Transport Manager at Southend) was appointed to advise the Corporation and on 3 March 1942 he submitted a Heads of Agreement. The trams were to be withdrawn after service on 8 April 1942 and replaced by buses on a cross-town route from Southchurch to Leigh. On 9 April J. F. (now Sir Frederick) Heaton (Chairman of Thomas Tilling) attended a meeting in Southend with Mr. Muscroft in response to the earlier MoWT directive. The joint scheme recently introduced at Brighton was considered to be a suitable model. However, following a visit to that town on 15 May it was concluded that conditions of transport in Brighton were not comparable to those in Southend. Proposals were made by both sides but again no agreement could be reached. It was also suggested that a short-term wartime agreement might be made which could be revised in peace time. Extensive discussions took place at a meeting on 24 July but these ended in stalemate.

Frustrated by the lack of progress J. Mathieson (Secretary of WMS) circulated a letter (dated 4 August) to all WMS shareholders to inform them of the present position. A joint committee was proposed involving no transfer of assets. The letter referred to a SCT counter-proposal apparently based on a scheme inaugurated in the north of England which was designed to protect the interests of particular operators rather than improving the public service. This scheme was not favoured by WMS.

Matters then came to a head following a series of articles published in the *Southend Standard* newspaper. The 6 August 1942 issue reported that W. Baxendale had been appointed General Manager at SCT and that it was hoped that this new appointment would lead to a working agreement. It was also reported that negotiations had been successfully completed at Plymouth in the previous month. In the same issue the circular letter to WMS shareholders was reproduced. Following the newspaper articles the co-ordination sub-committee submitted an interim report to the TRC which met on 11 August. In this it was deemed undesirable to enter into an agreement at a time when the local population had been severely depleted by Southend's wartime designation as an evacuation area such that the relative transport mileages and receipts were very different from normal. The appointment of a new General Manager was noted as an opportunity for progress to be made. The adopted sub-committee report was placed before the full Town Council meeting on 18 August.

Fig.4.7 *Whilst all this discussion about the future was ongoing, those residents remaining in Southend relied to an increasing extent on electric traction as this saved on fuel imports. Elderly trolleys like 118 (JN2818) an English Electric bodied AEC 661T dating from 1933 soldiered on after the war.* LTPS

The *Southend Standard* of 20 August featured a report of the Town Council meeting and included the full report of both the sub-committee and subsequent discussions. The differences between the two sides were explained and the SCT objections to a merger were reported. The next issue of the newspaper on 27 August featured a letter from G. Napthine, General Manager of WMS, which re-iterated that the proposed co-ordination scheme involved the formation of a joint committee and not a merger. As the example referred to (Keighley) had been called a Joint Committee but was in fact dominated by the company operator West Yorkshire who provided buses on behalf of both itself and Keighley it was perhaps not surprising that Southend councillors were not convinced of the benefits of the scheme, rightly fearing loss of municipal control.

COUNTY BOROUGH OF SOUTHEND-ON-SEA

REPORT

OF THE

TRANSPORT COMMITTEE

AS TO

The Proposed Co-Ordination of Transport Services

To be submitted to the Council at a Special Meeting to be held

ON

Tuesday, the 25th day of July, 1944

In order to find a solution, the Joint Committee continued to meet but now with input from the new SCT General Manager. On 2 February 1943 H. Muscroft requested release from his advisory role and his place was taken, perhaps more appropriately, by G. F. Craven, General Manager of Halifax Corporation where a Joint Omnibus Committee had been in place since 1 April 1929. Negotiations then continued using the Plymouth Joint Services scheme as a model. Eventually on 13 June 1944 the sub-committee reported that negotiations had been concluded and that the Heads of the proposed Agreement had been reached.

There would be a joint committee covering a co-ordination area bounded by a line drawn from a point to the west of Canvey Island, northwards from the Thames as far as Vange (Timberlog Lane) then northwards to Wickford, north-eastwards to Runwell and Battlesbridge and then eastwards following the River Crouch to the coast. It should be mentioned at this stage that Basildon New Town did not exist at this time (and had not even been designated, the South Essex New Town being planned for Chipping Ongar) and hence the western boundary was drawn quite widely. It had already been agreed that the pooling should be on a fifty-fifty basis between WMS and SCT. However, since ENOC was now a party to the scheme their proportion was fixed at 8.2%. Consequently the pooled receipts and mileage would be shared as SCT 45.9%, WMS 45.9% and ENOC 8.2%. The Agreement was to be in force for a period of five years and the Corporation was to lease to 'the Companies' the right to use the trolley vehicle equipment. The Report was adopted at a Special Meeting of the Town Council on 25 July, duly recorded in the Southend Standard two days later. The Regional Transport Commissioner sent a letter of congratulations to all parties – and no doubt privately breathed a huge sigh of relief at getting closure on this difficult matter. The first draft of the Agreement was dated 23 August 1944.

However, it soon became clear that the matter was not yet resolved as the question of the 'other operators' had yet to be considered. This was first raised at the TRC meeting on 3 October 1944. Approaches were made to the Benfleet, Canvey and City companies to enquire as to whether they would either be willing to enter the co-ordination scheme or dispose of their services within the co-ordination area to the involved parties. H. A. Bridge (for Canvey and Benfleet) replied that he saw no merit in Canvey entering the scheme since their operations were completely physically separate but that entry by Benfleet & District was a possibility. W. F. Mallender for the City Coach Company (of which H. A. Bridge was also a Director) noted that their main line Southend service was presently being worked in three sections due to wartime restrictions, viz: Wood Green – Brentwood, Brentwood – Wickford and Wickford – Southend. Loss of the latter section (to the co-ordination scheme) would render City's through service far less viable and moreover, since the City operation between London and Brentwood was operated as a 'consent' given by the London Passenger Transport Board for a through service between Wood Green and Southend, should part of this service be disposed of it might well be that the consent would be vitiated. Consequently City declined the offer to dispose of this section of their service.

Statements were then prepared based on previous financial returns showing the percentage pooling attributed to these operators should they enter the scheme, Canvey being excluded. The figures calculated were:

Benfleet & District:
3.83% or 3.61% if City Coach was included

City Coach Company:
6.34 % or 6.11% if Benfleet & District was included

The proposed scheme of co-ordination of transport services was approved by a large majority of the council at a special meeting on 8 January 1946 led by the Mayor. At the TRC meeting on 5 March it was agreed that an advertisement be placed in accordance with the requirements of the 1870 Tramways Act that formal notice be given of the Corporation intention to lease to WMS and ENOC the rights of user of the trolley vehicle equipment.

The first meeting of the newly established Southend Joint Transport Committee (SJTC) was held on Thursday 21 March 1946 at Porters (the Civic House and Mayors Parlour) in the presence of His Worship the Mayor. At this meeting some key decisions were made. It was agreed that SCT would operate 'the Companies' share of the trolley vehicle mileage and that in turn 'the Companies' would increase their share of motor bus mileage. This was in contrast to the Brighton scheme where it had been a condition that Brighton, Hove & District operated a proportion of the trolleybus services. The Porters meeting also considered the position of the 'other operators', viz City, Benfleet and Canvey. It was resolved that the Principal Agreement be introduced first and that a Supplementary Agreement then be entered into for the co-ordination of their services with the parties of the Agreement. At the next SJTC meeting on 2 April the 'Appointed Day' for the introduction of the co-ordination scheme was provisionally fixed for 1 May 1946. Thus it was that the final Agreement for *'The Co-ordination of Passenger Transport Services in and around the County Borough of Southend-on-Sea'* was signed by all three parties on 24 May 1946. It appeared that after many years of wrangling Southend bus services were to at last be co-ordinated into a rational network. First, however, some practicalities needed to be resolved.

Fig.4.8 The City Coach Company service from London (Wood Green) to Southend was highly profitable, justifying the purchase of several new Beadle bodied Leyland PD1As as soon as they were available after the war. The brand new and still gleaming LD15 (NVX312) loads at Tylers Avenue. When faced with the potential loss of the section to Wickford (co-ordination scheme) City felt impelled to issue a writ against the 1946 Agreement to protect their business. OS

Fig.4.9 This photo shows three of the players involved in the 1946 Agreement. On the 25 is SCT 250 (UG1033), an AEC Regent/Brush acquired from Leeds City Transport. Just about to overtake is a Benfleet & District Daimler CWA6/Brush utility on the 3, and a WMS Bristol J05G/ECW can just be seen heading west along London Road. ABC

First application needed to be made by SCT under Part V of the Road Traffic Act, 1930 for the running of Corporation omnibuses in that portion of the proposed co-ordination area which was outside the borough. Consent was given by the Regional Traffic Commissioner following a public enquiry on 6 June, but only for those services co-ordinated with WMS and ENOC, that is the parties to the Principal Agreement. However, the 'other operators' Canvey Motor Transport, Benfleet & District Motor Services, the City Coach Company plus Rayleigh UDC all lodged appeals against the decision. Moreover, a writ was issued by City with an injunction to restrict SCT from entering into or acting under terms of the Agreement which was *ultra-vires* (in excess of one's legal powers) the powers of the Corporation.

At the TRC meeting on 25 November the Corporation were informed that City had asked for a 9% share of the receipts, having previously been offered 6.34%. Then Benfleet & District was asked if they might instead prefer to enter into a scheme to apply to service 3 only, whilst the isolated Canvey Motor Transport operations should continue to be excluded for the time being. At the next TRC meeting on 18 March 1947 after much discussion it was finally resolved that having examined all the proposals the SJTC felt that it was inappropriate to enter into any Agreement at the present time. The agreement of 24 May 1946 to the idea of co-ordination had in retrospect been unduly optimistic and, due to the established position of the 'other operators', the whole scheme had to be placed in abeyance.

Fortunately there was one lasting consequence of the 24 May 1946 Agreement; the newly established SJTC continued to function. It was thus able to institute certain more localised co-ordination of services insofar as they did not directly affect the 'other operators' who were not party to the local scheme. On 1 October 1947 new services 25A/25B were established

by a link between WMS and SCT providing a Highlands Boulevard (Leigh) to Thorpe Bay through joint service. The Shoebury services were the next to be considered and this scheme was introduced on 7 December 1949.

Phase 5 Nationalisation and the Final Co-ordination Agreement

The landslide victory of the Labour party in the first post-war election established a government with a manifesto to nationalise all road, rail, air and sea transport. It immediately put into place the Transport Act of 1947 and the British Transport Commission (BTC) was formed. In a move that was to prove enormously significant within the road transport industry Thomas Tilling Ltd. voluntarily sold out to the BTC in September 1948. The BTC had already expressed its interest in purchasing some well known independent bus operators and this together with Tilling's sellout and the fear of compulsory purchase at less than market prices sent a shiver of fear through the private bus sector about their future. Thus it was no surprise that in December 1950 tentative negotiations started regarding the voluntary acquisition of the Bridge family business by the BTC. Following further discussions it was agreed that WMS would acquire the Benfleet and Canvey concerns from Bridge on 2 March 1951.

Fig.4.10 The swishing of the trolley-booms around Victoria Circus would cease within months of this photo, denying WMS the chance to become a trolleybus operator. The vehicle is 146 (BDA366) a Park Royal bodied Sunbeam MF2 acquired from Wolverhampton Corporation. LTPS

With the bus industry experiencing the biggest upheaval since the 1930 Transport Act the Southend TRC met regardless on 18 December 1951 to appoint representatives to discuss the further co-ordination of services. Their deliberations were to be again upset by events beyond their control. On 17 February 1952 WMS obtained control of the City Coach Company. With this final and momentous action all the major obstacles to the earlier co-ordination scheme disappeared. Not surprisingly the TRC agreed that each side should review the legal position and report back.

The BTC after a period of rapid acquisitions was now in a position to set about consolidating bus operating territories. That of most significance to our story took place when the Midland area of ENOC passed to United Counties on 1 May 1952 and in compensation ENOC assumed control of WMS from 18 May. The WMS Registered Office moved to Chelmsford on 1 June and new appointments were made. Former ENOC man J. S. Gavin became the new General Manager with L. E. Richards from WMS becoming Assistant General Manager.

Fig.4.12 *The 1954 Agreement denied WMS the chance to serve Basildon New Town. In ENOC days several former WMS vehicles were transferred to Basildon (BN) garage. In this view 2300 (DJN554) a Bristol KS5G/ECW is seen departing from the Town Centre Bus Station on town service 241.* *JRYC*

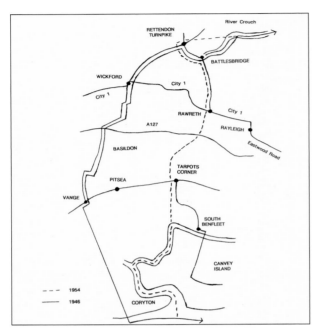

Fig.4.11 *The western boundaries of the co-ordination areas as proposed in 1946 (solid line) and 1954 (dashed line) are indicated on this map. The later boundary was moved so as to exclude the area to be occupied by Basildon New Town though also note that Rawreth and Rettendon have been included in the zone in the 1954 delineation.* *AGO*

In Southend the Transport Committee (TRC) was re-named the Passenger Transport Committee (PTC) on 18 November, its first act on 16 December being to approve the abandonment of trolleybuses, thus removing the last stumbling block to the co-ordination scheme previously mooted. Its second major decision was to agree on 23 June 1953 that any new Agreement should run for a period of 21 years rather than the 5 years suggested previously. Then on 28 September the PTC approved plans for a revision to the co-ordination area resulting in a zone of roughly 96 square miles bounded by Tarpots Corner, Rawreth (Carpenters Arms), Rettendon Turnpike and the River Crouch. Since the area of the original agreement would by this date have included part of the now rapidly growing Basildon New Town it was agreed to exclude it from the Co-ordination area and leave Basildon operations entirely in the domain of ENOC. Such a decision was greatly helped by the fact that ENOC now incorporated all the 'other operators' who would previously have objected to this, and that SCT had no interest in this distant area.

The final decision to implement the co-ordination plan had to be approved by the full Southend Town Council. A special meeting was arranged for 6 October. After a long and heated discussion the proposal was put to the vote. The Council was divided equally with 20 votes for and 20 votes against. By great good chance the Mayor Alderman Selby had been a previous Chairman of the TRC and he then used his casting vote to approve the plan. The sealing of the Agreement was approved on 8 December, the new Agreement being dated 1 January 1954. The 'Appointed Day' for the commencement of the scheme was to be decided by mutual consent. There then followed a series of meetings of the re-named Southend & District Joint Transport Co-ordination Committee (SDJTCC) to discuss the phases necessary to implement the scheme. The need to address promptly the apportionment of routes and mileages was considered on 21 January 1954, which meant that the planning and linking of services needed to be deferred until a later date. The apportionment of services was agreed at the 1 March meeting as follows:

To be operated by SCT
1, 4/A, 5/A/B, 7, 8/A, 9/A, 25A/B (39%), 28A/B, 63A/B.

To be operated by WMS
2/A/B/C, 3, 4B, 6, 9B, 10, 11, 12, 17, 18, 19/A, 21, 22, 23/A, 24, 25A/B (61%), 26/A, 27, 61, 62, 64, 251(*).
(*) portion within Co-ordinated area only

To be operated by ENOC
11(*), 19/A(*), 70(*)
(*) portion within Co-ordinated area only

The annual mileages to be operated were SCT 2,939,723 miles (37%) and WMS and ENOC 5,005,287 miles (63%).

The trolleybuses were withdrawn in stages culminating with the final run on 28 October 1954 and appropriately on the same day the SDJTCC agreed that the 'Appointed Day' should be Sunday 2 January 1955. At the WMS board meeting on 7 December it was reported that the BTC had approved that the properties, rolling stock and other assets of WMS be transferred to the ownership of ENOC with effect from 1 January 1955. Applications for ENOC service licences would then be made soon afterwards.

The Southend & District Joint Services therefore commenced on 2 January 1955 with the first departure being the 0430 service 2C to Pitsea. All revenues and expenses for the period up to and including 1 January were recorded under WMS these being legally transferred to ENOC at midnight even though the last arrival was actually not until 0023 on WMS service 2A from Romford.

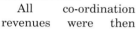

Fig.4.13 This view of Daimler CVD6/Massey SCT253 (DHJ428) catches the atmosphere of SCT and its operations at about the time of the Agreement. Massey's unique body styling, most accentuated on these Daimlers, was more characteristic of the thirties than the fifties. Combined with SCTs vivid livery and set against the delights of Southend's 'golden half-mile' between the Pier and the Kursaal we have the essence of holiday Southend. The Agreement changed where SCT buses were allowed to roam, though the 5A remained SCT worked. PJSA

All co-ordination revenues were then recorded as ENOC only. However, since WMS still held the road service licences the first two S&D Joint Services timetables still showed all three operators being involved. The process of transferring the WMS road licences to ENOC commenced on 12 January. *Chapter Two* covers subsequent developments.

Thus after a very lengthy gestation period an Agreement was at last implemented which would give a comprehensive and efficient bus service within Southend and adjoining areas. This Agreement went on to last just over 30 years only being terminated as a consequence of the impending deregulation of local bus services from 26 October 1986, the third piece of central government road passenger transport legislation to have such dramatic consequences for the travelling public and the provision of bus services in Southend.

Fig.4.14 SCT 258 (EHJ442), one of their distinctive AEC Regent III/Masseys is almost at its destination, Southend Central Station, having worked in on a 9 from Eastwoodbury. These were the final development of the curvaceous Massey body style favoured by SCT after the war, and with future deliveries Southend buses lost some of its slightly 'racy' charm. In the background an ENOC FLF, probably on a 2 or 11, waits in Victoria Station forecourt. Some mid-sixties fashions in both clothing and shop fronts provide a period setting. The lamp post is a reminder of earlier electric transport as it is a former trolleybus standard. AGOC

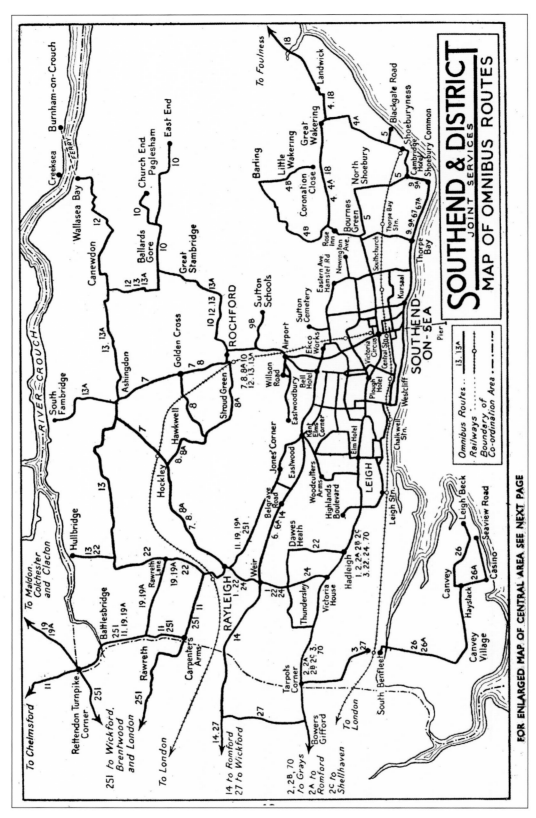

Fig.4.15 *The Southend & District Joint Services timetable dated 28 May 1955 included this route map of the SCT/WMS/ENOC services. By this date ENOC and WMS operations were no longer differentiated. Changes resulting from the co-ordination shown are the re-numbering of the sea-front services (to avoid clash with the ENOC Colchester service) whilst WMS 11 to South Fambridge became 13A. A cross-town facility was introduced with the extension of the 9/A over the 5A through to Shoeburyness. The full boundary area is shown.*

82

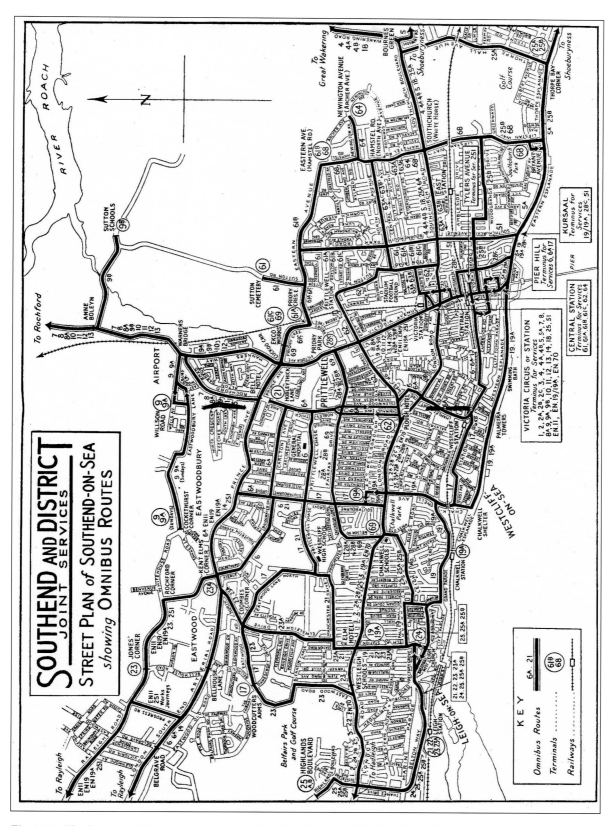

Fig.4.16 *The first map of the central area appeared in the 2 January 1955 timetable. ENOC services were specifically indicated though notice that the numbers 11 and 19/A appear twice as the conflicting WMS services have yet to be re-numbered.*

Chapter Five
Bus and Coach Services at June 1951

The 6 June 1951 timetable has been selected to show WMS services at their post-war peak just before the City Coach Company was absorbed in February 1952. The list shows the services operated and includes outline details of fares, running times and frequencies. In addition for some services notes of their antecedents are given, though for more details *see Chapter Two*. For details of the routes followed, the map from the front and back covers of the WMS bus timetable dated 24 July 1946 shown in *Fig.7.1* may be consulted. For details of the roads traversed within the central area please refer to the Southend & District Joint Services map *Fig.4.16*. Where sufficient photos are available depictions of different locations as well as types of buses used on each service over the years are shown.

The following information is presented:-

Period of operation: M Monday, T Tuesday, W Wednesday, Th Thursday, F Friday, S Saturday, Su Sunday, PH Peak Hours only.

Through fares: S – single, R – return, DR – day return shown in pre-decimal currency: e.g. 9d = approx. 4p; 2/4 = 2s 4d = 2 shillings and 4 old pence = approx. 11p.

Running time: of full route, in hours and minutes (if times are different in each direction, the longest approximate timing is given).

Frequency: (generalised).

Development of route: where appropriate.

SOUTHEND (Victoria Circus) – Leigh (Elm Hotel) – Hadleigh – Thundersley – RAYLEIGH (High Street)				
Daily	S: 10d	R: 1/3	39 mins	every 30 minutes

Re-numbered from service 2 in 4/22

Chapter Frontispiece Fig.5.1 This 1934 view is a most appropriate start to a chapter on bus services. The two major routes are represented here with a Benfleet & District Tilling-Stevens on service 3 to Benfleet and a WMS AEC Regent on service 1 to Rayleigh. These were the only directions that connected Southend to 'the rest of the world'. Both buses are high capacity double-deckers and both are fairly new. The whole scene encapsulates the period, the backdrop of the WMS headquarters at Victoria Arcade and the new Bridge family transport undertaking as described in the text. *JFP*

Fig.5.2 Some of the service numbers used by WMS are still in use today. The route from Southend to Rayleigh via Hadleigh was started in 1921 as service 2 being re-numbered 1 in April 1922. At the time of writing this number was still being used by Arriva Southend, although the service has been extended to Rayleigh Station and to Shoebury. Many years ago the crew of Daimler CK open topper HJ 4920 pose in front of their conveyance in Rayleigh High Street. Note their uniforms and caps and the bell punch ticket machine carried by the conductor. *AGOC*

Fig.5.3 *This picture epitomises WMS in the 1930s. JN2798, an AEC Regent with Park Royal highbridge bodywork of 1933, heads a line of AEC Regents, all with paintwork gleaming. Only the WMS keynote roof number box breaks the smooth lines of this modern looking bus which waits to depart for Rayleigh on service 1, one of the top-line routes.   JFH*

Fig.5.4 *Some twenty years later the final days of WMS operations just before control passed to ENOC are captured in this view in Rayleigh High Street. BJN114 is one of the ultimate batch of Bristol K5G/ECWs, these being delivered to WMS after the war. The period street furniture, fashions and cars help enliven the scene.   PJSA*

2 SOUTHEND (Victoria Circus) – Leigh (Elm Hotel) – Hadleigh – Tarpots – Pitsea – Vange – Corringham – Stanford-le-Hope – Orsett – GRAYS (War Memorial)

Daily   S: 1/10   R: 2/7   1hr 28 mins   every 60 minutes
jointly operated with ENOC service 70 (Southend, Victoria Station – Grays), daily, every 30 mins; and 84 (Tarpots Corner – Grays), daily, every 60 mins (combined frequency, with service 2B, every 15 minutes) alternate workings by ENOC and WMS.
Operated jointly with Borough Services Ltd. until 10/40.

Fig.5.5 MY2542 is a Short bodied AEC Regent, originally an AEC demonstrator which was acquired by Borough Services in March 1931. Upon absorption by ENOC in May 1933 it acquired fleet-number 3441. This view must date from shortly afterwards since the Borough service number 2 (the same as the WMS designation) is shown. ENOC did not allocate the number 70 until a few months later. The delightful animated street scene at Grays has a traffic-duty PC, gas-holder, open-staircase bus and two Green Line coaches. ABC

Fig.5.6 Service 2 was the only pre-war service that was jointly operated, initially shared with Borough Services service 70 and from 1940 with ENOC, their terminal being at Southend Victoria Station. The London Transport RT in the background shows Grays to be the location. The bus is 3639 (DEV475) a Bristol GO5G/Brush dating from 1936. DAJ

Fig.5.7 *In this classic early post-war view 1936 vintage Bristol GO5G JN6896 with original Brush bodywork complete with roof number box is seen in London Road, Pitsea en route for Southend. The bus was soon to be re-bodied by ECW and is shown in this form in Fig.6.28.   AGOC*

Fig.5.8 *An early 1950s view of service 2 at the Southend Victoria Station forecourt terminus catches these two classic WMS types together. However, the 1934 AEC Regent/Weymann is not all it seems. JN3717 was the only WMS AEC Regent to have had its body rebuilt by Portsmouth Aviation. In addition, its AEC petrol engine had been replaced by a Gardner 5LW oil unit. To the right JN6885 a 1936 Bristol JO5G with an ECOC B36R body which had also been rebuilt, this time by local company C. W. Beale, awaits a turn on service 18 to that most remote Essex outpost, Foulness Island.   ADP*

2^A SOUTHEND (Victoria Circus) – Leigh (Elm Hotel) – Hadleigh – Tarpots – Pitsea – Vange – Nevendon – Laindon – Homefields Garage – Alma Factory (or West Horndon) – Cranham – Upminster – ROMFORD (Market Place)

Daily   S: 2/4   R: 3/9   1hr 45 mins   every 30 minutes
every 60 minutes via Homefields Garage and Alma Factory and every 60 minutes via West Horndon. Certain journeys (Weekday PH) operate to Childerditch Lane.

Fig.5.9 Park End Road was the stand used when Romford market was in full swing on Wednesdays, Fridays and Saturdays so that buses and their passengers could keep out of the way of the pigs and cattle, still a feature into the early fifties. This photograph was taken on 15 May 1948. There were about half-a-dozen short workings from Romford mostly to Laindon (Fortune of War) but also a couple to Vange and Pitsea thus making this view even more interesting. Study of JN6895, a 1936 Bristol GO5G/Brush affords an opportunity to compare the effect of its body rebuild by Beadle with the unaltered Brush bodywork carried by JN6896 in Fig.5.7.   VCJ

Fig.5.10 The reason for running to far-off Romford is evident in this animated early 1950's scene. The huge market and many shops were a major attraction as the crowds of people testify. 1932 AEC Regent JN4745 had been re-bodied by ECW in 1949 producing a very smart machine. The destination display outlines the route very clearly as the bus turns from South Street into the Market Place on the final few hundred yards of its almost two hour long journey.   ABC

2^B SOUTHEND (Victoria Circus) – Leigh (Elm Hotel) – Hadleigh – Tarpots – Pitsea – Vange – Homesteads – Stanford-le-Hope – Orsett – GRAYS (War Memorial)

Daily   S: 1/10   R: 2/7   1hr 28 mins   every 60 minutes

jointly operated with ENOC (for details see service 2)

Service No. 2b.	**SOUTHEND, HADLEIGH, PITSEA, GRAYS, BARKING & EAST HAM.**												
Weekdays and Sundays.													
Leave.—	NS	NS	N S		A.M.	A.M.	A.M.	A.M.		A.M.	P.M.	P.M.	
SOUTHEND, Vic. Circus	6 20	6 20	6 40		7 20	8 20	9 20	1020		1120	1220	1 20	
Elms, Leigh		6 32			7 32	8 32	9 32	1032		1132	1232	1 32	
Water Works		6 34			7 34	8 34	9 34	1034		1134	1234	1 34	
Hadleigh, Church		6 39			7 39	8 39	9 39	1039		1139	1239	1 39	
Bread & Cheese Hill		6 44			7 44	8 44	9 44	1044		1144	1244	1 44	
Tarpots		6 49	7 3		7 49	8 49	9 49	1049		1149	1249	1 49	
Pitsea		6 58			7 58	8 58	9 58	1058		1158	1258	1 58	
Vange, Barge Inn	6 50	7 2			8 2	9 2	10 2	11 2		12 2	1 2	2 2	
Vange, Five Bells		7 8			8 8	9 8	10 8	11 8		12 8	1 8	2 8	
Homesteads		7 18			8 18	9 18	1018	1118		1218	1 18	2 18	
Stanford-le-Hope		7 23			8 23	9 23	1023	1123		1223	1 23	2 23	
GRAYS { a		7 43			8 43	9 43	1043	1143		1243	1 43	2 43	
{ d		7 45			8 45	9 45	1045	1145		1245	1 45	2 45	
Rainham		8 6			9 6	10 6	11 6	12 6		1 6	2 6	3 6	
Dagenham, Chequers		8 13			9 13	1013	1113	1213		1 13	2 13	3 13	
Barking		8 24			9 24	1024	1124	1224		1 24	2 24	3 24	
EAST HAM		8 30			9 30	1030	1130	1230		1 30	2 30	3	
Leave.—	P.M.	P.M.		P.M.	P.M.	P.M.		P.M.	P.M.	P.M.		P.M.	P.M.
SOUTHEND, Vic. Circus	2 20	3 20		4 20	5 20		6 20	7 20	8 20		9 20	10 20	
Elms, Leigh	2 32	3 32		4 32	5 32		6 32	7 32	8 32		9 34	10 32	
Water Works	2 34	3 34		4 34	5 34		6 34	7 34	8 34		9 34	10 43	
Hadleigh, Church	2 39	3 39		4 39	5 39		6 39	7 39	8 39		9 39	10 39	
Bread & Cheese Hill	2 44	3 44		4 44	5 44		6 44	7 44	8 44		9 44	10 44	
Tarpots	2 49	3 49		4 49	5 49		6 49	7 49	8 49		9 49	10 49	
Pitsea	2 58	3 58		4 58	5 58		6 58	7 58	8 58		9 58	10 58	
Vange, Barge Inn	3 2	4 2		5 2	6 2		7 2	8 2	9 2		10 2	11 2	
Vange, Five Bells	3 8	4 8		5 8	6 8		7 8	8 8	9 8		10 8	11SS 8	
Homesteads	3 18	4 18		5 18	6 18		7 18	8 18	9 18		1018	11SS18	
Stanford-le-Hope	3 23	4 23		5 23	6 23		7 23	8 23	9 23		1023	11SS23	
GRAYS { a	3 43	4 43		5 43	6 43		7 43	8 43	9 43		1043	11SS43	
{ d	3 45	4 45		5 45	6 45		7 45	8 45	9 45		1045	11SS45	
Rainham	4 6	5 6		6 6	7 6		8 6	9 6	10 6		11 6	12SS 6	
Dagenham, Chequers	4 13	5 13		6 13	7 13		8 13	9 13	1013		1113	12SS13	
Barking	4 24	5 24		6 24	7 24		8 24	9 24	1024		1124	12SS24	
EAST HAM	4 30	5 30		6 30	7 30		8 30	9 30	1030		1130	12SS30	
NS Not Sundays. **SS** Saturdays and Sundays only.													

Fig.5.11 Timetable

The 2B was one of the premier services of WMS running as it did from Southend to East Ham. As can be seen in this extract from the July 1932 timetable booklet an hourly frequency was offered every day, including Sundays. The route virtually paralled the London, Tilbury and Southend Railway's original route via Grays but of course ran through the centre of the settlements and offered a cheaper, if slower, journey. The market for such a service lay in the growth of Southend and the area towards Pitsea which was largely populated by people moving out from the East End. Some would then need to commute back to work whilst others would have parents and relations still living in the East End who would visit, by WMS 2B of course.

Fig.5.12 *The typical late pre-war and early post-war allocation to the busy 2B was a Bristol GO5G or K5G, one of the latter JN9543 seen here waiting time at Hadleigh Church. The trees, churchyard and shops remain of this scene though not the distinctive shelter cum direction-post cum street-lamp. Fig.5.82 shows this corner of Hadleigh in the early thirties. PJSA*

Fig.5.13 *Regent JN4745 seems to have been a favourite allocation to the 2 group. Looking at its clean lines no one would guess that it was about twenty years old, though no doubt the driver had other views. This period view was taken in Grays in the early fifties. ABC*

Fig.5.14 *The final face of WMS on the 2B is shown by FJN158, by then ENOC 1392, a Bristol KSW5G/ECW new in 1952. It is seen rounding Victoria Circus. Above the fleet number is a white circle, the garage code for Hadleigh, which later became HH, much easier to remember. The three line intermediate blind matched SCT displays, most ENOC buses in Essex having only two line 'via' blinds. RFM*

3 **SOUTHEND (Victoria Circus) – Leigh (Elm Hotel) – Hadleigh – Tarpots – SOUTH BENFLEET (War Memorial)**

Daily   S: 10d   R: 1/4   40 mins   every 15 minutes

Re-numbered from service 8 in 1/23. Incorporates timings ex-Benfleet & District service 3 from 3/51.

Fig.5.15 *South Benfleet War Memorial was the terminus of the 3 from its inception. It was the nearest bus turning point to the station and Canvey ferry (later bridge) that was allowed by Benfleet UDC. This evocative late 1920s scene catches passengers alighting and others making their way towards the station and ferry. The WMS bus appears to be HJ3319 a Daimler CK. JRYC*

Fig.5.16 *This view shows Canvey & District veteran 25 (GX131) working on 'mainland' service 3. The bus pre-dates the rugged wartime Bedford lorry and is not what it seems. Despite the AEC radiator (and engine) it is actually a Leyland TD1 which was new to Birch Bros. of Kentish Town in 1932. It then became TD85 in the London Transport fleet. Its Birch body, which originally had an open rear staircase has been considerably rebuilt. PJSA*

Fig.5.17 *The Benfleet & District service was a real 'money-spinner' and relief buses were a common sight. In this 1950 view taken in London Road, Southend B&D 15 (KEV535) a Brush utility bodied Daimler CWA6 new to the Bridge family business in 1945 is seen on a short working to Hadleigh Church. More number threes wait their turn behind. ABC*

Fig.5.18 *At the other end of the 3 service at South Benfleet (War Memorial) FOP462 loads for a return journey to Southend. This bus was one of the large batch of Daimler CWA6s delivered to Birmingham City Transport during the war quite a number of which moved south to Essex just five years later finding buyers in the Bridge family and SCT. CC*

Fig.5.19 *Towards the end of WMS operation of service 3 the Bristol K was the most likely allocation for this busy route. In this view one of the CJN batch of Bristol K5G/ECWs new in 1948 has a heavy load, to judge by the way it is 'sitting down' on its springs at the rear. Note the full side blind destination display matching that at the front.   PJSA*

4 **SOUTHEND (Victoria Circus) – Southchurch – Bournes Green – Little & Great Wakering – LANDWICK**

Daily   S: 6d   R: 9d   22 mins   every 60 minutes
Re-numbered from service 3 in 1/23.

Fig.5.20 *A nicely ani-mated period scene at Victoria Station catches a summer-dust-jacketed conductor taking a keen interest in his surround-ings from the platform, a small boy doing exactly the same but from the pavement edge and really only the driver doing any work. AJN823 was an ECW bodied Bristol K5G delivered in 1939 still in largely original condition. It is seen turning into Victoria Circus to start a service 4 to Landwick via Great Wakering. RFM*

Fig.5.21 *Weymann bodied AEC Regent JN5461 of 1935 had the distinction of being the last new AEC Regent bought by WMS, further double-deckers being Bristols. It was also rebuilt, in this case in 1946 by C. W. Beale. It is seen here working a 4 with a Beadle rebuilt AEC Regent behind. Despite both buses being lowbridge configuration JN5461 looks noticeably higher.* PJSA

4 ᴬ SOUTHEND (Victoria Circus) – Southchurch – Bournes Green – Little & Great Wakering – SHOEBURYNESS (Station)

| Daily | S: 7d | R: 1/1 | 24 mins | every 60 minutes |

Fig.5.22 *CJN323, one of the less common Bristol K6B/ECW, awaits departure for Shoeburyness LMS Station on a dull Sunday.* PJSA

Fig.5.23 UEV842 was new in 1952, a fine Bristol KSW5G/ECW one of no less than nineteen that were to bear the WMS name. The photographer has captured a smartly turned out nearly new bus at work on the 4A, yet garage staff have fitted a second-hand and inappropriate via point blind bearing the circled route number needed for buses without separate route number apertures.   RM

4ᴮ SOUTHEND (Victoria Circus) – Southchurch – Bournes Green – Barling – LITTLE WAKERING (Coronation Close)

Daily	S: 7d	R: 9d	26 mins	every 60 minutes

additional journeys on FS give a service every 30 mins.

Fig.5.24 Following the introduction of the Southend   co-ordination scheme in 1955, service 4B was worked by SCT.   In Broadway Market veteran AEC Regal 203 (JN823) of 1931 with English Electric bodywork which had been substantially rebuilt in the Corporation workshops awaits departure for Coronation Close, Little Wakering.   CC

5 SOUTHEND (Victoria Circus) – Southchurch – Bournes Green – North Shoebury – SHOEBURYNESS (Blackgate Road)

Daily   S: 6d   R: 9d   25 mins   every 15 minutes

main service terminates at Shoeburyness Station (23 mins), extended to Blackgate Road at weekday peak hours.

Re-numbered from service 4 in 1/23. Incorporates timings ex-Shoeburyness Motor Services from 2/36.

Fig.5.25   *WMS service 5 was originally Shoeburyness Motor Services raison d'etre as seen by the prominent route identification along the waistrail of this bus. Its profitability justified their purchase of brand new buses one of which is seen in this pre-delivery view. It is EV1925 a Duple bodied Dennis HV.   PJSA*

Fig.5.26   *Pre-war Bristol K5G/ECW AHJ402 of 1938 looks very smart and appears unrebuilt except for the fitting of the lower PV2 radiator. No doubt this is partly due to the clean lines of the ECW body style, despite it having six window bays. It is ready to provide the next 5 to Shoeburyness in this early post-war view.   PJSA*

Fig.5.27 *Another brand new bus but two decades later than the Dennis in Fig.5.25 overleaf is FJN161 the very last Bristol KSW5G/ECW to be delivered to WMS. It awaits departure for Shoeburyness on a sunny Sunday.   MLWC*

6   SOUTHEND (Pier Hill) – Clifftown Road – Westcliff Station – Hamlet Court Road – WESTCLIFF (Plough)

Daily   S: 3d   R: -   13 mins   every 15 minutes
Re-numbered from service 5 in 1/23.

Fig.5.28 *The crew, resplendent in their white summer dustcoats, proudly pose by their new bus outside the Royal Hotel at the end of the High Street. The photo clearly shows the sliding-roof arrangement specified by WMS for their saloons at this period. Further examples are shown in Figs.11.15 & 11.16. Dennis, Daimler and early AEC Reliance chassis were fitted with similar style bodies including those built by London Lorries, though this bus is believed to be by Strachan & Brown. The route between Pier Hill and the Plough Hotel was started by the WSMC on 19 July 1920 as service 1. It later became service 5 and then 6, a number which it then retained for some years.   PJSA*

6 B WESTCLIFF (Station) – Plough Hotel – Carlton Avenue or Prittlewell Chase – Prince Avenue – Kent Elm Corner – Eastwood – Belgrave Road – Rayleigh Weir – RAYLEIGH (High Street)

Daily   S: 8d   R: 1/-   32 mins   see next line

Westcliff – Eastwood every 15 mins, via Prittlewell Chase, Weekdays every 30 mins, Su every 60 mins; via Carlton Avenue, Weekdays every 30 mins. Eastwood – Rayleigh Weekdays 4/5 jnys

Fig.5.29   *JN9543 leaves its Pier Hill terminus (behind the Palace Hotel) for Rayleigh. It is a 1937 Bristol K5G/ECW that has been rebuilt by C. W. Beale. The destination blind has become folded obscuring the service number. But the location of the bus together Carlton Avenue as a via point on the blind indicates that this is a service 6B.*   *WJH*

Fig.5.30 DHJ21 is a Bristol K5G/ECW of 1948 now carrying its ENOC number 1307 but with WMS fleet-names. It waits at Pier Hill terminus behind the Palace Hotel to work a service 6. The 6B was grouped with the 6 in the 1951 timetable but in fact the services shared a common section only between The Plough Hotel and Westcliff Station. After co-ordination all buses ran through to Rayleigh as 6 via Prittlewell Chase as the 6A via Carlton Avenue. Thus this view shows the 6B after co-ordination. PJSA

7 SOUTHEND (Victoria Circus) – Bell Hotel – Rochford – Ashingdon – Hockley – RAYLEIGH (High Street)

Daily   S: 10d   R: 1/3   42 mins   see next line

Southend – Ashingdon   4 jnys/hour,   Ashingdon – Rayleigh   every 30 mins

Re-numbered from services 6/6A in 1/23. Incorporates ex-Rochford & District timings from 5/33

Fig.5.31   Despite it being a key route, good photos of WMS buses on service 7 have proved elusive. CJN321 was one of the final batch of K5G/ECWs delivered in 1948. This early 1950s view catches it on a sunny afternoon heading out of Broadway Market on a 7 short working to Rochford, Spa Hotel.   PJSA

Fig.5.32   This interesting view in the Prittlewell yard includes two ex-BH&D Dennis Lances that had been bought for contract use, the unique roofed ex-Southdown Tilling-Stevens UF4510 and an open-topper's roof. AEC Regent JN2800 (centre) shows ROCHFORD Bell Hotel on the blind, hence its inclusion here. It is one of the first batch of Park Royal bodied AEC Regents and dates from 1933. It has been rebuilt by ECW during the war gaining sliding windows but losing its roof number box in the process. It sits next to another similar AEC Regent allowing us to note the variation in application of WMS's livery.   RFM

8 **SOUTHEND (Victoria Circus) – Bell Hotel – Rochford – Hawkwell – Hockley – RAYLEIGH (High Street)**

Daily   S: 10d   R: 1/3   42 mins   every 30 minutes
service 8 replaced every 2 hours by service 8A.
Re-numbered from service 10 in 1/23 Incorporates timings ex Rayleigh Motor Services from 8/36

8ᴬ **SOUTHEND (Victoria Circus) – Bell Hotel – Rochford – Golden Cross – Stroud Green – Hawkwell – Hockley – RAYLEIGH (High Street)**

Daily   S: 10d   R: 1/3   42 mins   every 2 hours
service 8A replaces service 8 every 2 hours.

Fig.5.33 *The wide sweep of Rayleigh High Street in the late forties has much of interest which has now been lost, in particular the impressive cast-iron signpost and of course the WMS AEC Q and Bristol GO5G. It is unclear whether they are on service 7 or 8.   JRYC*

Fig.5.34 *WMS standard buses from before and after the war are caught together on the 7/8 stand in Broadway Market. Neither is working the full route. The AEC Regent/ Weymann JN4295 is a service 8 short to Rochford and the Bristol K5G/ECW, CHJ254, is on a service 7 short to Ashingdon Schools. JN4295 has been rebuilt by C. W. Beale and has had its roof number box painted over, an unhelpful move when no route number appears on the destination blind (compare Fig.5.43).   AMW*

Fig.5.35   There are no such problems here. The full blind display makes it very clear exactly where DJN556 a Bristol KS6B/ECW is going and exactly matches the standard displays on the SCT buses working this route after coordination.   PJSA

9   SOUTHEND (Victoria Circus) – Cuckoo Corner – Bell Hotel – Eastwoodbury (Wilson Rd) – COCKETHURST CORNER

Daily   S: 4½d   R: 7d   17 mins   see next line
Southend – Eastwoodbury every 30 mins; certain journeys operate via Ekco Works (M-F PH).
Eastwoodbury – Cockethurst Corner Su only 1-3 jnys

Fig.5.36   Despite appearances this is not a JO5G but WMS's sole Bristol L5G/ECW AJN826, new in 1939. Later saloons were either LWL5G or LS5G models. It waits in Broadway Market to work the short 9 to Eastwoodbury, taking just twelve minutes.   PJSA

Fig.5.37   Just passing Southend Victoria Station on service 9 from Eastwoodbury is JN 6897, a Bristol GO5G dating from 1936. It was one of eight with Brush bodies all of which were either rebuilt or rebodied after the war. This bus, JN6897 which later became ENOC 1230, had a thorough rebuild by Beadle which was in effect virtually a rebody as comparison with JN6896 of the same batch in original condition in Fig.5.7 will make clear.   RFM

9ᴬ   SOUTHEND (Victoria Circus) – Cuckoo Corner – Manners Way – COCKETHURST CORNER

| Daily | S: 4½d | R: 7d | 17 mins | see next line |

Southend – Eastwoodbury   every 30 minutes; certain jnys operate via Ekco Works (M-F PH)
Eastwoodbury – Cockethurst Corner Su only 1-3 jnys

Fig.5.38   The Weymann body on AEC Regent JN3718 of 1934 was rebuilt by Beadle in 1947. Comparison with Fig.5.37 above shows some similarities in front end treatment. It is seen departing Broadway Market on a service 9A in the early 1950s.   PJSA

9^B SOUTHEND (Victoria Circus) – Manners Way – Rochford Road – SUTTON (Schools)

9^B SOUTHEND (Victoria Circus) – Manners Way – Rochford Road – SUTTON (Schools)
Daily   S: 4d   R: 6d   13 mins   every 2 hours

Fig.5.39 *JN7499 was one of the 1936 batch of Bristol JO5G/ECW buses rebuilt by C. W. Beale in 1946/7 though no external changes are obvious. New service 9B to Sutton Schools started on 29 December 1948 the day on which this photograph was taken.   ABC*

10 SOUTHEND (Victoria Circus) – Manners Way – Rochford – Stambridge – Ballards Gore – PAGLESHAM (East End)
Daily   S: 1/-   R: 1/7   38 mins   every 2 hours
Combined frequency services 10/12 every 30 mins between Southend and Ballards Gore
Re-numbered from service 9 in 1/23

Fig.5.40 *Who could wish to be anywhere else? HJ7616, a wonderful Dennis E saloon has just hissed and purred through the remote marshes to the last place before Siberia, or so it seems. We now have a warm pint of Mann, Crossman and Paulin's best mild ale to look forward to inside the weather-boarded Ship & Compasses at Paglesham.   MLWC*

Fig.5.41 *This fairly standard Bristol saloon was, for WMS anything but. EJN 633 was one of three similar ECW bodied Bristol LWL5Gs delivered in 1951 which were the only half-cab single-deck buses bought by WMS after the war. Other saloons were purchased but they were either dual-purpose or coach variants based on the newly introduced under-floor layout. Most WMS bus services required double-deckers so the saloon intake was always somewhat limited and plenty of JO5Gs had survived from before the war. EJN633 had just arrived at Southend Victoria Station having worked in on service 10 and the destination blind has already been set for the return journey to Paglesham. These services to the thinly populated area between the rivers Roach and Crouch only required single-deckers.* WJH

| | SOUTHEND (Victoria Circus) – Bell Hotel – Rochford – Ashingdon – LARKS HILL (Leon Cottage) or – Stambridge – Larks Hill – Ashingdon – FAMBRIDGE (The Anchor)

Weekdays   S: 1/3   R: 1/4   43 mins   see next line
Southend – Ashingdon (Schools) M-F 2 jnys, Sat 1 jny. Southend – Larks Hill Th 2 jnys.
Southend – Fambridge Sat 2 jnys.
Ex Rochford & District in 5/33

Fig.5.42 *Rochford Square in the mid-thirties is complete with ornate drinking trough/street lamp. It is further enhanced by the presence, albeit temporary, of HJ8934, a Dennis E possibly working an 11 to/from Fambridge and carefully observed by a small dog.* AGOC

Fig.5.43 *The Ashingdon wire- and bungalow-scape has not changed that much in the intervening half-century that we cannot recognise this backdrop to 'standard' WMS AEC Regent/Weymann JN4747 pausing before a return working to Southend. Although the blind has a circle to display the service number the circle is empty, and the roof number box is painted over. The via points however indicate that JN4747 is working an 11 via Larks Hill rather than the more frequent service 8 hence its inclusion here.* MLWC

Fig.5.44 *The more usual allocation for the service 11 at this time was a Bristol JO5G/ECW saloon. JN8564 is seen here in Fairfax Drive opposite Prittlewell garage and has either just come off or awaits a turn on the 11 to Fambridge. In this case an appropriate blind complete with encircled route number has been fitted.* ENEG

12 SOUTHEND (Victoria Circus) – Manners Way – Rochford – Stambridge – Ballards Gore – Canewdon – CREEKSEA (Wallasea Bay)

Daily   S: 1/2   R: 1/9   42 mins   see next line

Southend – Canewdon (Loftmans Corner) every 60 mins. Canewdon – Wallasea Bay every 1-2 hours.
Combined frequency services 10/12 Southend and Ballards Gore every 30 mins.
Re-numbered from service 10A in 1925. Incorporates timings ex Rochford & District from 5/33.
Original service 12 was South Benfleet – Leigh Beck, abandoned in 1925.

Fig.5.45   Wallasea Island, here called Creeksea, is located in the relatively remote area between the rivers Roach and Crouch which still remains purely agricultural with few villages and low population density. WMS bought Bristol JO5Gs for these rural routes and here JN6889 confirms the point as it waits in Broadway Market before setting off for these backwaters.   AMW

Fig.5.46   EJN633 was one of three Bristol LWL5G/ECW buses bought in 1951 before WMS turned to under-floor engined buses with an LS intake the following year. It is seen here in ENOC days as 344 at Wallasea Island terminus in reality nothing more than a boatyard, cafe and maybe a walk down-stream along the sea wall to look at Burnham on Crouch across the river.   OS

17 **SOUTHEND (Pier Hill) – Clifftown Road – Westcliff Station – Chalkwell Avenue – Southbourne Grove – Prittlewell Chase – Coombes Corner – EASTWOOD (Woodcutters Arms)**
Daily   S: 5d   R: 8d   24 mins   every 10 minutes

Fig.5.47 CJN323 was one of only eight of the more powerful six cylinder Bristol-engined K6B/ECW bought by WMS. Given the fairly full load no doubt the driver appreciates the extra horse-power on this run. The location is Grove Terrace with Pier Hill as indicated by the reflective road sign on the right. The 17 terminus was just opposite the Ritz cinema and adjacent to the back of the Palace Hotel. The Nescafe hoarding covers what was the Holmes & Smith garage.   RFM

18 **SOUTHEND (Victoria Circus) – Southchurch – Little & Great Wakering – FOULNESS (Court End)**
Daily   S: 1/2   R: 1/9   40 mins   see next line
MTWTh, 2 jnys, F 4 jnys, Sat 9 jnys, Su 2 jnys.
Restrictions apply to passengers travelling to Foulness Island regarding War Department lands.

Fig.5.48 After the introduction of co-ordination some unusual operator/vehicle/service working combinations occurred which would have been impossible just a few years earlier. SCT 261 (EHJ445) an AEC Regent with stylish Massey lowbridge bodywork is one such example, here about to set off for Foulness Island on an 18, surely a bleak and inhospitable destination for such a refined vehicle.   ABC

Fig.5.49 *This view was taken at the other end of the High Street in the far less salubrious surroundings of Bradley Street just opposite the LNER goods yard. JN6882 a Bristol JO5G/ECOC of 1936 had been rebuilt by C. W. Beale in 1947 though without significant change to its external appearance. A trip to that most remote of Essex locations, Foulness Island is in prospect.   MLWC*

19   SOUTHEND (Kursaal) – Pier – Chalkwell Shelter – Pall Mall – LEIGH (Elm Hotel)

Daily (Summer only)	S: 6d	R: 9d	27 mins	every 20 minutes

Fig.5.50 *This wonderful pre-war view of 1927 Dennis E ML1582 (ex- LGOC and Admiral) just oozes period atmosphere with summer dust-coat and caps, 'informal' jackets and ties for passersby and of course hats for the ladies. Service 19 is perhaps rather over-promoting itself as a 'Grand 7 Mile Marine Tour' but the bus is as immaculate as the crew sporting a showroom shine to the paintwork and white-wall tyres. Its charms have already attracted a number of customers. DWKJ*

Fig.5.51. *The 'Grand Marine Drive' started in 1924 as service 6A, with Berliet open-sided toastrack vehicles (see Fig.2.8). It proved so popular that larger Daimlers with sun roofs and dual doors were introduced. This enlargement of a commercial postcard shows one of these, HJ4643, loading at the Pier stop. Just pulling away is an Edwards Hall Vulcan on their competing service H.   JRYC*

Fig.5.52. *This sea-front view has just about everything! Working a service 19 is GJ2005, an AEC Regent new to Tilling in 1930 with a Tilling body built at Peckham. This body was replaced in 1936 by another Tilling body but built at Hove. In 1942 it gained a third body this time by ECW at Irthlingborough. WMS bought GJ2005 from BH&D in 1949 for use on the sea-front service. As if this is not enough for one photograph, to the right may be seen a Ladies Mobile Toilet which had been converted from a former SCT trolleybus in 1950. And, as if this was not enough, the trolleybus was the very first AEC 663T built. It started in 1930 as a demonstrator, was re-bodied by English Electric, demonstrated again and in 1932 sold to SCT to become 116, JN2086. They later converted it from its original half-cab configuration and reduced its twin staircases and entrances to one of each at the rear. It was finally scrapped as late as 1967.   PJSA*

TIMES & FARES
for
Sea Front Services
Commencing 30 JUN 1947
Terminating 30th September, 1947

SERVICE
No. 19
SOUTHEND (KURSAAL)
WESTERN ESPLANADE
THE LEAS
CHALKWELL RLY. STATION
GRAND PARADE
PALL MALL
STATION ROAD
ELM HOTEL
SERVICE
No. 19A
SOUTHEND (KURSAAL)
WESTERN ESPLANADE
THE LEAS
CHALKWELL AVENUE
LONDON ROAD
ELM HOTEL

WESTCLIFF-ON-SEA
MOTOR SERVICES LIMITED

19A SOUTHEND (Kursaal) – Pier – Chalkwell Shelter – Chalkwell Ave – LEIGH (Elm Hotel)

Daily (Summer only)   S: 6d   R: 9d   25 mins   every 20 minutes

Re-numbered from service 6A in 7/47

Fig.5.53 *We are now at the other end of the sea-front, Chalkwell Shelter where the road turns inland towards Leigh. JN8566 is one of two brand new Bristol JO5Gs in this period scene which is enhanced by stylish cars, smart conductor and a very orange looking Belisha beacon. These ECW bodied cream liveried saloons with their sun-roofs were bought specially for sea-front use to replace the earlier toast-racks. This speaks volumes about the business to be had in those balmy days. But would WMS have bought them had they known that all this would end just two years later in September 1939?   MLWC*

Fig.5.54 *The sea front services 19 and 19A have been home to a variety of interesting buses over the years. This classic view is taken opposite the Kursaal Amusement Park. Note the wonderful bus stop sign advertising the route, and of course the helter-skelter. The centre-piece is GW6273, an AEC Regent which began life with Tilling in Brighton (6273) in 1932 with Tilling open rear staircase bodywork. In 1943 it was re-engined with a 5LW, 'rebuilt' though in practice re-bodied in 1943 by ECW, then converted to open top by BH&D in 1950 for sale to WMS. Remarkably, it survived long enough to be taken into stock by ENOC as 1140.   PJSA*

19^A **CHALKWELL (Station) – Chalkwell Avenue – WESTBOROUGH ROAD**
Weekday PH   S: 1½d   R: -   5 mins   see next line
Supplementary service M-F 14 jnys, Sat 4 jnys

21   **LEIGH (Station) – Elm Hotel – Manchester Drive – Prittlewell Chase – Southbourne Grove – Carlton Avenue – PRITTLEWELL (Hobleythick Lane)**
Weekdays   S: 4d   R: -   17 mins   every 30 minutes
Re-numbered from joint Borough service 72/WMS service B in 8/42.

Fig.5.55   This ECW Archive view was taken on 12 May 1939. The vehicle is AJN 826 the only Bristol L5G ever operated by WMS. When new it carried ECW B32R bodywork featuring more cream than usual on this style of body. The legal address carried was 17-21, London Road and the fleet-name was by then in the standard Tilling style, underlined 'Westcliff-on-Sea'. The seating capacity was later increased to 35. The destination blind setting is of particular interest here as it shows 'Westcliff (Somerset Crescent)' and is lettered service B which had been started in July 1934. This service was joint with Borough Services route 72 and was re-numbered 21 in 1942.   ECW/SJB

22   **LEIGH (Station) – Elm Hotel – Hadleigh – Dawes Heath – Rayleigh – Hambro Hill – HULLBRIDGE**
Daily   S: 1/-   R: 1/7   48 mins   see next line
service between Leigh (Station) and Leigh (Rectory Grove) irregular.
Leigh (Rectory Grove) – Rayleigh   every 60 minutes;   Rayleigh – Hullbridge every 30 minutes.
No terminal point shown in Hullbridge, later designated as The Anchor.
Re-numbered from WMS service E in 8/42 which incorporated former Rayleigh & District timings.

Fig.5.56   This view was taken at Hullbridge in 1958 in Eastern National days and shows 1344 (DJN 556), a former WMS Bristol KS5G/ECW standing at the 22 terminal point at The Anchor public house. The road to the left leads to the River Crouch and former ferry in a few hundred yards. The bus, approaching from the right of the photo, has had to drive past the pub car park and reverse back in.   JCG

23 LEIGH (Station) – Elm Hotel – Eastwood Road – Woodcutters Arms – Kent Elm Corner – EASTWOOD (Jones Corner)

Daily   S: 3d   R: 5d   18 mins   every 30 minutes
service between Leigh (Station) and Leigh (Rectory Grove) irregular.
Re-numbered from joint Borough service 71/Westcliff service G in 8/42.

23ᴬ LEIGH (Station) – Elm Hotel – Elmsleigh Drive – EASTWOOD (Coombes Corner)

Weekdays   S: 3d   R: 5d   11 mins   every 30 minutes
service between Leigh (Station) and Leigh (Rectory Grove) irregular.

Fig.5.57   The Leigh services of WMS have proved rather camera shy, though a fascinating bus on the 23 is shown in Fig.11.17. The best available for the short service 23A is this depot view. The Kent Elm Corner destination is incorrect as it actually applied to the 23. JN4294 was one of two AEC Regent/Weymanns rebodied by ECW. Comparison with JN4745 (Figs.5.10, 5.13) shows how the longer replacement radiator on the latter bus considerably enhanced and modernised its appearance.   PJSA

24 LEIGH (Church/Rectory Grove) – Thames Drive – Hadleigh – Rayleigh Road – RAYLEIGH (High Street)

Daily   S: 8d   R: 11d   25 mins   every 60 minutes
Leigh – Hadleigh (Victoria House) Weekdays every 30 minutes, Su every 60 mins.
Hadleigh (Victoria House) – Rayleigh   Daily every 60 minutes.
Re-numbered from WMS service C in 8/42.

Fig.5.58   In Hadleigh garage yard BHJ532 showing '24 LEIGH Rectory Grove' is as near as we can get to a WMS bus working this service. This 1939 Bristol K5G/ECW was destined to spend two war years with Thames Valley. Here it sits next to JN9541 the second K5G delivered to WMS. The difference in appearance is due to some remedial work by BH&D to JN9541's body and the fitment of a a larger windscreen and a PV2 lower radiator giving a noticeably more modern look to the front compared to BHJ532, a bus two years younger but which had not been rebuilt.   RFM

25^A LEIGH (Highlands Boulevard) – Thames Drive – Leigh Station – Leigh Road – Chalkwell Schools – Southend – Southchurch – Bournes Green – Thorpe Hall Avenue – THORPE BAY CORNER

| Daily | S: 8d | R: - | 40 mins | every 20 minutes |

Joint service with Southend Corporation Transport

25^B LEIGH (Highlands Boulevard) – Thames Drive – Leigh Station – Leigh Road – Chalkwell Schools – Southend – Eastern Esplanade – THORPE BAY CORNER

| Daily | S: 8d | R: - | 40 mins | every 20 minutes |

Joint service with Southend Corporation Transport
Services 25A/25B operated as a circular: Leigh – Southend – Thorpe Bay – Southend – Leigh, outward as 25A, returning as 25B and vice versa. Through running time 1 hr 23 minutes, through round trip single fare 1/4.

Fig.5.59 *The first joint working agreement between WMS and SCT was introduced in 1947 and involved services 25A and 25B. This fine view shows SCT 234 (BHJ808) a 1945 Duple re-bodied Daimler CWA6 on route 25B working through to Leigh, Highlands Boulevard. SCT provided most of the buses on this joint service. The bus has just passed the imposing facade of the erstwhile WMS garage at 33, London Road, which later formed the entrance to ENOC Southend (SD) garage.* PJSA

Fig.5.60 *To take us onto Canvey Island for the 26/A we need to cross the LT&S railway at Benfleet and then the Colvin Bridge. But buses from the mainland turned at Benfleet War Memorial, and those from the island had their own terminal on the mainland side of the bridge at the creek. Not until 1962 when the new railway underpass opened, did a through bus service start. So this view (taken from the station footbridge) is very welcome as it shows JN2799 a WMS AEC Regent/Park Royal actually making the link, albeit running PRIVATE. The volume of traffic at this bottleneck may be noted as well as the row of buildings, all demolished to make way for the new underpass.* VCJ

26 **SOUTH BENFLEET (Canvey Bridge) – Canvey Village – Haystack – CANVEY (Leigh Beck Farm)**

Daily   S: 5d   R: 8d   18 mins   every 10 minutes

Ex Canvey & District service 1 in 3/51

26ᴬ **SOUTH BENFLEET (Canvey Bridge) – Canvey Village – Haystack – CANVEY (Casino)**

Daily (Summer)   S: 4½d   R: 8d   18 mins   see next line

operated in accordance with traffic requirements

Ex Canvey & District service 1A in 3/51

Fig.5.61   Some idea of both the profitability of buses on Canvey, and the demands put on the operators (and the patience of passengers) during summer peak hours may be gained from this remarkable scene. Yes it is a queue and it stretches from the Daimler around Furtherwick Road at least as far as the Casino (white building), and possibly further on. Just what the crew's thoughts were, and whether an inspector was hiding somewhere to avoid harassed passengers is anyone's guess. The bus is one of the ex-Birmingham Daimler CWA6s of Canvey & District working a 1A duplicate, later to become service 26A.   JRYC

Fig.5.62   Canvey & District's standard bus after the war was the utility Daimler, but there were some other remarkable survivors. Seen at the South Benfleet (Canvey Bridge) terminal, with the bridge to the island visible in the background is a very interesting bus, AEC Regent 8 (VX4108) now carrying a Northern Coachbuilders utility body. The chassis dates from February 1930 and it was the very first Regent delivered to ENOC as 3020 then having Short bodywork. The road to its final guise is the subject of much controversy. The full story is given in Fact File 6. Although acquired by WMS it was withdrawn in December 1951 and so never returned to ENOC.   ABC

Fig.5.63 *GX131 is seen again, now at the Leigh Beck terminus, Point Cafe where no doubt the crew are imbibing strong 'busman's tea' whilst the 'young shaver' minds their bus. The turning circle in the background is still in use today and marks the end of the public road. Our last view of GX131 (see Fig.5.16) was of it on service 3. Since then it has lost its roof number box and protruding destination box, gained a smaller windscreen, simplified livery and has been renumbered to 4. It was scrapped in October 1949.* DWKJ

Fig.5.64 *We are back at the Benfleet terminus but this time in colour and later ENOC days as may just be discerned by the bus livery and fleet-name and the notice board in the background (the National part of the name just being visible). NVX302 started life with the City Coach Company as LD5 (see Fig.1.10 for a view of this bus with City, remarkably also in colour) before passing to WMS and then ENOC where it became 1122. It is a Leyland PD1A with bodywork by Roberts (of Wakefield) and dates from 1949.* PJSA

Fig.5.65 *WMS only operated the Canvey routes for a couple of years before coming under ENOC control. Those few years at the beginning of the decade saw so many changes through take-over and absorption that a fascinating variety of various former owner buses in several different liveries, fleet-names and numbers existed, but just for a year or two. This view at literally 'the end of the road' (see behind the bus) on Canvey sea-front catches all that. The Beadle bodied Leyland PD1A NVX311 is a former City Coach Company bus, operating an ex-Canvey & District route with now obsolete 'Westcliff-on-Sea' fleet-names but with ENOC fleet-number plate (1131) and garage code disc. Phew! And to cap it all, this bus was later exported to the USA.   WRL*

Fig.5.66 *Photographed on Canvey sea-front by the Labworth Cafe (right on sea wall) is this former Canvey & District Brush utility bodied Daimler CWA6 KHK864. The date is 1955. Although the bus now has number 1214 in the ENOC fleet it still carries 'Westcliff-on-Sea' fleet-names. Despite its two changes of owner it continues to work its old routes, probably fit for little else.   JCG*

27 **SOUTH BENFLEET (War Memorial) – Tarpots Corner – Pound Lane – Nevendon – WICKFORD**
Mondays   S: 8d   R: 1/2   30 mins   5 journeys
No terminal point shown in Wickford, later designated as White Swan on W27.
Ex Benfleet & District in 3/51 *(See Fig.6.54 for a photograph)*

WORKS CONTRACT SERVICES   AWRE BEA MEC

These were run as required, usually two or three times a day as appropriate to shifts and were not included in public timetables.

In the immediate post-war years a number of large scale industrial building projects were planned either side of the Thames Estuary, so located to benefit from having their own wharves for international shipping bringing in raw materials. The best known to the enthusiast is probably the Grain power station. Charles Banfield bought a large fleet of mostly Leylands to transport the huge numbers of (motor-car less) workers from their south London homes to the site every day.

But though less well known similar operations were also taking place north of the river. There was no single dominant bus or coach operator as with Banfield but a variety of established companies provided works buses from their areas to the construction sites. These included the Atomic Weapons Research Establishment (AWRE), based on Foulness Island, Middle East Crude (MEC) oil refinery at Shell Haven and the British Electricity Authority (BEA) at Tilbury (Power Station).

WMS got its share of this work and bought second-hand buses specifically for these contracts. They could be seen at usually extremely unsociable hours as they set off, and rarely at the construction sites for reasons of accessibility (no regular bus services for enthusiasts to get there!) and security. Prittlewell yard was, however, a favourite location and some wonderful machines could be photographed there. We include a selection though details of the contracts themselves have proved elusive. A couple of such workings although aimed at workers were for regular employees once the site was in operation. As such these were given route numbers and lasted into ENOC days and until mass car ownership made them unnecessary. One of your authors had the 'privilege' of conducting one such journey from Southend to Coryton oil refinery, a Bristol KSW5G on service 2C, in the last days of its operation and recalls the purpose built bus station and almost complete lack of passengers.

Fig.5.67 AWRE, the Atomic Weapons Research Establishment, located on Foulness Island was provided with a works service by WMS as shown on the blind of MVW970. This AEC Regent with Weymann bodywork had been acquired with the business of Benfleet & District. It was new to Sheffield Corporation in 1935 as their 104 (BWA 204). Before entry into Essex service the vehicle was extensively refurbished by Chas. W. Beale of Westcliff and re-registered. The fleet-number plate visible (1173) indicates ENOC ownership, despite the WMS fleet-name.   RFM

Fig.5.68 *Now passing its declining years with very early starts, a long nap, and just one more trip every day on contract services was veteran AEC Regent MV3394. This remarkable survivor had been new in 1932 as an AEC demonstrator, though one's reaction is that by the date of this photo in 1950 it best demonstrates how not to style a body, which was by MCCW. It had been bought by WMS in November 1933, was one of the buses loaned to London Transport during the war, working from Clay Hall garage (see Chapter Six) but other than this photograph has proved rather camera shy. HC*

Fig.5.69 *Although this view is against the sun and in ENOC days it continues the WMS contract theme. Both buses continued to carry 'Westcliff-on-Sea' fleet-names despite their ENOC ownership. Veteran 1929 all-Leyland TD1 1102 (WH1552) was acquired by ENOC with the Hicks Bros. of Braintree business. The bus looks quite original though the body had been rebuilt by Watson in 1948 and the Leyland petrol engine replaced by a Gardner 5LW. The Bristol K5G/ECW 1005 (BRX915) dates from 1939 and was new to Thames Valley Traction Co. as their 399. ENOC bought it in 1954 though it lasted just three years, all on contract work. PJSA*

Fig.5.70 *This is one of those 'spot the difference' puzzles. In 1949 WMS bought all six of Brighton, Hove and District's Tilling bodied Dennis Lances which had been new in 1935, five of them for works contracts, the sixth (NJ5976) being converted to an open-topper (see Figs.11.9-11.11). Despite appearances NJ5974 (above) and NJ5978 (below) were two of these Lances. Both had been re-engined by BH&D, NJ5974 with an AEC 7.7 and NJ5978 a Gardner 5LW. The AEC radiators were fitted by WMS. NJ5974 had been rebuilt for BH&D in 1947 by Portsmouth Aviation producing a very unusual mix of bus. Both are showing 'MEC' for the Middle East Crude site at Shell Haven. Now it is your turn to 'spot the differences'.   ENEG*

Fig.5.71 *NJ5978 awaits your perusal and comparison with sister bus NJ5974 above. For a third bus from this batch, see Chapter Eleven.   ABC*

Fig.5.72 *This is a most interesting photograph. FOP461 is a Daimler CWA6/Park Royal utility taken over with Canvey & District, and now carrying the WMS fleet-name. AVF354 is a Bristol GO5G/ECW new in 1936 to Eastern Counties as LG12, later HLG12 which was acquired by ENOC in April 1954, complete with 'bible boards' destination indicator. The photo can be dated to May/June 1954 as neither bus carries the numbers they were allocated under the July 1954 re-numbering scheme, viz. 1206 and 1001 respectively and AVF354 was only taken into stock in April. PJSA*

Fig.5.73 *AWRE Foulness is believed to be the location of these buses. Those of WMS include JN4747 and JN4748 and one other AEC Regent/Weymann. A City Coach Daimler CVD6/Roberts is the interloper. The first bus shows service 18 blinds so it seems likely that this is the service bus and the remainder contract buses, and the location the military compound at Court End. The variations in staff dress are noteworthy. The diagonal mark in the sky is not a blemish on the photography but a wind-sock. PJSA*

EXPRESS COACH SERVICES

In the timetable dated 6 June 1951 the express services did not have any specifically allocated numbers or letters. Accordingly the express services shown below have been listed in order of the letter designations that were introduced by WMS in January 1953 whilst under ENOC control. WMS had ceased to use their own letter designations in 1939. For further details see *Chapter Three*.

D **SOUTHEND (Pier Hill) – Westcliff – Leigh – Hadleigh – Wanstead – Walthamstow – Dalston – Islington – LONDON (Victoria Coach Station)**
Daily (Summer only)   2 hr 25 mins   4 jnys
S: 3/9 M-F 4/6 S+Su   DR: 4/6 M-F 6/3 S+Su   PR: 7/- M-F 8/9 S+Su

E **SOUTHEND (Pier Hill) – Westcliff – Leigh – Hadleigh – Tarpots Corner – Tilbury Ferry – Brighton – WORTHING (Southdown Coach Station, Marine Parade)**
MWSu (Summer only)   4 hr 30 mins   1 jny
S: 12/2   DR: 14/10   PR: 21/10
Ex Multiways, Westcliff-on-Sea, 4/40

F **SOUTHEND (Pier Hill) – Westcliff – Leigh – Hadleigh – Tarpots Corner – Tilbury Ferry – EASTBOURNE (Southdown Coach Station, Cavendish Place)**
ThSu (Summer only)   4 hr   1 jny
S: 9/8   DR: 12/7   PR: 18/4
Ex Multiways, Westcliff-on-Sea, 4/40

G **SOUTHEND (Pier Hill) – Westcliff – Leigh – Hadleigh – Tarpots Corner – Tilbury Ferry – FOLKESTONE (Lower Sandgate Road)**
ThSu (Summer only)   4 hr   1 jny
S: 9/8   DR: 12/7   PR: 18/4
Ex Multiways, Westcliff-on-Sea, 4/40

H **SOUTHEND (Pier Hill) – Westcliff – Leigh – Hadleigh – Tarpots Corner – Tilbury Ferry – HASTINGS (Fishmarket)**
TFSu (Summer only)   4 hr   1 jny
S: 9/8   DR: 12/7   PR: 18/4
Ex Multiways, Westcliff-on-Sea, 4/40

M **SOUTHEND (Pier Hill) – Westcliff – Leigh – Hadleigh – Rayleigh – Lowestoft – GREAT YARMOUTH (Wellington Road Omnibus Station)**
TThSu (Summer only)   5 hr   1 jny
S: 11/9   DR: 14/6   PR: 23/3
Ex Multiways, Westcliff-on-Sea, 4/40

Fig.5.74 *Typical of the vehicles used on the London express services in the late-thirties was JN6886, a Bristol JO5G with Eastern Counties dual-purpose 32-seat body. It is seen here in a pre-delivery view showing the attractive livery to the full.* ECW/BAC

Fig.5.75 *A rather quiet Victoria Coach Station is the location for this view of FJN165 one of the six 1953 deliveries of LS6G/ECW coaches. The blinds read LONDON VICTORIA and D WALTHAMSTOW ISLINGTON.   AGOC*

Fig.5.76 *Seen against the unmistakable backdrop of the East Cliff at Hastings, EHJ29 has worked the express service from Southend and is taking a well earned rest. It is a Bristol L6B with ECW's full-front coach body, the style sometimes known as 'Queen Mary' though what that monarch had done to deserve this is not clear, apart from being 'stately'. The service that EHJ29 has just worked traced its roots (should that be 'routes'?) back to Multiways of Westcliff-on-Sea.   PJSA*

From **LONDON** (Victoria) **ISLINGTON, DALSTON,** and **WALTHAMSTOW**

To **LEIGH-ON-SEA, WESTCLIFF-ON-SEA & SOUTHEND-ON-SEA**

		a.m.	a.m.	p.m.
*London—VICTORIA COACH STATION, Buckingham Palace Road ...	dep.	8.50	10.00	8.00
*Islington—The Green, Opposite Collin's Music Hall	,,	9.10	10.20	—
*Dalston—King Henry's Walk, Balls Pond Road	,,	9.20	10.30	—
*Walthamstow—Selborne Road, Hoe Street Station ...	,,	9.35	10.45	8.45
Leigh-on-Sea—Broadway West, The Public Library... ...	arr.	10.55	12.05	10.05
Westcliff-on-Sea—Holmes & Smith's Garage Opposite Palace Theatre	,,	11.05	12.15	10.15
Southend-on-Sea—Tylers Avenue	,,	11.10	12.20	10.20
Southend-on-Sea—Pier Hill Coach Station...	,,	11.15	12.25	10.25

* Passengers picked up only at these points.

NOTE—Passengers will not be picked up at Islington or Dalston on the 8 p.m. departure from Victoria.

— FARES —

Single **3/-**   Day Return **3/6**   Period Return **5/6**

Saturdays, Sundays and Bank Holidays, from Whit Saturday to the Second Sunday in September inclusive.

Single **3/6**   Day Return **5/-**   Period Return **7/-**

Children at Half the above Rates.

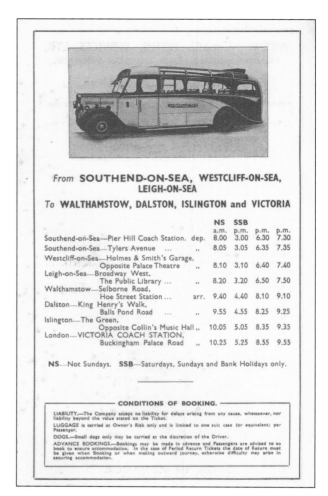

From **SOUTHEND-ON-SEA, WESTCLIFF-ON-SEA, LEIGH-ON-SEA**

To **WALTHAMSTOW, DALSTON, ISLINGTON** and **VICTORIA**

		NS	SSB		
		a.m.	p.m.	p.m.	p.m.
Southend-on-Sea—Pier Hill Coach Station. dep.		8.00	3.00	6.30	7.30
Southend-on-Sea—Tylers Avenue ...	,,	8.05	3.05	6.35	7.35
Westcliff-on-Sea—Holmes & Smith's Garage, Opposite Palace Theatre	,,	8.10	3.10	6.40	7.40
Leigh-on-Sea—Broadway West, The Public Library ...	,,	8.20	3.20	6.50	7.50
Walthamstow—Selborne Road, Hoe Street Station ...	arr.	9.40	4.40	8.10	9.10
Dalston—King Henry's Walk, Balls Pond Road ...	,,	9.55	4.55	8.25	9.25
Islington—The Green, Opposite Collin's Music Hall	,,	10.05	5.05	8.35	9.35
London—VICTORIA COACH STATION, Buckingham Palace Road	,,	10.25	5.25	8.55	9.55

NS—Not Sundays.   **SSB**—Saturdays, Sundays and Bank Holidays only.

— CONDITIONS OF BOOKING. —

LIABILITY.—The Company accept no liability for delays arising from any cause, whatsoever, nor liability beyond the value stated on the Ticket.

LUGGAGE is carried at Owner's Risk only and is limited to one suit case (or equivalent) per Passenger.

DOGS.—Small dogs only may be carried at the discretion of the Driver.

ADVANCE BOOKINGS.—Bookings may be made in advance and Passengers are advised to so book to ensure accommodation. In the case of Period Return Tickets the date of Return must be given when Booking or when making outward journey, otherwise difficulty may arise in securing accommodation.

Fig.5.77 *Two of the many publicity leaflets for the London express services issued by WMS are shown, both dating from the late thirties. For further examples see Fig.3.8.   AGOC*

WITHDRAWN SERVICES

Looking through the service listing in the 6 June 1951 timetable it will be seen that certain numbers are missing. This end piece fills these gaps and provides some additional information relevant to the WMS bus and coach service history.

Service numbers no longer used in June 1951

13   **Southend – Leigh – Eastwood – Prittlewell – Southend (Circular)**
Abandoned 6/27, covered by EHM 'Blue Bus' routes.

14   **Southend – Sutton – Shopland Corner**
Service passed to SCT in 1/33.

15   **Royal Red Pullman Saloon service – see below**

16   **Royal Red Pullman Saloon service – see below**

20   Numbers used for former TH&D services A and F (see *Fig.2.25*). Service 20A was incorporated into SCT joint service 25A/25B in 10/47 (see *Fig.5.59*).
The numbers 13 and 14 were used once again for new services to Hullbridge and Romford introduced on 30 May 1954 (see Fig.2.39).

ROYAL RED PULLMAN SALOONS

These were longer distance semi-limited stop services to London which latterly ran at regular intervals but which were not bookable. Tickets had to be purchased on board from the conductor. Some publicity material for these services is shown in *Figs.5.78 and 5.79*. For more details of their development please see *Chapter Two*.

15   Southend – London (Stratford Broadway)

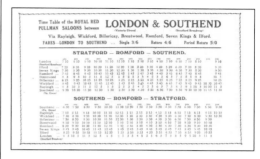

Fig.5.78   *The leaflet above shows the hourly service to Stratford following the extension from Seven Kings on 23 June 1930.*   AGOC

16   Southend – London (Wood Green)

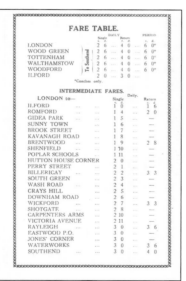

Fig.5.79 This is the first timetable, dated 18 June 1928, after the introduction of the hourly interval London to Southend service which was co-ordinated with New Empress City Saloons. Bus service 2B from Southend to East Ham was also marketed as a further Pullman saloon service.   AGOC

Fig.5.80 In this delightful commercial postcard period scene one of the four model 660 AEC Reliances (HJ9072/3, HJ9121/66) purchased by WMS makes its way along Brentwood High Street working a Royal Red Pullman Saloon service to Southend. JCC

Fig.5.81 The little bus at Rayleigh is from the Edwards Hall Motors fleet. (enlargement above) JRYC

More period scenes from postcards give us the opportunity to savour the early days of bus operation in Rayleigh High Street (upper) and at Hadleigh Church (lower). Neither bus is on a WMS service, though in time both the operating companies and their services would be taken over by WMS.

Fig.5.82 Waiting at Hadleigh, Church is a slightly larger Dennis owned by Thundersley, Hadleigh & District. The finger-post with circular bench provides an informal bus passenger waiting area. This would be recognised by the parish council and a wooden circular bus shelter built around the post, as shown in Fig.5.12. JRYC

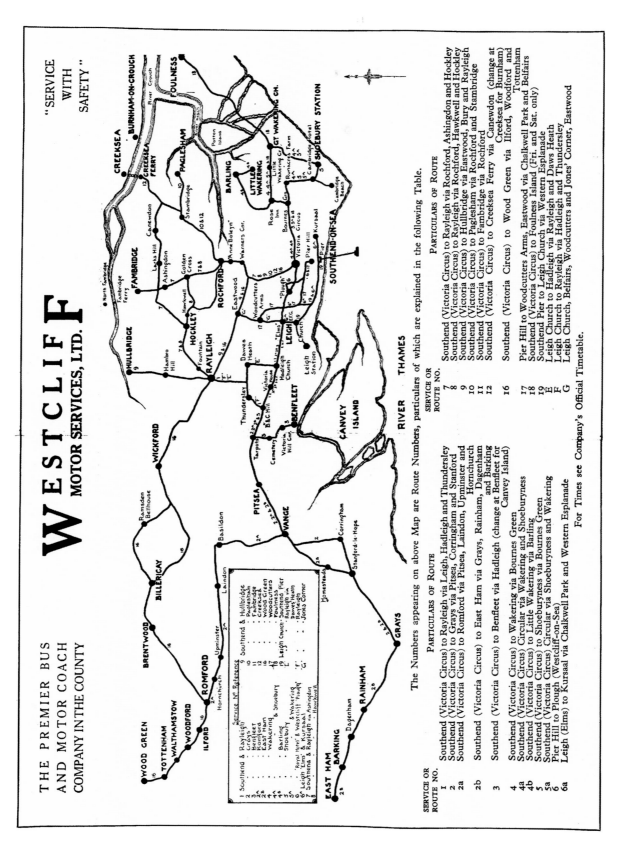

Fig.5.83 *This map has the advantage of identifying many intermediate points on the bus service routes helping us to identify the via points listed above under each service number in this chapter. It is taken from a pre-war guide book to Southend on Sea. It is remarkable to note that WMS served more islands than any other English bus company. These were Canvey, Wallasea, Foulness, Havengore and New England all of which are depicted, though not named, on this map.*

Fig.6.1 *How it all started. This Strachan & Brown pre-delivery photograph is of the first double-decker to be purchased by WSMC. It was a Daimler CK and would be registered HJ1759 on 23 March 1921. Little did anyone then know that this would be the beginning of forty years of WMS bus and coach service provision in south-east Essex.*   *ERO*

Chapter Six
Vehicle History and Fleet List 1951-1955

Any single photograph can be used to illustrate a number of points in several chapters. The difficulty of covering all the services listed in Chapter Five has meant that photos have been reproduced there that are equally important to this chapter. This has necessitated cross referencing back to the appropriate figure numbers so that the reader can fully appreciate the complex development of the WMS fleet.

Introduction

WMS was unusual amongst bus operators in that for most of its existence as a major group company it did not use fleet-numbers. However in its early independent years fleet-numbers were carried, these being displayed in a circle on the side of the lower deck. Their use was however somewhat sporadic. Fleet-number 1 (HJ1312) was allocated to a Daimler single-decker, whilst 11 (HJ1879) was carried by an open-top Daimler CK double-decker. The lowest registration numbers in the fleet were carried by a pair of Dodson bodied Daimler saloons acquired from the Southend Char-a-banc Company in 1923, these being 20 (HJ147) and 21 (HJ230). From photographic evidence the highest fleet-number reached would appear to have been 53.

Another major operator which relied solely upon registration numbers for vehicle identification was the East Kent Road Car Company. In many respects the development of their own distinct systems is very similar since the respective speeds of issue of registration numbers by their appropriate local licensing office followed a close correspondence. Thus any earlier vehicles registered within the first two letter combination would have been long withdrawn by the time that the second two letter series started thus readily eliminating any potential number clashes. The respective registration details are interesting to compare and are as follows:

East Kent: the County Borough of Canterbury commenced FN in January 1904, followed by JG in March 1929. The first three letter mark AFN was issued in November 1937.

WMS: Southend-on-Sea was created a County Borough on 1 April 1914 and started issuing registrations then. Thus HJ commenced in April 1914, followed by JN in May 1930. The first three letter mark AHJ was issued in December 1937 just one month later than Canterbury CBC.

Whilst the larger East Kent concern persevered with their system for many years by registering new vehicles in comparatively large blocks in numerical sequences, WMS seemed to have used a rather haphazard 'system'. Whether duplicate numbers were avoided by luck or by design is not known. Remarkably, there was only one instance of a clash between two three number

combinations. The example involved 608, viz. DHJ 608 a Bristol K5G, delivered new in 1949 and JTW 608 a Daimler CWG5, acquired with the business of Benfleet & District in 1951 and withdrawn two years later. However, since the Bristol was allocated to Southend whilst the Daimler spent all of its short working WMS life at Hadleigh this clash should not have presented too many operational problems.

There were, however, a number of instances where a three number registration clashed with the same component within a four number registration mark. Since the latter vehicles were always referred to as 'JN' with four digits then these too should not have presented too many problems. The instances, which mainly involved acquired vehicles, are listed below:

FOP461	JN 5461
BHJ532/3	JN 9532/3
KEV534-6	JN 9534-6
DJN560	JN 8560

However, this lack of fleet-numbers or of any numerical system of vehicle identification has rendered the accurate recording of the WMS fleet rather difficult, particularly during the early period when HJ registrations were being issued.

Livery

The Royal Red char-a-bancs were in an overall red livery. The WMS coach livery was cream and red whilst the buses were red and cream. During the 1930s the double-deckers carried three or four cream bands and additional lining out in black which resulted in a superior appearance. Later the colour scheme was simplified to just one cream band without further embellishment. A cream and red livery was also used for both single and double deck vehicles used on sea-front services.

Review of the WMS bus and coach fleet

This review is not intended to be fully comprehensive rather it is intended to relate the 'flavour' of the WMS fleet over the years. A 1951 – 1955 fleet list has been included in the present volume and the later portions of this review should be read in conjunction with this listing. This chapter also includes brief details of the development of the WMS bus garages in the area.

Because their mews premises were very cramped *(see Fig.2.2)* Holmes & Smith signed a 16 year lease on a motor garage at Pier Hill, Southend on 29 September 1913, which became their base. For further details *see Chapter Nine.*

Early days

At the time of the amalgamation *(see Chapter Two)* the Holmes & Smith (Royal Red) fleet consisted of four 20-seater Thornycroft 30hp char-a-bancs. One early vehicle owned was F5619 first registered on 10 May 1912 which later passed to Moore Bros. of Kelvedon on 27 July 1915. They disposed of it in 1918 and it was converted to a goods vehicle. Other vehicles were registered F5654 and F6956 (it should be remembered that Southend CBC did not issue registrations until 1914). The Southend-on-Sea Char-a-banc Company (Royal Blue) fleet consisted of three 28hp Dennis char-a-bancs seating 20 passengers *(see Fig.3.11)*.

Fig.6.2 *Holmes & Smith traded as 'The Royal Red'. This Thornycroft char-a-banc was later sold to Moores of Kelvedon. PJSA*

Westcliff-on-Sea Motor Char-a-banc Company Ltd. (WSMC)

In order to meet demand the Westcliff-on-Sea Motor Char-a-banc Co. Ltd. fleet was to have been expanded to 15 cars, by the acquisition of six new Daimler 40hp and two new Dennis 26hp char-a-bancs each with seats for 24 passengers. This marked the beginning of a long association with Daimler vehicles. However, the war curtailed activities with certain char-a-bancs being converted to run on town gas during this period and engaged on military transport duties. The char-a-banc fleet was increased through purchase of more Daimlers (HJ934-6) and some Dennis's including HJ577/9. One of the machines used on their first local town bus service 1 between Pier Hill and the Plough Hotel was HJ580 a Daimler saloon with pneumatic tyres first registered on 1 April 1920. Further Daimler saloon buses were taken into stock these being HJ1312/3 *(see Fig.2.7)*.

Fig.6.2a *The two Dennis 26hp char-a-bancs are seen together, HJ1385 nearest the camera. BAC*

To operate their early bus services to the outlying districts, the use of further saloons was originally envisaged. Due to extended delivery times agreement had to be secured on 8 October 1920 from Southend Council for the use of double-deckers. Two former London General Omnibus Co. Ltd. 'B type' open-top double-deckers were soon acquired. Because their London marks had been surrendered these were re-registered in Southend on 1 November 1920 as HJ1388/9, the latter formerly B200 (LC3838). The identity of the former is unknown. Another pair then followed, B92 (LN4792) and B1689 (LF8476). These became HJ1578/91 on 28 January 1921.

The first new double-deckers to be added to the WSMC fleet were registered on 23 March 1921. These were a pair of Daimler CKs with Strachan & Brown bodywork, HJ1759/60 *(see Fig.6.1)*. Reference to *Fig.8.3* shows one of these in service. A similar bus, HJ1879, followed soon afterwards. The single-deck fleet was boosted by more Daimler saloons, including HJ2055, this being registered on 10 October 1921, the last addition to the WSMC fleet.

Fig.6.3 *This was the last vehicle delivered to WSMC, HJ2055 seen here in a less than perfect photo which nevertheless captures the flavour of the mid-twenties with horse drawn traffic still much in evidence. PJSA*

Fig.6.4 This view of HJ1389 in later WMS days shows it as a saloon but still allows its origin as former LGOC B200 to be confirmed from the chassis frame and bonnet fleet numbers. *ERO*

Fig.6.5 This pre-delivery view is of one of the trio of Dennis double-deckers (HJ2312-4) that were the very first new vehicles to be taken into stock by WMS. *ERO*

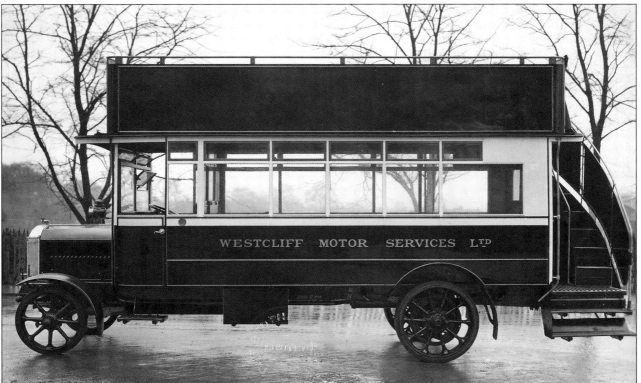

Westcliff-on-Sea Motor Services Ltd.

The first new buses delivered to WMS were HJ2312-4 a trio of Dennis E double-deckers with Dodson bodywork registered on 11 April 1922. Again we are fortunate to have both pre-delivery and in-service views available to illustrate this momentous event *(see Figs.6.5 and 6.6)*.

The char-a-banc fleet was supplemented by further Daimlers HJ3717/8 *(see Fig.3.12)*. As a consequence of this fleet expansion in 1922 a purpose-built bus garage

was opened at 33, London Road, Southend. Six unusual Berliet toast-racks (HJ3718/9, HJ3729/30 & HJ3811/2) arrived in 1924 to operate sea-front service 6A *(see Fig.2.8)*. Later toast-racks to join the fleet were based on the locally favoured Daimler chassis e.g. HJ4642/3, HJ4877 & HJ4981 *(see Fig.5.51)*. In 1924 WMS purchased a plot of land on the south side of Fairfax Drive, Prittlewell for the construction of a bus garage, which opened the following year.

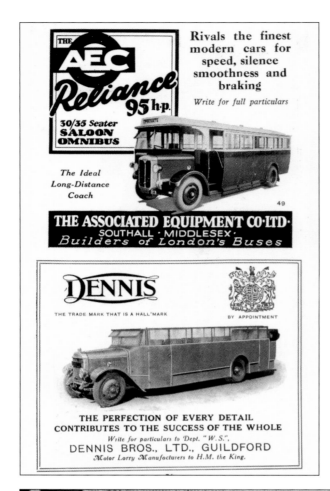

Fig.6.6 (right) *HJ2313, a Dodson bodied Dennis was the second new bus to be received by WMS. It is seen here in the snow working a 1 to Rayleigh, a service which had gained this number the previous year.* PJSA

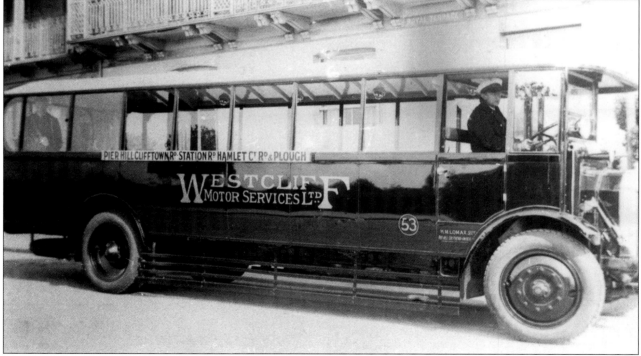

Fig.6.7 *This early view of a Dennis saloon on route 6 shows the impressive style of fleet-name carried in the early years, the side route-board and even a fleet-number, 53. The distinctive background is the balconies of the Royal Terrace then a departure point for WMS services and surviving today as part of a conservation area.* PJSA

Fig.6.8 *Despite the logo and red livery carried this Bristol char-a-banc HJ1310 is seen after sale by WMS. It is now owned by Deeds Motor Services who have neatly adapted the WMS coach tours logo to their own use.* **PJSA**

Fig.6.9 *Unfortunately no close-up photographs of the elusive WMS Guys have been found. This less than perfect view of Southend High Street on 27 February 1930 might just contain one in the shape of the diminutive normal control bus making its way from the Pier. In the absence of definite proof we can at least enjoy the period atmosphere: note the London Belle steamer advertisement.* **ERO**

Fig.6.10 *HJ7078, one of the 1927 intake of Associated Daimler char-a-bancs, is seen here laying over on a hot day, I wonder if the driver has just popped into the shop for a bar of Fry's chocolate? JFH*

Fig.6.11 *What a monster! This Associated Daimler model 802 (London Six) HJ7670 was one of only twenty ever built of which twelve went to the LGOC. The others were demonstrated to major operators including WMS who then acquired this one. It is seen outside the WMS Head Office at Victoria Arcade. Note that the driver's cab was open to all weathers, reflecting London practice. JFH*

Fig.6.12 *Seen at Grays on service 2 is HJ8592, a Daimler CF6 with Strachan & Brown body. The CF6 was the Daimler replacement for the ADC 423. It had a 5.76 litre engine and was made in both normal and forward control variants as well as a double-deck version. It became very popular with 531 examples being built between 1929 and 1931. Note the simple underlined 'Westcliff' fleet-name. JFH*

Fig.6.13 *Following the failure of the 'Welsh Pullman' service the coaches were transferred to the Ardley Bros. of Tottenham fleet. This view shows HJ9119 one of the six Tilling-Stevens coaches with London Lorries bodywork. JFH*

Fig.6.14 *Rounding the corner behind the Palace Hotel is HJ9189. This was a Daimler CF6 with London Lorries C24F body new in 7.29. It is in the cream and red coach livery. Note the garage parking costs then applicable. The Palace Hotel in the background has survived, refurbished into a hotel and apartments in 2009. ENEG*

Fig.6.15 *An official Dennis Bros. view of JN953 one of a batch of nine 32-seat EV saloons emphasises the clean lines of the body. Careful inspection of the roof over the canopy will reveal the mesh grid of a luggage rack. The registration indicates delivery in 1931 shortly after the introduction of the second series of Southend CBC marks. PJSA*

In 1926 a number of Guy vehicles joined the fleet (HJ5316-9, HJ5773/4) though unfortunately very little is known about them. They were thought to have been small capacity buses of about 14 seats bought to run on lightly used routes such as service 18 to Foulness. It is likely that these vehicles were Guy OWDs.

The 1926 Directors Report included a fleet list which showed that the fleet then stood at about 80 vehicles, indicating rapid growth. WMS submitted a further plan for an extension of the Fairfax Drive garage, but this was refused. The vacant land at the corner of Fairfax Drive and North Street (now Victoria Avenue), Prittlewell was later sold. For an early view of Fairfax Drive garage see *Fig.9.1.*

In March 1928 some further Associated Daimlers (ADC) were purchased examples being char-a-bancs HJ8048/9. A more remarkable purchase was an ADC 802 six-wheeled covered top 68 seat double-decker HJ7670 registered on 25 March. On 15 September the Temperance Billiards Hall was purchased by Olive Mary Bridge and was then transferred to WMS on 12 February 1929 for conversion into a coach station. For further details see *Chapter Two.*

WMS started a new service of Royal Red Pullman Saloons between Southend and Wood Green in June 1928 for which some new Dennis E saloons with 32-seat bodies including HJ7612-7, HJ8033-5 and HJ8933-6 were purchased. The vehicle intake in 1929 was very mixed. First to arrive during February and March was a batch of Daimler CF6 models (HJ8592-7) which were used on the Grays service. Also in March following their long experience with Daimler char-a-bancs a further double-decker from this manufacturer entered service in the shape of HJ8677, a Dodson bodied model CF6. During May and June 1929 WMS purchased six Tilling-Stevens (HJ8598, HJ8943, HJ9060/9, HJ9119/20) with 33-seat bodies by London Lorries of Kentish Town incorporating armchair seats and many high class fittings. These were used on their first venture into

the long distance coach scene when they introduced a service from London to Cardiff. The service started in September with the vehicles carrying 'Welsh Pullman' as the fleet-name *(see Fig.3.2).* Unfortunately competition on the route proved to be severe with the result that the service was soon withdrawn. The vehicles passed to the Ardley Bros. of Tottenham fleet.

In July four model 660 AEC Reliances were added to the fleet HJ9072/3, HJ9121 and HJ9166 *(see Fig.5.80).* The vehicle to be taken into stock which carried the highest HJ-mark was HJ9879, a Dennis F normal-control coach registered on 16 April 1930 *(see Fig.3.23 for an example).* This was followed, on 30 May by the registration of JN166 a Dennis EV saloon the first vehicle to feature the second series of Southend CBC registration marks.

Some further second-hand Dennis's were also acquired at around this time from the fleets of Yorkshire Woollen District and the London General Omnibus Company (former DE class), the latter being received in 1931. Some of these DE vehicles had started their lives in 1927 with Admiral of West Green then passing to the London Public Omnibus Co. Ltd and thence to LGOC in January 1930 *(see Fig.5.50).* Incidentally, the impressive Admiral garage passed to London Transport and was coded WG, the same code as the nearby ENOC Wood Green (WG) garage. The year 1931 saw the introduction of an extensive batch of vehicles. First to appear were more 32-seat Dennis EV saloons (JN951-9) to supplement the London service operations. Next in the registration series were JN960-2, Dennis Lances with 56-seat bodies by Park Royal. Two of these survived until 1950 later being fitted with Gardner 5LW engines and AEC radiators.

Following the takeover of Rochford & District at the end of 1931 two rather unusual vehicles joined the WMS fleet. The first was JN485, an AJS Pilot saloon, whilst the second was JN341, a Gilford 168OT double-decker. In 1932 some former Tilling-Stevens demonstrators

Fig.6.16 The three Park Royal bodied Dennis Lances were impressive machines. Contemporary with the newly introduced Leyland TD1 and AEC Regent models, of revolutionary design, they thus had strong competition. WMS had started with Dennis double-deckers, and tried Daimlers, but further orders went solely to AEC until Tilling involvement. WMS certainly got good value from their Lances, as they lasted into the 1950s, though much modified. For further photos of JN961/2 see Figs.11.6 to 11.8. PJSA

were acquired three C60A7 saloons (KJ2447/8, KJ2914) and one E60A6 double-decker (KJ2449) with Park Royal bodywork. The last vehicle was operated by the subsidiary Thundersley, Hadleigh & District for a while before being disposed of to Benfleet & District in 1937.

Fig.6.17   The 1932 intake of vehicles included some former Tilling-Stevens demonstrators including KJ2449 an E60A6 double-decker with Park Royal bodywork. Later on it ran for Benfleet & District. The roof route-number box was a feature of virtually all WMS double-deckers before the war.   STP

In 1929 AEC had introduced what was to prove a highly successful new model, the Regent. The first chassis was fitted with a camel-back (or camel-hump) style body, replaced a year later by a double-deck body of more conventional layout. For more details see *Fact File 6*. WMS started its link with the AEC Regent double-decker with the acquisition in 1932/3 of two former demonstrators HX2980 with Short bodywork *(see Fig.0.3)* and MV842 with Brush bodywork. Later in life HX2980 was re-bodied with an ECW H30/26R body in 1942 and later fitted with a Gardner 5LW engine. It was converted to open-top in 1950 and survived until 1956 having given twenty-four years valuable service *(see Figs.11.17 and 11.18)*. MV842 was later converted to a breakdown tender.

By 1931 the WMS fleet stood at about 115 vehicles. After experience with a Daimler CH6 double-decker demonstrator KV1396, *(see*

Fig.6.18   This pre-delivery view of the AEC Q JN3457 shows the revolutionary design of the bus to the full. At this time the roof number box had not yet been fitted.   AEC/JRYC

Figs.11.12 and 11.13) which despite carrying full WMS livery was not purchased, WMS developed a strong preference for the AEC product which became the staple diet for the immediate future. This saw the double-decker fleet enhanced by twenty-eight buses over the next three years. In 1933 two batches of Regents were received the first (JN2796-800) with high-bridge Park Royal bodies sporting roof destination boxes *(see Fig.2.25)*, whilst the second intake (JN3328-31) carried lowbridge Weymann bodies which were then to become the standard choice. Another former AEC Regent demonstrator was also added this being MV3394 which had a Metro-Cammell body *(see Fig.5.68)*. There followed a 'one-off', a most unusual purchase of a revolutionary new vehicle. First licensed on 4 October 1933 was JN3457 a side-engined AEC Q double-decker (chassis no. 761005) fitted with a 60-seat front-entrance Metro-Cammell body.

An Original Omnibus Company model of this vehicle exists showing it working service 2 to Grays. The compulsory purchase of those sections of other operator's routes that fell within the newly defined LPTB operating area could have meant a reduction in the size of the WMS fleet. This resulted in service 2B to East Ham being curtailed at Grays on 17 July 1934 but in fact no vehicles changed hands.

When Borough Services Ltd. was acquired by ENOC on 5 May 1933 *(see Figs.2.20 and 5.5)* their subsidiary operation Rayleigh Motor Services Ltd. was transferred to WMS *(see Chapter Two for the complete story)*. The RMS fleet of six vehicles *(see Fig.6.20)* was very mixed and comprised two Dennis, an AEC, an AJS, a Gilford and a 20-seat Bedford (AEV869) which had been purchased just prior to the takeover.

Three further batches of AEC Regents arrived in 1934 all with Weymann bodies and with registrations between JN3715 and JN4748 (see Figs.5.8 and 5.43). As in the previous year one less common example from the AEC range was taken into stock, this being JN4612 a 30 foot long 6-wheeled Renown model 664 with a 53-seat front entrance body. This had been exhibited by Short Bros. at the 1933 Commercial Motor Show in the livery of Whites of Cardiff. The stylish bodywork secured the silver medal of the Institute of British Carriage and Automobile Manufacturers at the Show. It was registered JN4612 by WMS on 20 July 1934.

On 28 December 1933 WMS obtained control of Thundersley, Hadleigh & District Motors Ltd which included a small garage at Oak Road, off London Road, Hadleigh. WMS continued to use this until 1951. The acquisition of Shoeburyness Motor Services on 3 January 1934 saw three vehicles added to the fleet, a pair of Duple bodied Dennis HV double-deckers (EV1925/6) (see Figs.2.17 and 5.25) and a Dennis Lancet with Duple C32R coachwork (AEV542). The Shoeburyness MS garage continued to be used until completion of business on 11 December 1935.

The final batch of Regents (JN5456-61) came in 1935 with an improved style of Weymann low-bridge body, together with three more AEC Q's (JN5782-4) though these were single-deckers with luxury Harrington coach bodies. They were numerically and probably chronologically the last Q models with petrol engines to be built having chassis numbers 762157-9. Remarkably one chassis has survived (see Chapter Ten). The London service was sold to the City Motor Omnibus Co. Ltd. in January 1935 together with 14 Dennis saloons. These included JN951-5/7-9 which became City D7-14 whilst the earlier examples between HJ7613 and HJ8933 became D1-6. After the Tilling Group gained control

of WMS in December 1934 future orders mainly focused on Bristol chassis since the manufacturing side of the Bristol Tramways Co. Ltd had also become part of the Tilling empire. The first Bristols received by WMS carried Eastern Counties bodies whilst the remainder were bodied by the re-named Eastern Coach Works (ECW). More details are included in the 1951-1955 Fleet List at the end of this Chapter.

The single-deck requirements were initially met by the delivery of Bristol JO5G saloons with Eastern Counties bodies. The 'O', '5' and 'G' in the designation indicated that the engine was a Gardner five cylinder oil (diesel) unit. The first batch to arrive, in 1936, was saloon buses JN6880-5. All of these saloons were later rebuilt by local firm C. W. Beale of Westcliff-on-Sea, although their external appearance was little changed (see Fig.5.49). The remainder of the batch, JN6886-9, had dual-purpose bodywork with cream and red livery,

Fig.6.20 One of the six vehicles acquired with the business of Rayleigh Motor Services Ltd. in 1933 was VX7189 a 20-seat Dennis 30 cwt. It is seen here ready to leave for Hullbridge on service 9. PJSA

Fig.6.21 *A solitary AEC Renown joined the fleet in 1934 JN4612. As an AEC exhibit at the Olympia Show its Short body had won a silver medal. It is seen here in original condition, no doubt the 'Pride of the Fleet'. It is complete with rear wheel spats and drop windows.* JRYC

Fig.6.22 *By the time of this post-war photo alterations to JN4612 reflected the practicalities of operations rather than showroom appearances. The wheel spats had gone and windows were now sliders. The livery application has changed though the lighter shade may be due to the rendering of red between ortho- and pan-chromatic film emulsion. One wonders whether the Renown was working the 4 to Landwick towards the end of its life because its high seating capacity was essential on this service. Or was it, perhaps, an example of 'put the least popular/reliable bus on a service where it won't have to work very hard'?* PJSA

Fig.6.23 JN5461, a Weymann bodied AEC Regent of 1935 vintage shows evidence of its rebuild by C. W. Beale. It is laying-over in Park End Road, Romford, the market day terminus of the 2A which would otherwise turn in the Market Place. Note the cream window surrounds, the 'Westcliff-on-Sea' fleet-name and the circle around the route number. JN5461 is set for a short working on the 2A to Vange (Gales Corner) via Laindon. VCJ

Fig.6.24 This splendid official view of JN6880 was taken on 3 April 1936 in a park at Oulton Broad near to the Lowestoft factory. It is a Bristol JO5G with B36R bodywork actually built by Eastern Counties before the body business was re-named Eastern Coach Works. Note the plain upper-case 'WESTCLIFF' style of fleet-name and that the legal address carried at this time was 18/20 Victoria Avenue. SJB/ECW

Fig.6.25 JN6889, a Bristol JO5G with Eastern Counties 32-seat dual-purpose bodywork was new in 1936. Unlike JN6887 it had escaped being requisitioned and is seen here at Victoria Coach Station after the war. It has just arrived from Southend. RFM

which allowed them to undertake bus or coach work. In later years they were repainted red and cream and relegated to bus work *(see Fig.5.45)*. JN6887 did not survive to be relegated as it was destroyed by enemy action.

The next intake with ECW bodies comprised JN7499-7501 *(see Figs.2.23 and 3.6)*. JN7500 was requisitioned and suffered considerable war damage. After withdrawal and sale its chassis was renovated, fitted with a new Thurgood C35F body and re-registered LRO981 in 1950 for Hillside Coaches of Markyate, Hertfordshire. It earned the distinction of being the only former Tilling company chassis ever to carry a Thurgood body.

A further batch of eight JO5G/ECW saloons arrived in 1937 (JN8560-7) all of which were later rebuilt by C. W. Beale, again with little change to their appearance. Some of these were delivered in a cream and red livery for sea-front service 6A *(see Fig.5.53)* though they were repainted to bus livery after the war. The final batch of Bristol JO5Gs amounted to nine saloons (JN9531-9) some of which were replacements for the vehicles lost in the Prittlewell garage fire.

Double-decker deliveries into the Tilling controlled WMS fleet were initially of the GO5G model. The first

batch of eight to be received in 1936 (JN6890-7) were bodied by Brush *(see Fig.5.7)*. By the time the war was over, these bodies were showing significant signs of wear. To prolong their life four (JN6890/1/5/7)) were sent to J. C. Beadle Ltd. of Dartford to be re-furbished. However, when they returned their appearance was more consistent with re-bodying than rebuilding as comparison of *Figs.5.7, and 5.37* shows. The remaining four GO5Gs (JN6892-4/6) were sent to ECW to have completely new bodies fitted. The first of the Beadle rebuilds was withdrawn in 1956 whilst the last of the ECW rebodied buses survived until 1960 having by then given 24 years service.

In 1937 another small batch of GO5Gs was delivered, JN8570-2, this time fitted with ECW open-top bodies finished in a cream with red livery for the sea-front service. In 1942, with the exigencies of war (closure of sea-front, no visitors, bus shortages etc) these buses were fitted with roofs by ECW which remained in place until 1949 *(see Fig.6.30)*. They were then permanently removed and the buses returned to the now busy sea-front service. After transfer to ENOC these open-toppers saw further service, ending up at Clacton on the route to Jaywick where they lasted until 1961 *(see Fig.6.31)*.

Fig.6.26 *What better way is there to herald the start of the Tilling era than to admire a WMS bus in full, original colour? The driver is just returning to JN8567, a Bristol JO5G/ECW saloon rebuilt by C. W. Beale. The scene is Broadway Market in ENOC days as evidenced by the fleet-number, 248. The Bristol in the background has already been repainted into ENOC green and cream.   FC*

Fig.6.27   The ECW body style shown on JN9532 incorporated slight variations from the earlier ECOC version, particularly the roof treatment. The use of more cream in the livery application considerably enhanced the overall appearance in the author's opinion. The bonnet is brushed aluminium, a short lived experiment to avoid oil damage to paintwork.   ECW/BAC

Fig.6.28   Bristol GO5G JN6896 proudly bears its new ECW body. Comparison with the 'before' Brush body (see Fig.5.7) shows just wheel hubs and registration number in common and it is hard to believe that it is the same bus. Because of the higher build of the G chassis and mid-mounted gearbox ECW's standard lowbridge body was mounted slightly higher than on a K. Fitting the lower PV2 radiator completed the illusion of a new bus.   WJH

Fig.6.29 *This evocative pre-war sea-front scene by Southend Pier shows JN8572 loading on service 19 for Leigh. Note the side-mounted board lettered 'SEA FRONT SERVICE' and the large informative bus stop.   OS*

Fig.6.30 *WMS's first ECW bodied Bristol GO5Gs had been delivered as open-toppers. Between 1942-9 they gained tops to allow their use in normal service, necessary whilst most of the Bristol K double-deckers were away on loan to other operators. In this early post-war view JN8570 demonstrates the rather ungainly appearance that resulted from this temporary expedient.   VCJ*

Fig.6.31 *On a gloriously sunny day during summer 1960 Bristol GO5G JN8570 (as ENOC 1244), now roof-less again, waits its turn in the queue at Jaywick Sands terminus before heading for Clacton. Unlike the Tilling bodied example in front, JN8570 has had its side and rear destination indicators painted over. This would be the penultimate summer it would serve the happy holidaymakers.* OS.

Fig.6.32 *WMS was privileged to receive the very first batch of ECW bodied Bristol K5Gs to be built. The unusual small window under the staircase on the offside is readily seen in this view of JN 9541 outside the Victoria Arcade. It appears to be a very warm day, and a conductor can be seen sampling the amenities of the Busmen's Social Club.* WJH

From 1937 the newly introduced Bristol K5G became the standard Tilling fleet double-decker. WMS was indeed privileged to receive the very first ECW body to be fitted to the new Bristol K5G chassis. This honour fell to JN9540 (chassis number 42.24) which carried a 55-seat low-bridge body featuring an unusual small window under the staircase on the offside. The complete batch was JN9540-4. For the coach fleet however non-Bristol types continued to be specified including a trio of 20-seat Leyland Cubs (JN7833, 7985/6) which joined the fleet in 1936.

There was a disastrous fire at Prittlewell garage on 5 March 1936 when ten vehicles were destroyed. The vehicles involved were seven single-deckers, comprising four Dennis F (HJ 9876/8/9, JN 878) and three Daimler CF (HJ8049, 8594, 9209) and three double-deckers which were one elderly Daimler CK (HJ3319), the unique ADC six-wheeler (HJ7670) and a fairly new AEC Regent (JN5460). This most unfortunate loss resulted in a number of replacement Bristols being ordered. To operate their prestigious range of 'Seeing Britain' extended coach tours quiet, petrol-engined AEC Rangers with luxurious 24-seat Duple bodies were purchased. The intake comprised JN 8584/5 (see Fig.3.7)

delivered in 1937 followed by AHJ843 in 1938 which was actually the last Ranger to be built. In 1936 there was a further influx of second-hand Tilling-Stevens in the shape of six Express model B10B2 forward-control char-a-bancs fitted with Harrington C30R coachwork featuring a fixed back and folding roof. The vehicles concerned were UF4507/9/10, 4827, 5021/2 which had been new in 1929 to Southdown Motor Services Ltd of Brighton, Sussex (see Fig.11.2).

In 1936 it was agreed that the London Road garage should be expanded and should also incorporate the Head Office. The adjacent premises at 35, London Road were acquired. These were purchased from Browns Garage and had previously been used to house the fleet of Multiways Ltd. Further purchases of the properties at 17/21, London Road followed. These subsequently became the Head Office. A new garage building was then constructed at the rear of the intermediate properties which fronted London Road and thus connected numbers 17/21 (the new exit) with 33/35 (the new entrance). The building was completed in 1937 the Head Office being transferred from 18/20, Victoria Avenue to 17/21, London Road from 2 September.

Fig.6.33 *An elderly couple 'take the weight off their feet' as they wait for their bus to depart from Romford Market Place on service 2A. The vehicle is AHJ 402 one of the fourteen low-bridge ECW bodied Bristol K5G's delivered to WMS before the war and which were to give such sterling service, and not just to WMS, AHJ402 being loaned to Thames Valley Traction Co. Ltd from 1940-1. LTPS*

Fig.6.34 *Seen on a private hire job is JN 7986, one of the three ECW bodied Leyland Cub bought by WMS. In the absence of an equivalent Bristol chassis many Tilling companies chose Cubs, notably Crosville.* **PJSA**

In 1938 the first vehicle to carry a three letter Southend CBC registration mark was received, Bristol K5G AHJ401, the first of a batch of three. This was followed shortly afterwards by a pair of AEC Regals with Duple coach bodies, AHJ404/5. Remarkably AHJ404, or at least the chassis and a few other parts of it, survived into the new millennium in a new home on the Mediterranean island of Malta *(see Chapter Ten)*.

The 1939 intake of vehicles was quite mixed. It comprised five Bristol K5G/ECW (AJN823-5 and BHJ532/3), illustrated in *Figs. 2.22, 5.20 and 5.58*. AJN825 has survived re-painted into traditional WMS red and cream livery; just look at the front cover in case you had forgotten how splendid it looks! For a view of AJN825 in original in-service condition *(see Fig.10.6)*.

The other 1939 Bristol was AJN826, the sole L5G/ECW to be operated by WMS, post-war examples being LWL variants. It is shown in *Figs.5.36 and 5.55*. It was about this time that the Tilling style 'Westcliff-on-Sea' fleet-name with enlarged end letters and central underlining was introduced. This replaced the former 'Westcliff' or 'WESTCLIFF' lettering styles, although the latter was still found on the front bulkhead or destination indicator as seen by comparison of *Figs. 5.55 and 6.24*. The remainder of the 1939 intake was of AEC Regals with Duple bodywork for the extended tours fleet. The first entered service as BHJ132, but the other four had a somewhat 'secret' existence, of which more later.

In October 1939 WMS considered the possibility of building a new garage at Hadleigh to take the place of their existing small Oak Road garage; for details of which see *Chapter Nine*.

With the declaration of war coastal areas that were considered to be at risk from potential invasion were subject to strict controls. Southend was declared an 'evacuation area' and children were evacuated to families all across Britain. Many residents left as both tourism jobs disappeared and the risk

of bombing raids increased. The population of Southend declined from 140,000 to a low point of about 30,000. It thus became a virtually deserted ghost town populated only by the military and essential workers. Half of the WMS workforce of four hundred employees joined the forces. A number of WMS vehicles were requisitioned by the War Department, starting with AEC Regals AHJ405 and BHJ132 on 14 December 1939 and 2 July 1940 respectively. Other vehicles included HJ9170/87, JN210, JN5782-4, JN6887, JN7500, JN8568/9 and also KJ2448 and AEV542. Many were never returned. The AEC Regal/Duple had become the preferred choice for the coach fleet so in order to prevent the requisition of these coaches by the War Department when the final four examples of the 1939 intake were delivered they were carefully hidden away in brown undercoat, reputedly behind a bricked up wall, throughout the duration of the war. They were eventually registered BJN116-9 in 1946 when they finally entered revenue service.

As a result of the decline of population from 1940 there were surplus vehicles which were available for loan to needy operators. WMS were also able to assist ENOC following bomb damage to their Duke Street, Chelmsford premises in May 1943. Details of the vehicles loaned are shown on *page 147*. This information has been obtained from original WMS documents and some of the dates quoted differ from those published elsewhere.

A total of 27 vehicles was loaned during 1941 including all but one of the Bristol K5Gs with JN9544 remaining the sole example at work in Southend. Some of the vehicles loaned received their new operators fleet-names and fleet-numbers though they were always shown as 'on hire'. In other cases their 'Westcliff-on-Sea' fleet-names were retained.

Fig.6.35 *One of the Bristol K5G/ECWs loaned to Thames Valley was JN 9541 where it gained temporary fleet-number 106. It is seen here at Slough Station on route 22 to Maidenhead. On the nearside it carries an 'on hire' notice.* **JFP/OS**

Buses Loaned During the Period 1940 to 1945.

On loan to Thames Valley Traction Co. Ltd

JN 9541	106	27/11/40 to 30/12/41
JN 9542	107	28/11/40 to 10/2/42
JN 9543	108	18/11/40 to 10/2/42
AHJ 401	101	25/11/40 to 10/2/42
AHJ 402	102	25/11/40 to 21/12/41
BHJ 532	104	26/11/40 to 5/2/42
BHJ 533	105	27/11/40 to 5/2/42

Vehicles were allocated to Reading and Maidenhead, used mainly on route 1 (Reading – Maidenhead) and 22 (Maidenhead – Slough), also used on 1A and 23.

On loan to Bristol Tramways & Carriage Co. Ltd

JN 961		30/5/42 to 14/12/42
JN 962		30/5/42 to 14/12/42
JN 6890	3720	6/2/42 to 14/6/45
JN 6895	3721	10/2/42 to 4/10/45
JN 6896	3722	6/2/42 to 7/9/45
JN 9540	3719	3/1/41 to 22/11/44
AJN 823	3716	1/1/41 to 27/6/45
AJN 824	3717	1/1/41 to 20/6/45
AJN 825	3718	3/3/41 to 22/11/44

On loan to Western National Omnibus Co. Ltd

JN 961	23/12/40 to 29/5/42
JN 962	23/12/40 to 29/5/42
JN 4744	16/2/42 to 27/12/42
JN 4745	16/2/42 to 28/12/42

On loan to Eastern Counties Omnibus Co. Ltd

JN 3230	22/11/40 to 5/6/45
JN 4295	1/12/40 to 13/7/45
JN 4748	1/12/40 to 3/8/45

JN 4748 was used at Cambridge.

On loan to London Passenger Transport Board (garages allocated shown)

JN 2797	GM	25/10/40 to 27/12/40
JN 2798	CL	25/10/40 to 27/12/40
JN 2800	T CL	25/10/40 to 27/12/40
JN 3229	U AR	25/10/40 to 27/12/40
MV 3394	T CL	25/10/40 to 27/12/40

Fig.6.36 AJN 824 an ECW bodied K5G is seen on hire to Bristol Tramways in sylvan surroundings. On the destination blind Weston-Super-Mare is just visible. Note the classic wartime advice to 'Save fuel – for the factories'. OS

Fig.6.37 In a similarly tree shrouded bus station, but on the other side of the country JN 4748 is seen at work in Drummer Street Bus Station, Cambridge. Eastern Counties had three of these Weymann bodied AEC Regents on loan from WMS. In modern terminology we would say that ECOC have retro-fitted 'bible-boards', in themselves a retrograde way of showing destinations. PJSA

As a wartime measure Bristol JO5G JN 7499 was converted to perimeter seating and was fitted with a built-in gas producer unit, though this was only in use for a very short time. The greater portion of Fairfax Drive garage was requisitioned by the War Department with effect from 18 January 1943 at a rental of £250 per annum, fortunately at a time when many vehicles were away on loan to other operators. Towards the end of the war the population of Southend began to rise again reaching about 110,000 and WMS needed to call in its bus loans.

A fleet composition was published dated 4 September 1945 showing a fleet strength of 102 vehicles:-

Bristol JO5G	28	AEC Renown	1
Bristol L5G	1(a)	AEC Q	1
Bristol GO5G	11	AEC Regal	6
Bristol K5G	13(a)	AEC Ranger	3
AEC Regent			
(Gardner)	27	Leyland Cub	3
Dennis Lance	2	Tilling-Stevens	6

(a) referred to as LO5G and KO5G respectively

When peace returned many vehicles were in a general state of neglect due to wartime maintenance restrictions. Although some new vehicles were ordered, as an immediate stop gap measure an extended programme of re-bodying, re-building and engine changes of existing vehicles was begun in order to extend their working lives. With the WMS garage staff being rather depleted during wartime it had became necessary from 1942 onwards to send many vehicles for body attention to the local firm of Charles W. Beale of Westcliff. This organisation also undertook a more extensive rebuilding programme from 1946 which included many Bristol JO5G saloons as discussed above. Some Weymann bodied AEC Regents were also found to be in need of body repair after the rigours of war work and low maintenance and were sent to C. W. Beale. The roof number boxes were retained but painted over (see JN4295 Fig.5.34, JN4746 Fig.6.39 and JN4747 Fig.5.43). In the case of JN4744 the roof must have required substantial remedial work leading to the incidental removal of the number box which together with the replacement of the pre-war AEC radiator by a Bristol PV2 resulted in a distinctly different appearance for this bus (see Fig.6.38).

AEC Regent body rebuilds were also undertaken by John C. Beadle Ltd. of Dartford, though the resulting appearance was often more like a completely new body than a rebuild. Not surprisingly the styling had several common features with the WMS Bristol GO5Gs similarly treated by Beadle. The buses concerned were JN3228 (see Fig.6.39), JN3229, JN3716 and JN3718 (see Fig.5.38). Inspection of Fig.6.39 allows comparison of the rebuilt products. Here the Beadle product shows a sloping front panel and new destination box, those by C. W. Beale, however, retaining the roof number box and several other original features.

Fig.6.38 *Local firm C. W. Beale rebuilt and repaired a number of buses for WMS where the bodies had worn far more rapidly than the chassis and the latter were judged to have more useful life left. Weymann bodied AEC Regent JN4744 of 1932 was selected for such a rebuild in 1946 unlike its sister buses JN4745 and JN4294 which went to ECW for a complete rebody (see Figs.5.13 and 5.57). Comparing the photos suggests why the ECW rebodied buses lasted until 1961 whereas JN4744 was withdrawn in 1954. Note also the unusual replacement radiator, which on close inspection appears to be an AEC less badge and central vertical bar   WJH*

In 1949 four 1936 Brush bodied Bristol GO5Gs (JN6892/3/4/6), were sent to Lowestoft to be fitted with new ECW bodies *(see Fig.6.28)* as were two 1934 Weymann bodied AEC Regents JN4745 *(see Figs.5.10 and 5.13)* and JN4294 *(see Fig.5.57)*. The old Weymann body from the latter vehicle was sold to J. W. Campbell & Sons Ltd. of Pitsea who mounted it on a new Albion CX37 chassis. The completed vehicle was registered PPU187 and was eventually acquired by ENOC in February 1956 and numbered 1020 (for further details and a photograph see *Campbells, Fact File No. 3*).

The Hampshire firm of Portsmouth Aviation was contracted to rebuild the Weymann body of AEC Regent JN3717 dating from 1934 *(see Fig.5.8)* in 1947. This was to remain a unique WMS choice but two further Portsmouth Aviation rebuilds joined the fleet in the form of Dennis Lances NJ5974 and NJ5978 from Brighton, Hove & District *(see Figs.5.70 and 5.71)*. The extensive workshops of BH&D were called upon in 1949 when WMS sent four early Bristol K5G/ECWs for refurbishment, JN9540-2/4. A programme of engine changes was undertaken with Gardner 5LW and AEC oil engines replacing the earlier petrol units; details are given in the 1951-1955 Fleet List.

Following the election of the Labour government in 1945 (with a mandate for nationalisation) the British Transport Commission was formed on 1 January 1948, and the LPTB became the London Transport Executive. In September 1948 the Tilling Group, of which WMS was an operating unit, decided to sell out voluntarily to the BTC. There followed a programme of freehold land and property valuations for all the operating Companies. In the case of WMS these included the following valuations:

Fairfax Drive, Prittlewell	£19,000
Hoe Street, Walthamstow	£7,910
Broadway, Hadleigh	£4,500
London Road, Southend	£106,872
Oak Road, Hadleigh	£3,500
Pier Hill, Southend	£17,500

Fig.6.39 *This view, taken at Fairfax Drive yard after the ENOC re-numbering, allows comparison of the results of rebuilding the Weymann bodies on two 1934 AEC Regents by different companies. JN3228 (1162) was sent to Beadle and JN4746 (1170) to C. W. Beale, both about 1946/7. The Beadle is the more comprehensive, now looking more like a Beadle than Weymann body. Work by Beale appears to be more repair than reconstruction and the Weymann shape remains. By ENOC days both buses had by been relegated to contract work, the BEA destination indicating not British European Airways but the British Electricity Authority and their power station then under construction at Tilbury. JCG*

Fig.6.40 *JN9542 was one of four pre-war Bristol K5Gs that were rebuilt by BH&D gaining the lower PV2 radiator. It is seen passing the Holmes & Smith premises next to the WMS coach station at Pier Hill. The presumed running number holder is clearly visible under the front nearside window. RFM*

Immediately after the war London Transport found itself desperately short of vehicles. The blitz had taken its toll, and the RT programme was running behind schedule. The vehicle shortage had been partially alleviated by the hiring of coaches from local fleets but there was still a shortfall. In consequence the newly-formed LTE turned to the BTC for help. BTC constituent companies had started to receive substantial numbers of new buses, most of the double-deckers being ECW bodied Bristol Ks. It was agreed that some 20-25% of these buses should be delivered directly from ECW to London Transport. The vehicles were fitted with a London Transport roundel on the front radiator and garage code and running number stencil holders. The words 'London Transport' were carried in the ultimate destination blind and a special 'lazy' blind used in the via box indicating the terminals and route number. Three vehicles from WMS were allocated to operate in London and they had the distinction of being the only vehicles there which did not carry fleet-numbers.

The complete information about periods of hire, routes worked, and garage allocations is shown below:

CJN 324 to London Transport   12/2/49
          Leyton (T) garage   16/2/49 – 26/1/50
          Route 38 Victoria Station to Chingford

CJN 325 to London Transport   26/2/49
          Holloway (J) garage   2/3/49 – 1/1/50
          Route 19 Finsbury Park
          to Upper Tooting
          Riverside (R) garage   1/1/50 – 23/2/50
          Route 72 Hook to East Acton

CJN 326 to London Transport   4/3/49
          Holloway (J) garage   4/3/49 – 1/1/50
          Route 19 Finsbury Park
          to Upper Tooting
          Riverside (R) garage   1/1/50 – 3/3/50
          Route 72 Hook to East Acton

Fig.6.41 This photo shows not a wartime loan but one in the immediate post-war period, on 11 February 1950 to be precise. CJN326, a Bristol K5G/ECW new in 1948, is running number R11 on route 72. It operated from two London Transport garages seen here operating from its second location, Riverside. Note the 'lazy' blind display showing the route terminals only that was carried by these loans and the London Transport display in the final destination blind. The other characteristic, the LT roundel on the radiator grille is obscured by the radiator blind. ABC

Fig.6.42 As soon as its body was completed in 1948 Bristol K5G CJN324 was sent direct from ECW to London Transport. It is seen operating from Leyton (T) garage on route 38 being passed by another loaned Bristol K on route 36. FWI/ LTPS

Fig.6.43 Another post-war loan to London Transport was of Bristol K5G/ECW CJN325. This fine view shows the London Transport crew returning to their vehicle at Plimsoll Road, Finsbury Park for their next trip on route 19. CJN325 ran in London for just under one year during which time it worked both from Holloway (J) and Riverside (R) garages.   PJSA

New vehicles received by WMS in the immediate post war period were mainly double-deckers in the form of several batches of K5Gs as well as a few K6Bs powered by 6-cylinder Bristol AVW engines.

Returning to the London area, the WMS Walthamstow garage premises ceased to be used after December 1948. For more details about operations in E.17 see *Chapter Three*.

In 1949 the first Bristol Lodekka prototype (chassis number LDX.001) entered service with Bristol Tramways as C5000 (LHY949). It achieved standard seating and a central gangway on the upper-deck together with low-bridge height through a radical chassis layout. The vehicle was loaned to many BTC companies for evaluation including WMS where it was used on service 5 to Shoeburyness.

In 1950 five Bristol KS (a development of the K type) models were added *(see Fig.5.56 for DJN556 a KS5G)*. These were followed in 1951 by a batch of seven of the eight-foot wide version designated the KSW, six being KSW5G (EJN627-32) and one a KSW6B DJN560. The only saloon buses to arrive were three ECW bodied Bristol LWL5Gs *(see Figs.5.41 and 5.46)*. Changes to the coaching fleet saw the withdrawal of the former Southdown Tilling-Stevens char-a-bancs in December 1949 being replaced

by an intake of eleven Bedford OBs with Duple Vista bodies *(see Figs.3.18 and 6.49)*, supplemented by a trio of Bristol L6Bs with ECW full-front 'Queen Mary' style coachwork *(see Fig.5.76)*. Around this time conversion of part of Prittlewell garage into overhaul workshops commenced.

Fig.6.44 The standard post-war Tilling product was the 7' 6" wide Bristol K type with completely re-designed Eastern Coach Works lowbridge bodywork. WMS took 26 of these with both Gardner and Bristol engines. DHJ607 is a K5G new in 1949 seen here on the 5 at Shoeburyness.   PJSA

Fig.6.45 The prototype Bristol Lodekka, Bristol Tramways C5000 (LHY949) is seen here on evaluation with WMS. It was exclusively employed on service 5. Production examples of the Bristol LD5G arrived in 1954.   PJSA

Fig.6.46 The takeover of Benfleet & District and Canvey & District added a substantial number of former Birmingham City Transport Daimler CWA6's to the WMS fleet.   In this view Park Royal bodied FOP417 is seen working its old haunts to Benfleet after being re-painted into WMS red livery. This bus later passed to SCT receiving fleet-number 243. Other examples are shown under service 26 in Chapter Five.   JFH

During 1950 the two 'one off' WMS AEC double-deckers were disposed of, the Renown (JN 4612) being sold in January followed by the Q (JN3457) in March.

Several second-hand vehicles were also purchased, all from Brighton, Hove & District. These arrived in 1949/50 in the shape of six Dennis Lance double-deckers NJ5974-9 *(see Figs.5.70, 5.71)*. One of these, NJ5976 had been converted to open-top in Brighton *(see Figs.11.9-11.11)*. This was accompanied for sea-front service by three open-top AEC Regents which had been new to Thomas Tilling in Brighton in 1930 GJ2004/5 *(see Fig.5.52)* and 1932 GW6273 *(see Fig.5.54)*.

In March 1951 the Benfleet & District and Canvey & District concerns were taken over, which added thirty-one double-deckers to the WMS fleet. Seven of the acquisitions were AEC Regents, one of which had originated with ENOC, VX4108 *(see Fig.5.62)*, whilst another three were re-registered examples which had started life with Sheffield Corporation *(see Figs.11.25-11.31)*. The remaining twenty-four buses were all Daimler CWs though with AEC engines, re-kindling memories of the earlier years when Daimler char-a-bancs were favoured

by WMS. Many of these vehicles had only recently been acquired by Benfleet/Canvey from Birmingham City Transport. The Benfleet/Canvey acquisition caused the only clash of three number registrations in the WMS fleet, this being between JTW608 and DHJ608. However, the duplication only lasted until March 1953 when the acquired Daimler was taken out of service.

WMS gained two garages with the Bridge family businesses, the Canvey & District garage at Leigh Beck and the Benfleet & District garage in London Road, Hadleigh situated close to Victoria House *(see Chapter Nine)*. This latter garage had also accommodated some of the vehicles from the Superior Coaches fleet, a Bridge subsidiary based in Tottenham which was associated with the Ardley Bros. business, *(see Chapter Three)*. Since the Superior coach fleet required a new base, the Bridge family acquired the Oak Road garage which had become surplus to WMS requirements, the seven vehicle output being transferred to WMS's newly acquired London Road, Hadleigh garage. Thus the Superior and WMS vehicles effectively swapped locations.

On 17 February 1952 the City Coach Company sold out to the BTC who placed it under WMS control. A total of 105 vehicles was acquired by WMS the details of which are given in *City Fact File Number 1*. Later in May 1952 the Midland section of ENOC was transferred to the United Counties Omnibus Co. Ltd. As compensation control of WMS passed to ENOC although WMS was the larger company by both numbers of buses owned and revenue but the area served was much smaller. The WMS Head Office was registered at New Writtle Street, Chelmsford from 10 June 1952. Subsequent fleet changes reflected the new corporate regime. The last vehicle delivered in full WMS red livery was Bristol KSW5G FJN159, and the last vehicle repainted red was AEC Regent JN3718. However, two batches of vehicles that had been ordered by City were registered in Southend by WMS. The first batch of six Leyland Titans FJN201-6 arrived in chocolate brown City livery complete with City fleet numbers, whilst the other batch of six Burlingham-bodied Leyland Royal Tigers FJN208-12/8 were delivered to WMS painted cream and green.

From 1953 WMS vehicles were delivered in ENOC Tilling green and cream livery with 'Westcliff-on-Sea' fleet-names though fleet-numbers were still not carried

in accordance with the established tradition. An early green repaint recorded was Bristol GO5G JN6897, followed shortly by the entire fleet of Bedford OB coaches which were all dealt with in the ENOC paint-shops in Rayne Road, Braintree. The very last Southend CBC registration issued was carried by Bristol LS6G coach, FJN169 *(see Fig.5.75 for FJN165).*

Fig.6.47 FJN211 was one of six Burlingham bodied Leyland Royal Tigers ordered by the City Coach Company but delivered directly to WMS with Southend CBC registrations. This view shows it as ENOC 135. PJSA

Fig.6.48 The six all-Leyland PD2/12s ordered by City had been painted in City colours by Leyland complete with City fleet-names. This was how they were delivered to WMS thus ensuring the City name was perpetuated for a few more years. In this view LD21 (FJN202) turns into Tylers Avenue garage at the end of its long run. Chapter Nine allows the still extant gabled houses visible in Baltic Avenue behind the bus to be located in present day Southend (see Fig.9.20). MLWC

Later Bristol KSW deliveries were then registered in Essex generally forming parts of larger ENOC batches of vehicles. These continued to appear in green with 'Westcliff-on-Sea' fleet-names and lacking fleet-numbers. The Essex registrations used were UEV, UVX, VNO and WNO. As far as City was concerned although a couple of City vehicles were repainted red, later repaints were into green but with 'Westcliff-on-Sea' fleet-names though retaining their City fleet-numbers producing an interesting if short-lived mix of styles. Because the main Wood Green – Southend City service (which later became service 251) was held in such high esteem by the travelling public, many of the six-wheel Leyland LT class retained their chocolate brown City livery. To supplement the service a number of ENOC Leyland PD1s including 3983/7-91 (MPU44/8-52) were drafted in for this service. These gained script style City fleet-names. Hicks Bros. 80 (MEV174, Leyland PS1/1) and 81/2 (MNO193/4, Leyland PD1) were also used by WMS and gained City fleet names thus concentrating Leylands at former City garages.

In March 1953 ex-Benfleet & District Daimler JTW 608 was withdrawn thus eliminating the only three number registration clash with DHJ608. Dennis Lance NJ5974 was converted to a painters' shop for use at the London Road, Southend garage. Daimler FOP413 was withdrawn following a collision with a railway bridge.

In January 1954 City, Hicks and WMS employees transferred to ENOC employment. Then the

Fig.6.49 *The classic combination of Bedford OB chassis with Duple Vista 29-seat coachwork created an ideal small coach for short tours and excursions. This view shows DJN553 when numbered 214 in the ENOC fleet but still carrying WMS fleet-names. It is at Euston Square Coach Station.* PJSA

Fig.6.50 *In ENOC green and cream but with WMS fleet-names, an almost brand new Bristol KSW5G/ECW UVX666 basks in the 1954 sunshine at Victoria Circus on service 5, just before the abandonment of trolleybuses. It later gained fleet-number 1400, then 2357 with ENOC. It is interesting to note that the destination blind shows SHOEBURYNESS LMS. RLY. STN. When this bus was delivered to WMS the LMS has been absorbed into British Railways for no less than six years!* RFM

unbelievable happened: WMS vehicles started to carry fleet-numbers once again! New deliveries carried numbers in the 'National' series 4215-9 using transfers rather than cast metal plates. The vehicles were WNO480/1 Bristol KSW5G and WVX444/6/7 Bristol LS5G saloons. Among the last vehicles to be received by WMS prior to the re-numbering were the new design Bristol Lodekka LD5Gs from the first production 100th Sanction series (chassis nos. 100.030/1). The vehicles were XVX26/7 numbered 4227/8.

Finally it is worth recording that the last two examples of the extensive WMS AEC Regent fleet JN4294 & JN4745 were finally withdrawn in 1961 after 28 years yeoman service. These had been new in 1934, re-bodied by ECW in 1949, fitted with Gardner 5LW engines, and numbered 1166/9 in 1954 (see *Figs.5.10, 5.13 and 5.57*). The very last pre-war vehicle of WMS stock to be withdrawn by Eastern National was Bristol K5G AHJ402 *(see Figs.5.26 and 6.33)* latterly carrying fleet number 1264, which was retired in 1962.

Fig.6.51 *XVX26 was one of three Bristol LD5G Lodekkas delivered to WMS in 1954 before the ENOC July re-numbering. It is seen here at Pier Hill on service 6. But look very closely and it will be seen that it is carrying a fleet-number! During the final months of ENOC control, vehicles allocated to WMS not only had Essex CC registrations but were also allocated fleet-numbers in the 'National' series which had begun way back in 1919 starting at 2001. The number carried by XVX26 was 4227. FC*

Fig.6.52 *FJN163 was a Bristol LS5G saloon with unusual dual-purpose and dual-door bodywork based within a bus rather than coach shell. It has arrived at Tylers Avenue on City replacement service 251 and has run via Battlesbridge rather than the normal route via Shotgate. It carries its new ENOC fleet-number 379. PJSA*

A comprehensive re-numbering scheme which consolidated the ENOC, City, Hicks and WMS stock took place on Sunday 18 July 1954. Vehicles were arranged by blocks of chassis manufacturers generally in chassis number order but with many exceptions and with the largest manufacturer Bristol last. Single-deckers were numbered from 100 and double-deckers from 1100. Just as the re-numbering was taking place WMS received two further vehicles. Bristol LS5G saloon YPU138 arrived carrying the new number, whilst the third Lodekka XVX28 arrived un-numbered, later becoming 1436.

Following the re-numbering WMS received six further Lodekkas one LD5G and five LD6Bs and another LS5G. Although these vehicles carried ENOC fleet-numbers they were actually owned by WMS until the close of service on 1 January 1955 when all WMS rolling stock and other assets were transferred to ENOC.

To help balance the respective fleet totals when the Southend Co-ordination Scheme came into effect in 1955 WMS sold seven of the former Benfleet & District Daimler CWA6s to Southend Corporation *(see Fig.10.8)* one of which was purely as a source of spares.

The unused plot of land at Broadway, Hadleigh was eventually sold to Benfleet Garages Ltd. (a Bridge family subsidiary) with a condition that the land was not to be used for the operation or maintenance of public service vehicles.

ENOC carried out a further re-numbering on Sunday 9 August 1964 which included many former WMS vehicles. The last 'real' WMS vehicle, which had been registered in Southend, to be withdrawn was FJN161 in January 1971, whilst the last vehicles delivered new to WMS to end their careers were the Bristol Lodekkas XVX23-31 which became 2408-10/01/2/5/6/11/2 and were taken out of stock in September 1971 (2408-10) and March 1973 (2405/6) respectively.

Fig.6.53 *XVX30 waits at the Hamstel Road terminus of service 64. This Bristol LD6B was delivered after the ENOC re-numbering had taken place gaining fleet-number 1442, but had 'Westcliff-on-Sea' fleet-names. It remained in WMS legal ownership for only a brief time. JCG*

Fig.6.54 *What a splendid way to finish, a Westcliff bus in full colour, albeit ENOC Tilling green and cream. Posed outside the former Benfleet & District garage at Hadleigh, then used by ENOC (HH), DHJ610 is an ECW bodied Bristol K6B delivered to WMS in 1949. In ENOC ownership it carried fleet-number 1325 and then 2253 in the 1964 scheme. I took this photograph in March 1966, on an Eastern National Enthusiasts Group coach tour I had organised, after carefully setting the destination blind to the Mondays only service 27. Although the bus had only about a year of service left the now much enlarged Hadleigh garage is still used by First Essex Buses as their only Southend district base.   AGO*

Tailpiece: The twilight of two very special AECs JN3457 and JN4612

Fig.6.55 *On 15 May 1949, near the end of their lives these two very special buses are parked together. Given that they remained unique and that WMS's subsequent purchases from the AEC double-deck catalogue were all Regents, were they a success? The pair was withdrawn several years before similar vintage Regents though in most cases these had been rebuilt or rebodied and re-engined. Even so, the AEC Q and Renown gave about twenty years of service, a good record for non-standard buses. VCJ*

Notes on the Fleet List 1951 to 1955

This fleet list provides a profile of the WMS fleet following the takeover of Benfleet & District and Canvey & District in March 1951 until the January 1955 ENOC acquisition of WMS. Since fleet-numbers were generally not carried vehicles have been listed in age order although certain batches have been reported in numerical order for convenience of layout.

The coverage is based on an official WMS list dated 31 December 1950 when the fleet strength stood at 147 vehicles. The AEC Renown JN4612 and AEC Q JN3457 had both been withdrawn during 1950, in January and March respectively. The two remaining original Dennis Lance double-deckers had been withdrawn in August 1950 (JN961) and October 1950 (JN962). Seven further vehicles were delivered after the July 1954 re-numbering with ENOC fleet-numbers but 'Westcliff-on-Sea' fleet-names. These have been listed separately.

All vehicles passed to the ownership of the Eastern National Omnibus Company Limited at the close of service on 1 January 1955.

Dates of acquisition are shown for buses not purchased new with the exception of the Canvey & District and Benfleet & District buses which were all acquired with the take-over of these businesses in March 1951.

Notes & Abbreviations Used

Operator names:	BH&D	Brighton, Hove & District
	B&D	Benfleet & District
	LT	London Transport
Body builders	ECOC	Eastern Counties Omnibus Company
	MCCW	Metro-Cammell Weymann
	ECW	Eastern Coach Works
	NCB	Northern Coach Builders
Body re-furbishers/ re-builders:	C. W. Beale	C. W. Beale, Westcliff-on-Sea
	Ports Avn	Portsmouth Aviation

In addition many vehicles received bodywork attention at C. W. Beale between 1942-6 before being further rebuilt or re-bodied at a later date. These have not been specifically listed. Vehicles in this category include JN6892 and JN6896.

Body type:	H	Highbridge	L	Lowbridge
	O	Open-top	B	Saloon bus
	C	Coach	DP	Dual-purpose
	FC	Full front coach		
Entrance position:	F	Front	R	Rear
	C	Centre	D	Dual

Eastern National (ENOC) fleet re-numbering Sunday 18 July 1954

Vehicles included in the fleet list but not shown below were withdrawn before the ENOC fleet re-numbering took place in July 1954. Vehicles taken over from the City Coach Company are not included. Refer to *Fact File 1* for full details.

The fleet re-numbering was carried out in blocks of chassis types and in chassis number order hence registration numbers and fleet numbers may not necessarily be in sequence. However, there were numerous exceptions to this general rule as will be noted with the FOP series of Daimlers.

Numbering scheme:	100	Single-deckers
	1100	Double-deckers

Eastern National (ENOC) second fleet re-numbering Sunday 9 August 1964

Numbering scheme:	3xx series	Bristol LS/MW coaches
	11xx series	Bristol L/LL/LWL saloons
	12xx series	Bristol LS saloons
	22xx series	Bristol K double-deckers
	23xx series	Bristol KS/KSW double-deckers
	24xx series	Bristol LD double-deckers

Westcliff-on-Sea Motor Services Ltd.   Fleet List 1951-5 with ENOC renumbering of 18 July 1954

Reg No	ENOC No. (1954)	Chassis type	Date new	Chassis No.	Body builder	Refurbish't by	Refurb/ rebody date	Seating capacity	Replacement engine	Notes
GJ2004	1148	AEC Regent	1930	661558	ECW		1942	O33/26R		Ex-Brighton, Hove & District 6004 in -/50
GJ2005	1147	AEC Regent	1930	661557	ECW		1942	O33/26R		Ex-Brighton, Hove & District 6005 in 7/49
VX4108		AEC Regent	1930	661128	NCB		1944	H30/26R		Ex-Canvey & District; new to ENOC as 3020
HF7435	1156	AEC Regent	1931	6611549	NCB		1944	H30/26R	Gardner 5LW	Ex-Benfleet & District; new to Wallasey Cpn as 63
HF7437		AEC Regent	1931	6611550	NCB		1944	H30/26R		Ex-Benfleet & District; new to Wallasey Cpn as 64
HX2980	1150	AEC Regent	1931	6611006	ECW		1942	O30/26R	Gardner 5LW	Ex-AEC demonstrator, 4/32
GW6273	1140	AEC Regent	1932	6611776	ECW		1943	O30/26R	Gardner 5LW	Ex-Brighton, Hove & District 6273 in 9/50
MV3394		AEC Regent	1932	6611729	MCCW	C.W.Beale	1943	H27/24R	Gardner 5LW	Ex- AEC demonstrator, 11/33
WN4761		AEC Regent	1933	6611898	NCB		1944/5	H30/26R	Gardner 5LW	Ex-Canvey & District; new to South Wales as 261
JN2796		AEC Regent	1933	6612055	Park Royal	C.W.Beale	1945	H30/26R	Gardner 5LW	
JN2797		AEC Regent	1933	6612056	Park Royal	C.W.Beale	1945	H30/26R	Gardner 5LW	
JN2798		AEC Regent	1933	6611981	Park Royal	C.W.Beale	1946	H30/26R	Gardner 5LW	
JN2799		AEC Regent	1933	6611982	Park Royal	ECW	1942	H30/26R	Gardner 5LW	
JN2800		AEC Regent	1933	6611983	Park Royal	ECW	1945	H30/26R	Gardner 5LW	
JN3228	1162	AEC Regent	1934	6612149	Weymann	Beadle	1947	L27/26R	Gardner 5LW	
JN3229	1163	AEC Regent	1934	6612150	Weymann	Beadle	1947	L27/26R	Gardner 5LW	
JN3230		AEC Regent	1934	6612151	Weymann	ECW	1943	L26/26R	Gardner 5LW	
JN3231		AEC Regent	1934	6612148	Weymann	WMS	1943	L26/26R	Gardner 5LW	
JN3715		AEC Regent	1934	6612063	Weymann	C.W.Beale	1946	L26/26R	Gardner 5LW	
JN3716	1161	AEC Regent	1934	6612064	Weymann	Beadle	1947	L27/26R	Gardner 5LW	
JN3717	1165	AEC Regent	1934	6612069	Weymann	Ports Avn	1947	L26/26R	Gardner 5LW	
JN3718	1164	AEC Regent	1934	6612460	Weymann	Beadle	1947	L27/26R	Gardner 5LW	
JN4294	1166	AEC Regent	1934	6612730	ECW		1949	L27/28R	Gardner 5LW	
JN4295	1167	AEC Regent	1934	6612731	Weymann	C.W.Beale	1946/7	L26/26R	Gardner 5LW	
JN4744	1168	AEC Regent	1934	6612887	Weymann	C.W.Beale	1946/7	L24/24R	Gardner 5LW	
JN4745	1169	AEC Regent	1934	6612888	ECW		1949	L27/28R	Gardner 5LW	
JN4746	1170	AEC Regent	1934	6612889	Weymann	C.W.Beale	1946/7	L24/24R	Gardner 5LW	
JN4747	1171	AEC Regent	1934	6612890	Weymann	C.W.Beale	1946/7	L24/24R	Gardner 5LW	

Reg	Fleet	Chassis	Year	Body	Body No.	Rebody builder	Rebody year	Layout	Engine	Notes
JN4748		AEC Regent	1934	Weymann	6612891			L24/24R	Gardner 5LW	
JN5456		AEC Regent	1935	Weymann	6613554			L27/25R	Gardner 5LW	
JN5457		AEC Regent	1935	Weymann	6613555			L27/25R	Gardner 5LW	
JN5458		AEC Regent	1935	Weymann	6613556	C.W.Beale	1946	L27/25R	Gardner 5LW	
JN5459		AEC Regent	1935	Weymann	O6613557	C.W.Beale	1946	L24/24R		
JN5461		AEC Regent	1935	Weymann	O6613559	C.W.Beale	1946	L24/24R		
MVW971	1172	AEC Regent	1935	Weymann	O6613544	C.W.Beale	1947	H29/28R	Gardner 5LW	Ex-B&D; new as Sheffield C.T. 104 BWA 204. Re-reg by B&D
MVW970	1173	AEC Regent	1935	Weymann	O6613548	C.W.Beale	1947	H29/24R	Gardner 5LW	Ex-B&D; new as Sheffield C.T. 100 BWA 200. Re-reg by B&D
NPU170	1174	AEC Regent	1935	Weymann	O6613635	C.W.Beale	1947	H28/28R	Gardner 5LW	Ex-B&D; new as Sheffield C.T. 226 BWA 826. Re-reg by B&D
NJ5974		Dennis Lance	1935	Tilling	126087	Ports Avn	1947	H30/26R	AEC A217	Ex-Brighton, Hove & District 6311 in 10/49
NJ5975		Dennis Lance	1935	Tilling	126088			H30/26R	Gardner 5LW	Ex-Brighton, Hove & District 6312 in 10/49
NJ5976		Dennis Lance	1935	Tilling	126089			O30/26R	Gardner 5LW	Ex-Brighton, Hove & District 6313 in 8/49
NJ5977		Dennis Lance	1935	Tilling	126090	Ports Avn	1947	H30/26R	AEC A217	Ex-Brighton, Hove & District 6314 in 9/49
NJ5978		Dennis Lance	1935	Tilling	126091			H30/26R	Gardner 5LW	Ex-Brighton, Hove & District 6315 in 12/49
NJ5979		Dennis Lance	1935	Tilling	126092	Ports Avn	1947	H30/26R	Gardner 5LW	Ex-Brighton, Hove & District 6316 in 10/49
JN6880	223	Bristol JO5G	1936	ECOC	JO5G.123	C.W.Beale	1946/7	B36R		
JN6881	224	Bristol JO5G	1936	ECOC	JO5G.124	C.W.Beale	1946/7	B36R		
JN6882	225	Bristol JO5G	1936	ECOC	JO5G.125	C.W.Beale	1946/7	B36R		
JN6883	226	Bristol JO5G	1936	ECOC	JO5G.126	C.W.Beale	1946/7	B36R		
JN6884		Bristol JO5G	1936	ECOC	JO5G.127	C.W.Beale	1946/7	B36R		
JN6885	227	Bristol JO5G	1936	ECOC	JO5G.128	C.W.Beale	1946/7	B36R		
JN6886	228	Bristol JO5G	1936	ECOC	JO5G.129	C.W.Beale	1946/7	DP32R		
JN6888	229	Bristol JO5G	1936	ECOC	JO5G.131			DP32R		
JN6889	230	Bristol JO5G	1936	ECOC	JO5G.132			DP32R		
JN6890	1223	Bristol GO5G	1936	Brush	GO5G.102	Beadle	1947	L27/26R		
JN6891	1224	Bristol GO5G	1936	Brush	GO5G.103	Beadle	1947	L27/26R		
JN6892	1225	Bristol GO5G	1936	ECW	GO5G.104		1949	L27/28R		
JN6893	1226	Bristol GO5G	1936	ECW	GO5G.105		1949	L27/28R		
JN6894	1227	Bristol GO5G	1936	ECW	GO5G.106		1949	L27/28R		
JN6895	1228	Bristol GO5G	1936	Brush	GO5G.107	Beadle	1947	L27/26R		
JN6896	1229	Bristol GO5G	1936	ECW	GO5G.108		1949	L27/28R		
JN6897	1230	Bristol GO5G	1936	Brush	GO5G.109	Beadle	1947	L27/26R		
JN7499	231	Bristol JO5G	1936	ECW	JO5G.232	C.W.Beale	1946/7	B36R		

Reg	Fleet No	Chassis	Year	Chassis No	Body	Prev Operator	Acquired	Type	Notes
JN7501	232	Bristol JO5G	1936	JO5G.234	ECOC			DP28R	
JN7833		Leyland Cub	1936	5983	ECW			C20F	
JN7985		Leyland Cub	1936	6775	ECW			C20F	
JN7986		Leyland Cub	1936	6776	ECW			C20F	
JN8560	242	Bristol JO5G	1937	JO5G.380	ECW	C.W.Beale	1946/7	B35R	
JN8561	243	Bristol JO5G	1937	JO5G.381	ECW	C.W.Beale	1946/7	B35R	
JN8562		Bristol JO5G	1937	JO5G.382	ECW	C.W.Beale	1946/7	B35R	
JN8563	244	Bristol JO5G	1937	JO5G.383	ECW	C.W.Beale	1946/7	B35R	
JN8564	245	Bristol JO5G	1937	JO5G.395	ECW	C.W.Beale	1946/7	B35R	
JN8565	246	Bristol JO5G	1937	JO5G.396	ECW	C.W.Beale	1946/7	B35R	
JN8566	247	Bristol JO5G	1937	JO5G.397	ECW	C.W.Beale	1946/7	B35R	
JN8567	248	Bristol JO5G	1937	JO5G.398	ECW	C.W.Beale	1946/7	B35R	
JN8570	1244	Bristol GO5G	1937	GO5G.171	ECW			O30/26R	
JN8571	1245	Bristol GO5G	1937	GO5G.172	ECW			O30/26R	
JN8572	1246	Bristol GO5G	1937	GO5G.173	ECW			O30/26R	
JN8584		AEC Ranger	1937	665091	Duple			C24F	
JN8585		AEC Ranger	1937	665092	Duple			C24F	
JN9531		Bristol JO5G	1937	JO5G.537	ECW			B32R	
JN9532		Bristol JO5G	1937	JO5G.538	ECW			B32R	
JN9533		Bristol JO5G	1937	JO5G.539	ECW			B32R	
JN9534		Bristol JO5G	1937	JO5G.540	ECW			B32R	
JN9535		Bristol JO5G	1937	JO5G.541	ECW			B32R	
JN9536		Bristol JO5G	1937	JO5G.542	ECW			B32R	
JN9537		Bristol JO5G	1937	JO5G.543	ECW			B32R	
JN9538		Bristol JO5G	1937	JO5G.544	ECW			B32R	
JN9539		Bristol JO5G	1937	JO5G.545	ECW			B32R	
JN9540	1252	Bristol K5G	1937	42.24	ECW			L27/28R	
JN9541	1253	Bristol K5G	1937	42.25	ECW			L27/28R	
JN9542	1254	Bristol K5G	1937	42.26	ECW			L27/28R	
JN9543	1255	Bristol K5G	1937	42.27	ECW	C.W.Beale	1947	L27/28R	
JN9544	1256	Bristol K5G	1937	42.28	ECW			L27/28R	
AAP829	1247	Bristol GO5G	1937	GO5G.181	BH&D	BH&D	1950	H30/26R	Ex-Brighton, Hove & District 6329 in 11/53
AHJ401	1263	Bristol K5G	1938	45.20	ECW			L27/28R	

Reg	Fleet No	Chassis	Year	Chassis No	Body	Seating	Engine	Notes
AHJ402	1264	Bristol K5G	1938	45.21	ECW	L27/28R		
AHJ403	1265	Bristol K5G	1938	45.22	ECW	L27/28R		
AHJ404	145	AEC Regal	1938	6623042	Duple	C32F	AEC 7.7 ex-LT	
AHJ405	146	AEC Regal	1938	6623043	Duple	C32F	AEC 7.7 ex-LT	
AHJ843		AEC Ranger	1938	665101	Duple	C24F		
AJN823	1267	Bristol K5G	1939	47.85	ECW	L27/26R		
AJN824	1268	Bristol K5G	1939	47.86	ECW	L27/26R		
AJN825	1269	Bristol K5G	1939	47.87	ECW	L27/26R		
AJN826	277	Bristol L5G	1939	48.064	ECW	B35R		
BHJ132	147	AEC Regal	1939	6623098	Duple	C30F	AEC 7.7 ex-LT	
BHJ532	1272	Bristol K5G	1939	53.087	ECW	L27/28R		
BHJ533	1273	Bristol K5G	1939	53.088	ECW	L27/28R		
BJN116	148	AEC Regal	1939	6623400	Duple	C30F	AEC 7.7 ex-LT	Delivered 1939 stored during war first registered 1946
BJN117	149	AEC Regal	1939	6623401	Duple	C30F	AEC 7.7 ex-LT	Delivered 1939 stored during war first registered 1946
BJN118	150	AEC Regal	1939	6623402	Duple	C30F	AEC 7.7 ex-LT	Delivered 1939 stored during war first registered 1946
BJN119	151	AEC Regal	1939	6623403	Duple	C30F	AEC 7.7 ex-LT	Delivered 1939 stored during war first registered 1946
FOP340	1195	Daimler CWG5	1943	11328	Duple	H30/26R	AEC 7.7	Ex-Canvey & District; new to Birmingham C.T. as 1340
FOP360	1196	Daimler CWA6	1944	11531	Duple	H30/26R		Ex-Canvey & District; new to Birmingham C.T. as 1360
FOP364	1197	Daimler CWA6	1944	11542	Duple	H30/26R		Ex-Canvey & District; new to Birmingham C.T. as 1364
JTW608		Daimler CWG5	1944	11364	Duple	H30/26R		Ex-Benfleet & District
JVW480		Daimler CWA6	1944	11564	Duple	H30/26R		Ex-Benfleet & District
JVW561	1198	Daimler CWA6	1944	11530	Duple	H30/26R		Ex-Benfleet & District
FOP385	1201	Daimler CWA6	1945	12018	Park Royal	H30/26R		Ex-Benfleet & District; new to Birmingham C.T. as 1385
FOP413		Daimler CWA6	1945	12040	Park Royal	H30/26R		Ex-Benfleet & District; new to Birmingham C.T. as 1413
FOP416	1202	Daimler CWA6	1945	12050	Park Royal	H30/26R		Ex-Canvey & District; new to Birmingham C.T. as 1416
FOP417	1203	Daimler CWA6	1945	12056	Park Royal	H30/26R		Ex-Benfleet & District; new to Birmingham C.T. as 1417
FOP429	1199	Daimler CWA6	1945	11994	Duple	H30/26R		Ex-Canvey & District; new to Birmingham C.T. as 1429
FOP431	1200	Daimler CWA6	1945	12015	Duple	H30/26R		Ex-Canvey & District; new to Birmingham C.T. as 1431
FOP452	1204	Daimler CWA6	1945	11925	Duple	H30/26R		Ex-Benfleet & District; new to Birmingham C.T. as 1452
FOP459	1205	Daimler CWA6	1945	12233	Park Royal	H30/26R		Ex-Benfleet & District; new to Birmingham C.T. as 1459
FOP461	1206	Daimler CWA6	1945	12234	Park Royal	H30/26R		Ex-Canvey & District; new to Birmingham C.T. as 1461
FOP462	1207	Daimler CWA6	1945	12257	Park Royal	H30/26R		Ex-Benfleet & District; new to Birmingham C.T. as 1462
FOP465	1208	Daimler CWA6	1945	12295	Park Royal	H30/26R		Ex-Benfleet & District; new to Birmingham C.T. as 1465

Westcliff-on-Sea Motor Services Ltd. Fleet List 1951-4 with ENOC renumberings of 18 July 1954 and 9 August 1964

Reg No	ENOC No. (1954)	Chassis type	Date new	Chassis No	Body builder	ENOC re-number (1964)	Seating capacity	Notes
KEV534	1209	Daimler CWA6	1945	12390	Brush		H30/26R	Ex-Canvey & District
KEV535	1210	Daimler CWA6	1945	12394	Brush		H30/26R	Ex-Canvey & District
KEV536	1211	Daimler CWA6	1945	12399	Brush		H30/26R	Ex-Canvey & District
BJN111	1275	Bristol K5G	1946	W3.116	ECW		L27/28R	
BJN112	1276	Bristol K5G	1946	W3.117	ECW		L27/28R	
BJN113	1277	Bristol K5G	1946	W3.118	ECW		L27/28R	
BJN114	1280	Bristol K5G	1946	62.061	ECW		L27/28R	
KHK863	1212	Daimler CWA6	1946	12672	Brush		H30/26R	Ex-Canvey & District
KHK864	1214	Daimler CWA6	1946	12674	Brush		H30/26R	Ex-Canvey & District
KNO71	1213	Daimler CWA6	1946	12673	Brush		H30/26R	Ex-Canvey & District
KNO72	1215	Daimler CWA6	1946	12675	Brush		H30/26R	Ex-Canvey & District
CHJ250	1286	Bristol K5G	1947	64.096	ECW	2214	L27/28R	
CHJ251	1287	Bristol K5G	1947	64.097	ECW	2215	L27/28R	
CHJ252	1289	Bristol K5G	1947	64.170	ECW	2217	L27/28R	
CHJ253	1290	Bristol K5G	1947	64.171	ECW	2218	L27/28R	
CHJ254	1292	Bristol K5G	1947	66.048	ECW	2220	L27/28R	
CHJ255	1298	Bristol K6B	1948	66.087	ECW	2226	L27/28R	
CHJ256	1299	Bristol K6B	1948	66.088	ECW	2227	L27/28R	
CJN299	203	Bedford OB	1948	83357	Duple		C29F	
CJN321	1305	Bristol K5G	1948	68.136	ECW	2233	L27/28R	
CJN322	1306	Bristol K5G	1948	68.137	ECW	2234	L27/28R	
DHJ21	1307	Bristol K5G	1948	68.138	ECW	2235	L27/28R	
DHJ22	204	Bedford OB	1948	86302	Duple		C29F	
DHJ23	205	Bedford OB	1948	90066	Duple		C29F	
DHJ24	206	Bedford OB	1948	94371	Duple		C29F	
CJN323	1308	Bristol K6B	1948	68.187	ECW	2236	L27/28R	
CJN324	1309	Bristol K5G	1948	72.056	ECW	2237	L27/28R	
CJN325	1310	Bristol K5G	1948	74.044	ECW	2238	L27/28R	

162

CJN326	1311	Bristol K5G	1948	74.045	ECW	2239	L27/28R
CJN327	1312	Bristol K6B	1949	74.071	ECW	2240	L27/28R
CJN328	1313	Bristol K6B	1949	74.072	ECW	2241	L27/28R
DHJ607	1323	Bristol K5G	1949	76.016	ECW	2251	L27/28R
DHJ608	1324	Bristol K5G	1949	76.017	ECW	2252	L27/28R
DHJ609	1333	Bristol K5G	1949	76.133	ECW	2261	L27/28R
DHJ610	1325	Bristol K6B	1949	76.024	ECW	2253	L27/28R
DHJ611	1330	Bristol K6B	1949	76.085	ECW	2258	L27/28R
DHJ612	1326	Bristol K6B	1949	76.025	ECW	2254	L27/28R
DHJ623	208	Bedford OB	1949	103966	Duple		C29F
DHJ624	209	Bedford OB	1949	104564	Duple		C29F
DHJ625	210	Bedford OB	1950	121146	Duple		C29F
DJN548	211	Bedford OB	1949	121213	Duple		C29F
DJN551	212	Bedford OB	1950	138314	Duple		C29F
DJN552	213	Bedford OB	1950	140148	Duple		C29F
DJN553	214	Bedford OB	1950	140536	Duple		C29F
DJN554	1343	Bristol KS5G	1950	80.063	ECW	2300	L27/28R
DJN556	1344	Bristol KS5G	1950	86.064	ECW	2301	L27/28R
DJN557	1345	Bristol KS5G	1950	86.065	ECW	2302	L27/28R
DJN558	1346	Bristol KS6B	1950	80.136	ECW	2303	L27/28R
DJN559	1347	Bristol KS6B	1950	82.042	ECW	2304	L27/28R
EHJ27	322	Bristol L6B	1950	79.144	ECW		FC31F
EHJ28	323	Bristol L6B	1950	79.145	ECW		FC31F
EHJ29	324	Bristol L6B	1950	81.109	ECW		FC31F
DJN560	1350	Bristol KSW6B	1951	84.019	ECW	2307	L27/28R
EJN627	1361	Bristol KSW5G	1951	84.132	ECW	2318	L27/28R
EJN628	1362	Bristol KSW5G	1951	84.133	ECW	2319	L27/28R
EJN629	1363	Bristol KSW5G	1951	84.134	ECW	2320	L27/28R
EJN630	1367	Bristol KSW5G	1951	86.003	ECW	2324	L27/28R
EJN631	1368	Bristol KSW5G	1951	86.004	ECW	2325	L27/28R
EJN632	1380	Bristol KSW5G	1952	86.005	ECW	2337	L27/28R
EJN633	344	Bristol LWL5G	1951	85.140	ECW	1132	B39R
EJN634	345	Bristol LWL5G	1951	85.141	ECW	1133	B39R

Reg	Fleet	Chassis	Year	Chassis No	Body	Body No	Type	Notes
EJN635	346	Bristol LWL5G	1951	85.142	ECW	1134	B39R	
EJN636	360	Bristol LS6G	1952	89.030	ECW	300	C39F	
EJN637	361	Bristol LS6G	1952	89.031	ECW	301	C39F	
EJN638	362	Bristol LS6G	1952	89.032	ECW	302	C39F	
EJN639	363	Bristol LS6G	1953	89.043	ECW	303	C39F	
EJN640	364	Bristol LS6G	1953	89.044	ECW	304	C39F	
FJN156	1386	Bristol KSW5G	1952	92.007	ECW	2343	L27/28R	
FJN157	1387	Bristol KSW5G	1952	92.024	ECW	2344	L27/28R	
FJN158	1392	Bristol KSW5G	1952	92.025	ECW	2349	L27/28R	
FJN159	1393	Bristol KSW5G	1952	92.042	ECW	2350	L27/28R	
FJN160	1404	Bristol KSW5G	1952	94.039	ECW	2361	L27/28R	
FJN161	1405	Bristol KSW5G	1952	94.040	ECW	2362	L27/28R	
FJN162	378	Bristol LS5G	1953	93.088	ECW	1204	DP41D	
FJN163	379	Bristol LS5G	1953	93.089	ECW	1205	DP41D	
FJN164	369	Bristol LS6G	1953	89.129	ECW	309	C39F	
FJN165	370	Bristol LS6G	1953	89.130	ECW	310	C39F	
FJN166	371	Bristol LS6G	1953	89.131	ECW	311	C39F	
FJN167	374	Bristol LS6G	1953	93.035	ECW	312	C39F	
FJN168	375	Bristol LS6G	1953	93.066	ECW	313	C39F	
FJN169	376	Bristol LS6G	1953	93.067	ECW	314	C39F	
FJN208	137	Ley PSU1/15	1952	520753	Burlingham		C39C	ordered by City Coach, delivered new to WMS
FJN209	138	Ley PSU1/15	1952	520754	Burlingham		C39C	ordered by City Coach, delivered new to WMS
FJN210	134	Ley PSU1/15	1952	520337	Burlingham		C39C	ordered by City Coach, delivered new to WMS
FJN211	135	Ley PSU1/15	1952	520342	Burlingham		C39C	ordered by City Coach, delivered new to WMS
FJN212	133	Ley PSU1/15	1952	520250	Burlingham		C39C	ordered by City Coach, delivered new to WMS
FJN218	136	Ley PSU1/15	1952	520348	Burlingham		C39C	ordered by City Coach, delivered new to WMS
UEV830	1394	Bristol KSW5G	1952	92.082	ECW	2351	L27/28R	
UEV840	1395	Bristol KSW5G	1952	94.011	ECW	2352	L27/28R	
UEV841	1396	Bristol KSW5G	1952	94.012	ECW	2353	L27/28R	
UEV842	1397	Bristol KSW5G	1952	94.017	ECW	2354	L27/28R	
UVX664	1398	Bristol KSW5G	1952	94.018	ECW	2355	L27/28R	
UVX665	1399	Bristol KSW5G	1952	94.019	ECW	2356	L27/28R	
UVX666	1400	Bristol KSW5G	1952	94.020	ECW	2357	L27/28R	

Reg No	ENOC No.	Chassis type	Date new	Chassis No.	Body builder	ENOC re-number	Seating capacity	Notes
VNO867	1415	Bristol KSW5G	1953	94.079	ECW	2372	L27/28R	
VNO868	1416	Bristol KSW5G	1953	94.080	ECW	2373	L27/28R	
VNO472	1417	Bristol KSW5G	1953	98.073	ECW	2374	L27/28R	
VNO473	1418	Bristol KSW5G	1953	98.074	ECW	2375	L27/28R	
VNO474	1421	Bristol KSW5G	1953	98.094	ECW	2378	L27/28R	
VNO475	1422	Bristol KSW5G	1953	98.095	ECW	2379	L27/28R	
VNO476	1419	Bristol KSW5G	1953	98.078	ECW	2376	L27/28R	
VNO477	1420	Bristol KSW5G	1953	98.079	ECW	2377	L27/28R	
VNO478	1423	Bristol KSW5G	1953	98.104	ECW	2380	L27/28R	
VNO479	1426	Bristol KSW5G	1953	98.140	ECW	2383	L27/28R	
VNO480	1427	Bristol KSW5G	1953	98.141	ECW	2384	L27/28R	Carried fleet-number in National series 4215
VNO481	1428	Bristol KSW5G	1953	98.173	ECW	2385	L27/28R	Carried fleet-number in National series 4216
WVX444	388	Bristol LS5G	1953	97.156	ECW	1211	B43D	Carried fleet-number in National series 4217
WVX446	386	Bristol LS5G	1953	97.134	ECW	1209	B43D	Carried fleet-number in National series 4218
WVX447	387	Bristol LS5G	1953	97.135	ECW	1210	B43D	Carried fleet-number in National series 4219
XVX26	1432	Bristol LD5G	1954	100.030	ECW	2401	H33/25R	Carried fleet-number in National series 4227
XVX27	1433	Bristol LD5G	1954	100.031	ECW	2402	H33/25R	Carried fleet-number in National series 4228
XVX28	1434	Bristol LD5G	1954	100.068	ECW	2405	H33/25R	No fleet-number on delivery
YPU138	391	Bristol LS5G	1954	101.017	ECW	1213	B43D	Delivered with new fleet-number

Westcliff-on-Sea Motor Services Ltd. Vehicles delivered after the ENOC fleet re-numbering in July 1954 and renumbered on 9 August 1964

Reg No	ENOC No. (1954)	Chassis type	Date new	Chassis No.	Body builder	ENOC re-number (1964)	Seating capacity	Notes
XVX23	1439	Bristol LD6B	1954	101.160	ECW	2408	H33/25R	National fleet-number 4212 not carried
XVX24	1440	Bristol LD6B	1954	101.161	ECW	2409	H33/25R	National fleet-number 4213 not carried
XVX25	1441	Bristol LD6B	1954	101.162	ECW	2410	H33/25R	National fleet-number 4214 not carried
XVX29	1437	Bristol LD5G	1954	100.090	ECW	2406	H33/25R	
XVX30	1442	Bristol LD6B	1954	101.163	ECW	2411	H33/25R	
XVX31	1443	Bristol LD6B	1954	101.164	ECW	2412	H33/25R	
YPU139	392	Bristol LS5G	1954	100.187	ECW	1214	B43D	

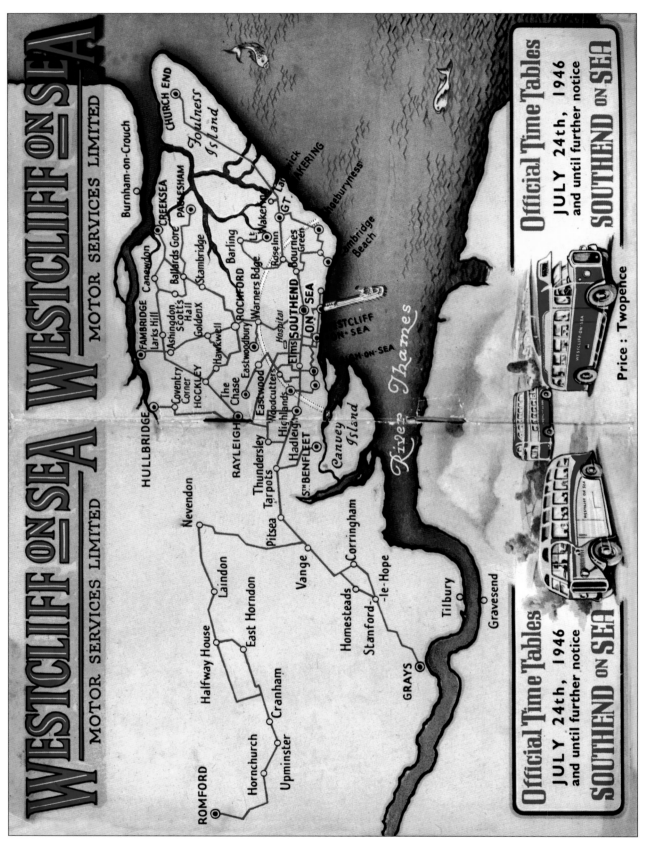

Fig.7.1 *This striking cover artwork is taken from the 24 July 1946 issue within the 'Eleventh Series'. The lavish use of colour on a good quality art paper is all the more surprising given the austerity, rationing and shortages of all sorts experienced in these immediate post-war years.*

Chapter Seven
Timetables

WMS timetables, information and publicity leaflets were, as with most transport companies, not simply a means of disseminating information to passengers and prospective passengers though this was of course their primary role. They were a key part of the creation of what we would today call the 'corporate image'. The other parts were the livery of the buses and coaches, the style of fleet-name, uniform and design of buildings. Other chapters allow the reader to judge these aspects for themselves. We have become increasingly aware of how important image is in our evaluation of place, period of time and indeed the quality and operation of a company. When we think of the thirties, a key period of growth for WMS, thoughts of streamlining in many aspects of design come to mind from vehicles to buildings by way of household appliances. Southend-on-Sea as a resort was promoted by the competing railway companies serving it in poster publicity. Today these posters fetch very high prices and form a field of study for academics, as well as attractive books of reproductions.

All this is by way of saying that the humble bus timetable and coach tour leaflet can offer us more than simply facts about WMS operations. Bus company posters have survived in much smaller numbers than those of their railway cousins. They did not merit the big name artists whose work so often defines an era, the exception being of course London Transport. Your author has a fairly comprehensive collection of WMS timetables and publicity material. This book provides an ideal opportunity to make this available in reproduction to a wider audience.

The developing styles of WMS bus timetable booklets that have been issued over the years may be followed through from the fussy but functional of the twenties, to the art deco of the thirties and then back to a more reserved presentation after the war. Some artwork may seem quite remarkable to our eyes but was clearly considered eye-catching and effective at the time of production. Material of this sort which can help us understand how a bus company wanted to present itself to its public is rarely given adequate coverage in books about bus companies. We have taken the opportunity to correct this and offer what can only be a selection, but a fairly representative one for your enjoyment. In addition a selection of the smaller operators absorbed by WMS is shown. Comparison of styles with the WMS timetables provides a useful yardstick of how important it was for the successful 'big company' to foster its image through design. For a complete listing of all WMS timetables the reader is referred to an article in *Essex Bus News*, no. 450 (October 2001).

The printers of the timetables were:

1923 – 1924	J. A. Godfrey & Sons Ltd., Southend-on-Sea
1924 – 1925	British Publishing Co. Ltd., Gloucester
1926 – 1933	Index Publishers Ltd., Dunstable
1933 – 1941	Washburn & Sons Ltd., Southend-on-Sea
1942 – 1952	H. Clark & Co. Ltd., London E.C.2

In the period until 1936 timetables were generally issued at monthly intervals, thereafter twice a year covering summer and winter services. During the Second World War issues were very much curtailed. When peace resumed two issues per year appeared until 1948, following which only an annual issue was produced which covered both winter and summer services. From 1923 until 1941 the timetables were of pocket booklet size 4¼″x5¼″, from 1942 were slightly larger 4¾″x7¼″, then from 1953 were standard BTC style with dimensions of 5½″x8½″.

Many leaflets and pamphlets were also issued to a wide variety of designs, examples of which may be found reproduced throughout this volume.

TIMETABLE STYLES

For ease of differentiation these have been divided into thirteen series by the author. Some dates are not known since a complete continuous run of timetables is not available thus the dates for each series show only those known to the author. All timetables published between 1923 and 1935 featured an advertisement on the lower half of the front cover as well as on the back cover. In judging the colours shown in the reproductions please make allowances for fading over the years.

First Series   February 1923 to February 1924

Cover: black print on red card. Front: upper 'Westcliff Motor Services, Limited.' name; lower letter-print advert (no photos); Back: full page letter-print advert (not reproduced here) for Ramuz, house, land and estate agent. Many adverts included through booklet. Centre-pages 'Reserved for new map of bus routes' printed across centre pages. 32 pages, 4¼"x5¼".
August 1923 illustrated: Front cover, title page, index, services 6A/12 timetables.

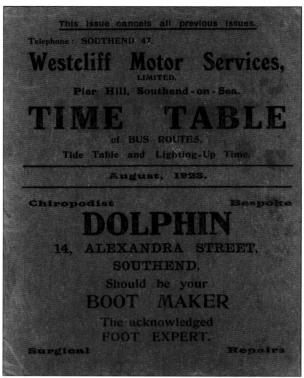

This issue cancels all previous issues.

Telephone: SOUTHEND 47.

Westcliff Motor Services,
LIMITED.

Pier Hill, Southend-on-Sea.

TIME TABLE
of BUS ROUTES.

Tide Table and Lighting-Up Time.

August, 1923.

Chiropodist   Bespoke

DOLPHIN
14, ALEXANDRA STREET,
SOUTHEND,

Should be your

BOOT MAKER
The acknowledged
FOOT EXPERT.

Surgical   Repairs

RIDE ON AIR.

GRAND

MOTOR COACH TOURS AND TRIPS
BY

The Westcliff Motor Services
LIMITED.

(ROYAL RED COACHES)

The whole of the Company's fleet
is now fitted with pneumatic tyres.

Head Office :
PIER HILL, SOUTHEND-ON-SEA
'Phone 47.   H. BROWN, Secretary.

London Agents :
COX SHIPPING AGENCY, Ltd.,
11/13, Charing Cross, S.W. 1.   Phone 7001 Gerrard
Messrs. LAMB, Ltd., Walthamstow, E. Phone 1111 Walthamstow
50, High Road, Wood Green. Phone 1956 Hornsey.
387, Euston Road, N.W. Phone 4978 Museum.

5

Service No. 6a.

Chalkwell Avenue, The Leas,
Swimming Bath and Pier.

First Bus leaves Chalkwell Avenue (London Road end) 10 a.m.,
and every 40 minutes till 9.20 p.m.

First Bus leaves Pier at 10.20 a.m. and every 40 minutes
till 9.40 p.m.

No. 12 Service.	BENFLEET and LEIGH BECK.		
Leave Leigh Beck—		**Leave Benfleet—**	
A.M. 6 40	P.M. 3 0	A.M. 7 10	P.M. 3 30
7 40	3 30	8 20	4 0
8 20	4 0	9 0	4 35
9 0	4 45	9 30	5 30
9 30	5 20	10 0	5 55
10 0	6 0	10 35	6 40
10 30	6 30	11 0	7 0
11 0	7 0	11 30	7 25
11 30	7 30	12 0	8 0
12 0	7 55	P.M. 12 30	8 25
P.M. 12 30	8 25	1 15	9 10
1 15	9 0	2 5	9 40
1 40	9 35	2 30	10 10
2 30	10 40	3 0	11 15

All Buses will wait for Trains when possible.

29

Second Series   August 1924 to January 1927

Cover: on white art paper. Front: upper red 'Westcliff-on-Sea Motor Services, Ltd.' design box around black and white photo of double-decker, lower black and white advert box. Back: full page black and white photo advert. Many adverts in booklet. 32 pages, 4¼"x5¼".
May 1925 illustrated: Front cover, back cover, t/t page services 12/13/14, t/t page service 17.

Cover: on white art paper. Front: upper red 'Westcliff-on-Sea Motor Services, Ltd.' & 'Edwards Hall Motors, Ltd.' names in design box around black and white photo of saloon, front lower black and white advert box. Back: full page black and white advert box for Motor Coaching Tours. Many adverts in booklet. Centre pages route map. 48 pages, 4¼"x5¼".
July 1927 illustrated: Front cover, back cover, service list page, t/t page service 10.

WESTCLIFF MOTOR SERVICES, Ltd.
Local Booking Offices.
HEAD OFFICE :—Pier Hill, Southend-on-Sea ; 'Phone 47.
Kiosk, Bottom of Holland Road, The Leas, Westcliff-on-Sea.
Messrs. Holmes & Smith Ltd., Seaforth Road, Westcliff-on-Sea ; 'Phone Southend 97, also at their Depot opposite the New Palace Theatre, Westcliff ; 'Phone Southend 1136.
Messrs. Brown's Motors Ltd., 35 London Road, Southend-on-Sea. 'Phone Southend 1185.
Mr. E. Read, Tobacconist, 39 Broadway, Leigh-on-Sea.
Mr. Follett, Post Office, 773 London Road, Westcliff-on-Sea (opposite Chalkwell Park Gates).
Lomax Bros., 381 London Road, Westcliff-on-Sea. 'Phone Southend 1434.
Messrs Balls Bros., Fishmongers, 180 Hamlet Court Road, Westcliff-on-Sea
Messrs A. L. Edwards & Son, Tobacconists, (opposite Queen's Hotel), Westcliff
The Victoria Garage (opposite Leigh Cemetery), Leigh-on-Sea

1

Service. No. 10.   SOUTHEND, ROCHFORD, STAMBRIDGE AND PAGLESHAM.
Weekdays and Sundays.

LEAVE	AM		P.M.				PM		SS
VICTORIA CIRCUS	915	1115	1 15	515	515	715	915		
Rochford	930	1130	1 30	330	530	730	930		
Stambridge	940	1140	1 40	340	540	740	940		
Ballard's Gore	945	1145	1 45	345	545	745	945		
PAGLESHAM	a 955	1155	1 55	355	555	755	955		

LEAVE	A.M.		P.M.		PM		PM		SS
PAGLESHAM	1015	1215	215	415	615	815	1015		
Ballard's Gore	1025	1225	225	425	625	825	1025		
Stambridge	1030	1230	230	430	630	830	1030		
Rochford	1040	1240	240	440	640	840	1040		
VICTORIA CIRCUS	1055	1255	255	455	655	855	1155		

SS Sast. and Suns. only.

Fourth Series   September 1928 to October 1930

Cover: on white art paper. Front: upper red 'Westcliff-on-Sea Motor Services Ltd.' in design box; front lower black and white advert with photo unboxed. Back: full page boxed black and white advert for Motor Coaching Tours. Many adverts in booklet. Centre pages route map. 48 pages, 4¼″x5¼″.

August 1930 illustrated: Front cover, back cover, service list page, t/t page Blue Bus services D/E.

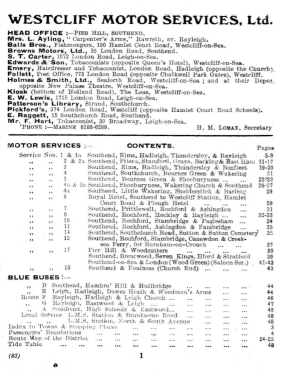

Fifth Series   April 1931 to July 1933

Cover: on white art paper. Front: upper black and white 'Westcliff on Sea Motor Services Ltd.' around drawing (red) of saloon between 'Safety service' lettering in black in design box; front lower boxed black and white advert with photo. Back: full page boxed black and white advert for Motor Coaching Tours. Many adverts in booklet. Centre-pages route map. 96 pages, 4¼"x5¼".
July 1932 illustrated: Front cover, back cover, service list page, t/t page for Pullman Saloon service 16.

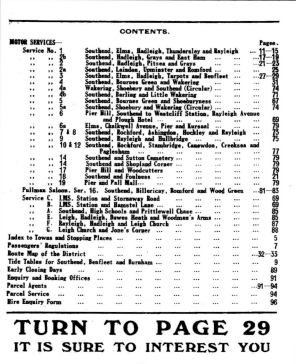

TURN TO PAGE 29
IT IS SURE TO INTEREST YOU

3

FELIXSTOWE. Comfortable Board Residence.   Large Airy Rooms. 2 mins. Sea Front.   Mrs. Wallis, Glenlyn, Constable Road.

Pullman Saloon Service.   Service 16.
Between SOUTHEND (Victoria Circus) ROMFORD & LONDON (Wood Green)
Buses leaving at 30 mins past the hour proceed via Ramsden Bell House.
Daily.

81

Sixth Series   August to September 1933

Buff cover with 'Westcliff-on-Sea' name and a bus in black and white. No example available for illustration.

Seventh Series   December 1933 to January 1936

Cover: all-red print on eau-de-nil paper. Front: red and white 'Westcliff on Sea Motor Services Ltd.' around drawing of saloon between 'Safety service' lettering in red in design box (as Fifth Series); front lower boxed letter-press advert. Back: full page boxed photo advert (red) for Palace Hotel. Many adverts in booklet. Centre-pages route map. 64 pages plus further four printed on pink paper showing Shoeburyness MS, Rayleigh MS, Thundersley, Hadleigh & District MS timetables as un-paginated insert. 4¼"x5¼".
June 1934 illustrated: Front cover, back cover, service list page, t/t page for service 2A.

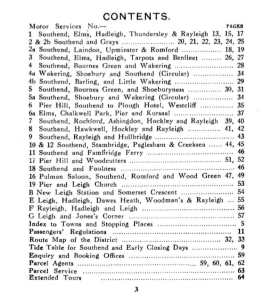

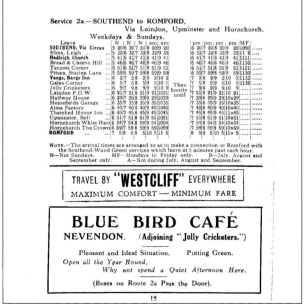

173

Eighth Series   January 1936 to October 1937

Cover: cerise/crimson print on primrose art paper. Full page design. Front: 'Westcliff-on-Sea Motor Services Limited' underlined logo device above line drawing of Southend Pier with AEC Regal exiting circle device. Back: unboxed advert for 'Travel in comfort by our luxury coaches' centred around photo of Bristol JO5G coach. Just three adverts in booklet. Centre-pages route map. Fare tables included. Timetables now landscape format. 96 pages, 4¼″x5¼″.
August 1936 illustrated: Front cover, back cover, service list page, t/t page for service 6.

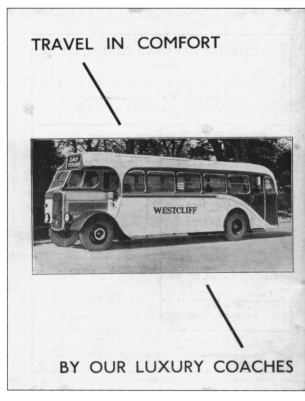

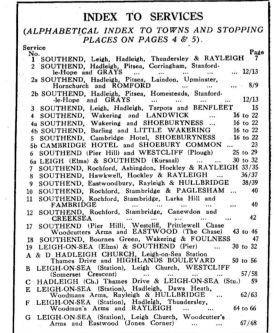

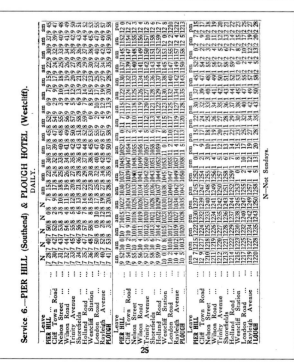

Ninth Series   June 1938

Cover: orange-red print on cream art paper. Full page boxed design. Front: 'Westcliff-on-Sea Motor Services Limited' underlined logo device above photo of AEC Ranger divided from lower artwork of Southend Pier (as Eighth Series) by 'Official Timetables' bar. All printing in orange/red. Back: boxed deco style advert for 'Comfort and safety if you travel by Westcliff-on-Sea Motor Services Ltd' device, linked by vertical lines. No adverts in booklet. Centre-pages route map. Fare tables included. Timetables now landscape format. 112 pages, 4¼"x5¼".

June 1938 illustrated: Front cover, (for back cover see Tenth Series), service list page, t/t pages for services E and 6B.

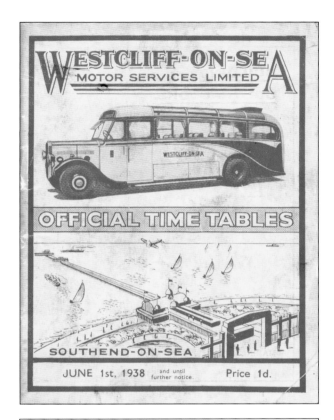

INDEX TO SERVICES

(ALPHABETICAL INDEX TO TOWNS AND STOPPING PLACES ON PAGES 4 & 5).

6

Service "E"—LEIGH-ON-SEA & HULLBRIDGE,
Via Hadleigh, Daws Heath, Woodman's Arms and Rayleigh.

76

Service 6b.—WESTCLIFF STATION & RAYLEIGH STATION,
via Prittlewell Chase, Prince Avenue and Arterial Road

39

Tenth Series   October 1938 to October 1941

Complete redesign of front cover. Front: 'Westcliff-on-Sea Motor Services Limited' logo above full page artwork of country road scene with three buses, winding to Southend Pier at bottom. Red and green print on cream art paper. Back: as Ninth Series. No adverts in booklet. Centre-pages route map. Fare tables included. Timetables now land-scape format. 128 pages, 4¼"x5¼".

May 1939 illustrated: Front cover, back cover, service list page, t/t page for services 2 and 2B.

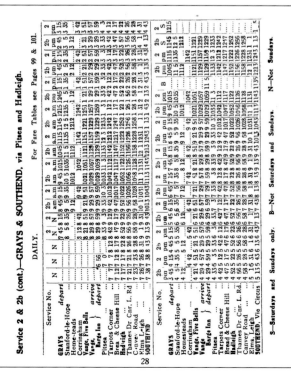

Eleventh Series   August 1942 to June 1951

For an illustration of front and back covers of the 24 July 1946 timetable booklet, *see Frontispiece, Fig.7.1*. Complete redesign of booklet to larger size and of artwork to wrap-around both covers, bled-off to page edge. 'Westcliff-on-Sea Motor Services Limited' logo printed on front and back above landscape format artwork of map of routes. Coach, bus and saloon drawn at base of map which lacks service numbers. Full colour printing on art paper. No adverts in booklet. Re-design of timetable layout to Tilling standard (landscape) with route divided from timetable by boxes within an encompassing box. Blue ink used. No adverts. 116 pages, 4¾"x7¼".

March 1947 illustrated: service list page, t/t page for services 7/8 and 10/12, fare-table for service 2A.

NUMERICAL INDEX TO STAGE CARRIAGE SERVICES

Service No.	Route	Page No.
1	Southend-on-Sea, Leigh-on-Sea, Hadleigh, Thundersley and Rayleigh	4/5
2	Southend-on-Sea, Leigh-on-Sea, Hadleigh, Pitsea, Vange, Corringham, Stanford-le-Hope and **Grays**	14/17
2A	Southend-on-Sea, Leigh-on-Sea, Hadleigh, Pitsea, Vange, Laindon, East Horndon, Upminster, Hornchurch and Romford	6/13
2B	Southend-on-Sea, Leigh-on-Sea, Hadleigh, Pitsea, Vange, Homesteads, Stanford-le-Hope and **Grays**	14/16
3	Southend-on-Sea, Leigh-on-Sea, Hadleigh, Tarpots and Benfleet	18/19
4	Southend-on-Sea, Bournes Green, Wakering and Landwick	20
4A	Southend-on-Sea, Bournes Green, Wakering and Shoeburyness	21
4B	Southend-on-Sea, Bournes Green, Barling and **Little Wakering**	22
5	Southend-on-Sea, Bournes Green and Shoeburyness (Direct)	24/25
6	Southend-on-Sea (Pier Hill) and **Westcliff-on-Sea** (L.M.S. Railway Station)	26/31
6B	**Westcliff-on-Sea** (L.M.S. Railway Station) and Rayleigh (High Street)	26/31
7	Southend-on-Sea, Rochford, Ashingdon, Hockley and Rayleigh	32/39
8	Southend-on-Sea, Rochford, Stroud Green, Hawkwell, Hockley and Rayleigh	32/39
9	Southend-on-Sea and Eastwood (Willson Road)	40/45
9A	Southend-on-Sea and Eastwood (Avro Road)	40/45
10	Southend-on-Sea, Rochford, Stambridge and Paglesham	46/49
11	Southend-on-Sea, Rochford, Ashingdon, Stambridge Larks Hill and **Fambridge**	51
12	Southend-on-Sea, Rochford, Stambridge, Canewdon, Loftmans Cnr. and Creeksea (Wallasea Bay Yacht Stn.)	46/49
17	Southend-on-Sea (Pier Hill), Westcliff-on-Sea, Prittlewell Chase and Eastwood (Woodcutters Arms Hotel)	52/55
18	Southend-on-Sea, Bournes Green, Wakering and Foulness	57
19	Southend-on-Sea (Pier), Western Esplanade, Chalkwell Avenue, Ridgeway, Pall Mall, Elm Hotel, **Leigh-on-Sea**	58/59
19A	Southend-on-Sea (Kursaal), Western Esplanade, Chalkwell Ave., London Rd., Elm Hotel, **Leigh-on-Sea**	58/59
20A	Leigh-on-Sea (L.M.S. Railway Station) and **Leigh-on-Sea** (Highlands Boulevard)	60/63
21	Leigh-on-Sea (L.M.S. Railway Station), Leigh Church and **Westcliff-on-Sea** (Somerset Avenue)	64/65
22	Leigh-on-Sea (L.M.S. Railway Station), Leigh Church, Hadleigh, Daws Heath, Woodmans Arms, Rayleigh and Hullbridge	66/67
23	Leigh-on-Sea (L.M.S. Railway Station), Leigh Church, Belfairs Golf Course and Eastwood (Jones' Corner)	74/75
23A	Leigh-on-Sea (L.M.S. Railway Station), Leigh Church, Elms Leigh Drive and Eastwood (Coombes's Corner)	74/75
24	Leigh-on-Sea (L.M.S. Railway Station), Thames Drive and Rayleigh (High Street)	76/79

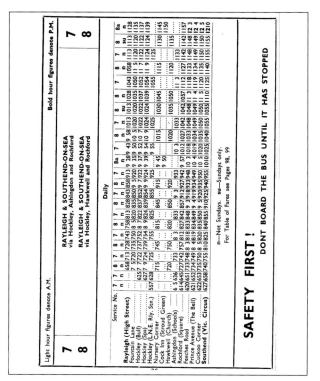

(Timetable pages reproduced: Service 2A fare-table — SOUTHEND-ON-SEA & ROMFORD Via Hadleigh, Pitsea, Laindon, Upminster and Hornchurch; Services 7/8 — RAYLEIGH & SOUTHEND-ON-SEA via Hockley, Ashingdon and Rochford / via Hockley, Hawkwell and Rochford; Services 10/12 — SOUTHEND-ON-SEA & PAGLESHAM Via Rochford and Stambridge / SOUTHEND-ON-SEA & CREEKSEA (Wallasea Bay) Via Rochford, Stambridge and Canewdon.)

SAFETY FIRST!   DON'T BOARD THE BUS UNTIL IT HAS STOPPED

Twelfth Series   June 1952

Standard Tilling size and layout retained. Complete redesign of cover artwork to separate front/back. Covers: Cream base over-printed in red with black lettering. Front: stylised design with 'Westcliff on Sea Motor Services Limited' above and 'Timetables' below printed diagonally across artwork of folded paper. Back: 'Westcliff on Sea Motor Services Limited' logo in black and white on deep red ground with stylised saloon and double-decker design in centre of page. Two adverts in booklet. Tilling layout for timetables. No route map included. Blue ink. Timetable contains un-numbered services previously operated by City Coach Co. Fare tables included. 184 pages, 4¾"x7¼".
June 1952 illustrated: Front cover, back cover, service list page, t/t pages for services 27 and 80.

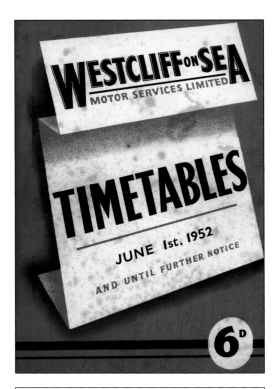

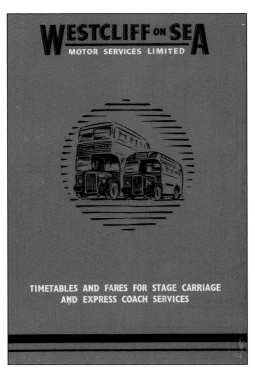

NUMERICAL INDEX TO STAGE CARRIAGE SERVICES

Service No.	Route	Page No.
1	Southend-on-Sea, Leigh-on-Sea, Hadleigh, Thundersley and **Rayleigh** ...	8/9
2	Southend-on-Sea, Leigh-on-Sea, Hadleigh, Pitsea, Vange, Corringham, Stanford-le-Hope and Grays	10/18
2A	Southend-on-Sea, Leigh-on-Sea, Hadleigh, Pitsea, Vange, Laindon, Upminster, Hornchurch and **Romford**	20/33
2B	Southend-on-Sea, Leigh-on-Sea, Hadleigh, Pitsea, Vange, Homesteads, Stanford-le-Hope and Grays	10/18
2C	Southend-on-Sea, Leigh-on-Sea, Hadleigh, Pitsea, Vange, Corringham, Shellhaven	19
3	Southend-on-Sea, Leigh-on-Sea, Hadleigh, Tarpots and **South Benfleet**	34/35
4	Southend-on-Sea, Bournes Green, Wakering and **Landwick**	36
4A	Southend-on-Sea, Bournes Green, Wakering and **Shoeburyness Station**	37
4B	Southend-on-Sea, Bournes Green, Barling and **Little Wakering**	38
5	Southend-on-Sea, Bournes Green and Shoeburyness (Direct) ...	40/41
6	Southend-on-Sea (Pier Hill) and **Westcliff-on-Sea** (Railway Station) ...	42/47
6B	Westcliff-on-Sea (Railway Stn.) and **Rayleigh** (High St.) ...	42/47
7	Southend-on-Sea, Rochford, Ashingdon, Hockley and **Rayleigh** ...	54/63
8	Southend-on-Sea, Rochford, Hawkwell, Hockley and **Rayleigh** ...	54/63
8A	Southend-on-Sea, Rochford, Hall Road, Hockley and **Rayleigh** ...	54/63
9 & 9A	Southend-on-Sea and Eastwood (Willson Road) ...	64/69
9B	Southend-on-Sea and Sutton (School) ...	70
10	Southend-on-Sea, Rochford, Stambridge and **Paglesham** ...	71/78
11	Southend-on-Sea, Rochford, Ashingdon, Stambridge, Larks Hill and **Fambridge**	79
12	Southend-on-Sea, Rochford, Stambridge, Canewdon, Loftmans Corner and Creeksea (Wallasea Bay Yacht Station)	71/78
17	Southend-on-Sea (Pier Hill), Westcliff-on-Sea, Prittlewell Chase and Eastwood (Woodcutters Arms Hotel) ...	80/87
18	Southend-on-Sea, Bournes Green, Wakering and **Foulness**	88
19	Chalkwell Station and Westborough Road	89
19	Southend-on-Sea (Kursaal), Western Esp., Chalkwell Avenue, Ridgeway, Pall Mall, Elm Hotel, **Leigh-on-Sea**	90
19A	Southend-on-Sea (Kursaal), Western Esplanade, Chalkwell Avenue, London Road, Elm Hotel, **Leigh-on-Sea**	90
21	Leigh-on-Sea (Railway Station), Leigh Church and **Prittlewell** (Hobleythick Lane) ...	101/102
22	Leigh-on-Sea (Railway Station), Leigh Church, Hadleigh, Daws Heath, Woodmans Arms, Rayleigh and **Hullbridge**	103/108
23	Leigh-on-Sea (Railway Station), Leigh Church, Belfairs Golf Course and Eastwood (Jones' Corner) ...	109/117
23A	Leigh-on-Sea (Railway Station), Leigh Church, Elmsleigh Drive and Eastwood (Coombe's Corner) ...	109/117
24	Leigh-on-Sea (Church and Station), Thames Drive and **Rayleigh** (High Street)	118/122
25A	Highlands Boulevard, Southchurch and **Thorpe Bay** ...	124/133
25B	Highlands Boulevard, Eastern Esplanade and **Thorpe Bay**	124/133
26	Leigh Beck Farm (Canvey Island), Haystack and South Benfleet (Canvey Bridge)	134/137
26A	Casino (Canvey Island), Haystack and **South Benfleet** (Canvey Bridge)	137
27	South Benfleet, Pound Lane, Nevendon and **Wickford**	137
80	Pitsea (Station Lane), Vange, Corringham, Stanford and **East Tilbury** (Bata Shoe Factory) ...	138
—	Southend-on-Sea (Tylers Avenue), Eastwood, Rayleigh, Wickford, Billericay, Brentwood, Romford, Ilford, Woodford, Walthamstow, Tottenham and London (Wood Green) ...	139/140
—	Brentwood, Billericay, Ramsden, Wickford and **Shotgate**...	141/142
—	Brentwood and Hutton (Bracken Bank) ...	142
—	Laindon (Railway Station), Billericay, Little Burstead and **Brentwood** ...	143/144
—	Laindon (Railway Station), Dunton, Bulphan, Herongate, Brentwood, Kelvedon, Stondon, Blackmore and Ongar (Two Brewers)...	145/156
—	Brentwood and Little Warley	157
—	Laindon (Railway Station), Billericay, Great Burstead and **Brentwood** ...	157
—	Laindon (Railway Station) and Pipps Hill (Circular) ...	158/159
—	Billericay (Sun Corner) and **Billericay** (Sunnymede Estate)	160
—	Laindon Hotel (Rectory Road) and **Wickford**	160
—	Brentwood (Woodman Road), Doddinghurst, Hook End and **Stowdon**	161
—	Laindon (Railway Station) and **Langdon Hills** (Crown Hotel) ...	162

Light figures denote A.M.							Bold figures denote P.M.			
27		**SOUTH BENFLEET & WICKFORD** Via Tarpots Corner								**27**

Mondays only

Benfleet	de.	9 25	1035	1145	1 0	2 7				
Tarpots Corner	,,	9 33	1043	1153	1 8	2 15				
Pound Lane	,,	9 36	1046	1156	1 11	2 18				
Harrows Inn	,,	9 43	1053	12 3	1 18	2 25				
Cricketers	,,	9 46	1056	12 6	1 21	2 28				
Tye Corner	,,	9 49	1059	12 9	1 24	2 31				
Wickford	arr.	9 55	11 5	1215	1 30	2 37				
Wickford	dep.	10 0	1110	1230	1 35	3 0				
Tye Corner	,,	10 5	1115	1235	1 40	3 5				
Cricketers	,,	10 9	1119	1239	1 44	3 9				
Harrows Inn	,,	1012	1122	1242	1 47	3 12				
Pound Lane	,,	1019	1129	1249	1 54	3 19				
Tarpots Corner	,,	1022	1132	1252	1 57	3 22				
Benfleet	arr.	1030	1140	1 0	2 5	3 30				

This service will not operate on Easter Monday, Whit Monday, August Bank Holiday nor on any other occasion upon which Wickford Market may not be held.

80		PITSEA (Station Lane) & EAST TILBURY (Bata Wks.) Via Vange, Corringham and Stanford	**80**

Daily, when Bata Works are open

Pitsea (Station Lane)	...depart	6 43 a.m.
East Tilbury	...arrive	7 18 a.m.
East Tilbury	...depart FX5	10 p.m.
East Tilbury	...depart F05	30 p.m.
Pitsea (Station Lane)	...arrive FX5	45 p.m.
Pitsea (Station Lane)	...arrive F06	5 p.m.

Connections are available at Pitsea for Southend, Leigh, Hadleigh, Tarpots and Benfleet.

F0—Fridays only.   **FX**—Fridays excepted.

Thirteenth Series   January 1953 to May 1955

New standard BTC group size, previous layout retained. Complete redesign of cover artwork to standard ENOC format. Green base with two white nested box outlines. Inner box outline links photos of double-decker and coach. Outer encloses 'Westcliff-on-Sea' logo appears below 'Eastern National' logo at top of cover. Front and back covers identical. WMS services prefixed by 'W' in timetables which cover all ENOC, ex-City and ex-Hicks services. One advert in booklet. Fold-out route map affixed inside back cover includes all service numbers. Blue ink. No fare tables included. 216 pages, 5½″x8½″.

May 1953 illustrated: Front cover, service list page for WMS routes, t/t pages for services W1, W26/A.

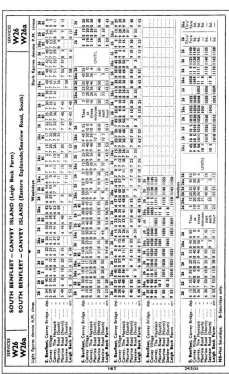

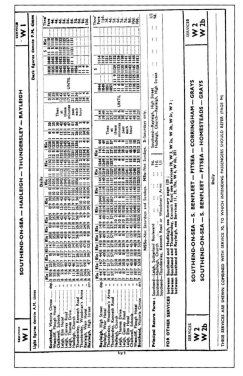

Other Operators Timetables

Thundersley, Hadleigh & District Motors, Limited. Time-Table of Public Motor Service. January 1921

Cover: black lettering on blue-green thin card, title above advert below plus 12 pages, 3¾" x5½". Black print. Includes their single route plus LT&S (Midland Railway). More than half is adverts.

Canvey & District Motor Transport Co. Ltd. Time & Tide Table for May 1939

Cover: black lettering on eau-de-nil paper, title above advert plus 16 pages. 4"x5½". Content is half timetables, half adverts.

Benfleet & District Motor Services, Ltd. Time Table, Fare Table from 13th May to 30th September 1934.

Cover: black print on light green card. Logo and bus line drawing in box above advert space box below. Back cover box advert for B&D. Further four pages on light green card totalling six pages of time/fare-tables. 4″x5″. No adverts.

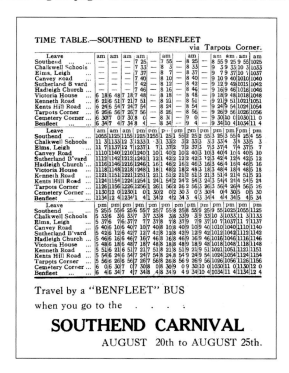

Rochford & District Motor Services, Limited. Time Table of Services. Commencing 1st November 1931.

A primrose card of 5″x12¼″ folded into four. Front contains 'cover' and fare-tables, back contains the timetable.

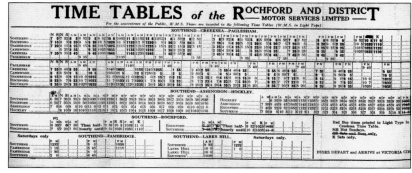

National Omnibus & Transport Co. Ltd (Chelmsford, Colchester, Clacton depots). Time Table. 3rd June 1921

Cover: orange lettering on orange thin card plus 68 pages, 2¾"x5½". Black print. Landscape format timetables. More than 50% contents are adverts.

The Borough Services, Ltd.   Southend-Colchester Time-Table, 1st June 1932

Cream paper printed in red, 'flyer' style folded to 4"x5½". Front: company logo and details; Back: timetable.

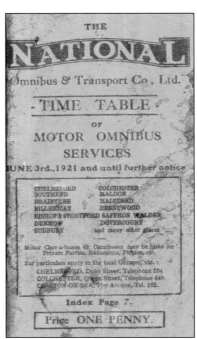

SOUTHEND - COLCHESTER

		a.m.	a.m.	a.m.	p.m.	p.m.	p.m.	p.m.	p.m.	p.m.	X. S.O. p.m.
SOUTHEND	Depart	7 45	8 40	10 30	12 40	1 30	3 0	5 30	7 30	8 0	
Rayleigh	"	8 10	9 5	10 55	1 5	1 55	3 25	5 55	7 55	8 25	
Battlesbridge	"	8 23	9 16	11 6	1 16	2 6	3 36	6 6	8 6	8 36	
Woodham " Whalebone "	"	8 33	9 24	11 14	1 24	2 14	3 44	6 14	8 14	8 44	
Bicknacre " Swan "	"	8 43	—	11 23	1 33	—	3 53	6 23	—	8 53	
Danbury " Eve's Corner " ...	"	8 48	—	11 28	1 38	—	3 58	6 28	—	8 58	
Woodham Mortimer ...	"	8 55	—	11 35	1 45	—	4 5	6 35	—	9 5	
Stowe Maries ...	"	—	9 32	—	—	2 21	—	—	8 22	—	
Cold Norton ...	"	—	9 37	—	—	2 26	—	—	8 28	—	
Latchingdon A.A. Box	"	—	9 44	—	—	2 31	—	—	8 35	—	
Mundon " White Horse "	"	—	9 50	—	—	2 36	—	—	8 40	—	
Maldon " Ship & Anchor " ...	"	9 5	10 0	11 45	1 55	2 45	4 15	6 45	8 50	9 15	
Gt. Totham " Compasses " ...	"	9 25	10 20	12 1	2 15	3 5	4 35	7 5	—	9 35	
Tiptree, Factory Corner	"	9 35	10 30	12 10	2 25	3 15	4 45	7 15	—	9 45	11 10
Birch Post Office	"	9 50	10 45	12 25	2 40	3 30	5 0	7 30	—	10 0	11 25
COLCHESTER	Arrive	10 5	11 0	12 40	2 55	3 45	5 15	7 45	—	10 15	11 40
											S.O.T.
COLCHESTER	Depart	8 0	10 25	11 15	12 45	3 0	4 30	5 15	8 0	—	10 30
Birch Post Office ...	"	8 15	10 40	11 30	1 0	3 15	4 45	5 30	8 15	—	10 45
Tiptree Factory Corner	"	8 30	10 55	11 45	1 15	3 30	5 0	5 45	8 30	—	11 0
Gt. Totham " Compasses " ...	"	8 40	11 5	11 55	1 25	3 40	5 10	5 55	8 40	B	
Maldon " Ship & Anchor " ...	"	9 0	11 25	12 15	1 45	4 0	5 30	6 15	9 0c	9 0	
Woodham Mortimer ...	"	9 10	11 35	—	1 55	4 10	—	6 25	9 10	—	
Danbury " Eve's Corner "	"	9 17	11 42	—	2 2	4 17	—	6 32	9 17	—	
Bicknacre " Swan " ...	"	9 22	11 47	—	2 7	4 22	—	6 37	9 22	—	
Mundon " White Horse "	"	—	—	12 22	—	—	5 37	—	—	9 7	
Latchingdon A.A. Box	"	—	—	12 27	—	—	5 42	—	—	9 13	
Cold Norton ...	"	—	—	12 34	—	—	5 49	—	—	9 20	
Stowe Maries ...	"	—	—	12 39	—	—	5 54	—	—	9 25	
Woodham " Whalebone "	"	9 31	11 56	12 46	2 16	4 31	6 1	6 46	9 31	9 33	
Battlesbridge ...	"	9 39	12 4	12 54	2 24	4 39	6 10	6 55	9 39	9 43	
Rayleigh	"	9 50	12 15	1 5	2 35	4 50	6 22	7 5	9 50	9 55	
SOUTHEND	Arrive	10 10	12 40	1 25	2 55	5 10	6 40	7 25	10 10	10 15	

S.O.—Saturdays Only.   C.—Connects at Maldon with Cold Norton Service 19B.

X.—Contingent upon Theatre Journey T.   B.—Connects at Maldon with Colchester 'Bus.

Eastern National (Eastern Section). Wartime Issue, 12th February 1942

Cover: black lettering, green artwork on cream paper, lettering around saloon set against clock face, 96 pages, 4″x5½″. Cover and timetable for service 70 Southend to Grays reproduced.

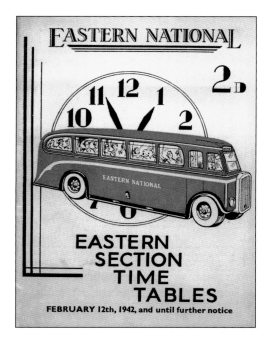

City Coach Company Ltd. Summer 1950

Brown lettering on cream paper, 20 pages, 4¾″x7½″. Cover, time table for service 1 and map reproduced.

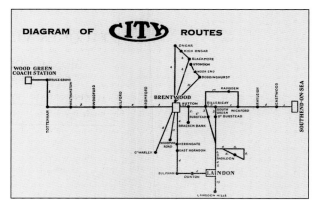

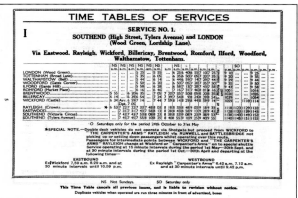

Fig.8.1 (above) A solid-tyred Daimler CK from the early twenties is posed for this view, with sun glinting nicely on the Bell Punch worn by the conductor. PJSA

These two views show the hardy souls responsible for issuing the early tickets illustrated in this chapter.

Fig.8.2 (left) A Borough conductor on the Leigh service enjoys a smoke whilst keeping his hand firmly on the Gilford's radiator cap, perhaps for a little warmth as suggested by the great coat and lack of leaves on the tree. Once again a Bell Punch is firmly strapped in place to cancel the tickets we now so much prize. He is smartly turned out complete with cap and badge, large PSV badge (No.353) and cash bag. PJSA

Chapter Eight
Tickets

In the early years of bus operation Bell Punch tickets were extensively used. The conductor would carry a rack which contained a range of numbered coloured tickets of different values for the fare to be paid. After removal from the rack the conductor would validate the ticket with the Bell Punch machine. A hole would be punched either at the stage boarded or at the stage paid to travel to (as stipulated by the operators requirements) which would be accompanied by a ringing sound made by the machine bell. Observation of the conductor standing against the radiator of Daimler HJ 1759 in *Fig.8.3* shows the Bell Punch machine and also a rack of tickets poking out of the cash bag *(see tickets 1 to 6 below)*.

Henry Roy Setright patented his first automatic totalisator machine in 1922. Later he moved from Australia to England where he established a base in Hackney, London and then in 1931 introduced the mechanical Setright Fare Register, which was commonly known as the Insert Setright. WMS was amongst the first few bus operators to adopt this ticket machine. The printing capacity was initially limited to five features. The instrument did not use a paper roll, instead various types of card ticket could be carried in the conductors rack. One end of these 'narrow' 28 mm wide tickets would be inserted into the machine for printing with the appropriate fare *(see ticket 7)*.

Since the WMS machines printed the class, separate blank tickets for single, return etc. were not required. The WMS Insert Setrights recorded and printed fares in 3d increments from nil (X) to 4/9d. This higher range was necessary for use on the Southend – London (Wood Green) Pullman Saloon service (maximum fare 4/6d return) which later passed to City *(see Chapter 2)*. Initially a series of three ticket blanks was used, a plain white and two with 'surcharge' overprints: 1d (yellow, later primrose), and 2d (green). The plain white ticket was used for round incremental 3d fares for which the machine printed the fare *(see ticket 7)*. The 'surcharge' tickets were used for other denominations either for the fare shown, when the X designation was printed, or in combination where the summated fare was indicated *(see tickets 8 & 9)*. Later the plain white ticket was replaced by a 3d (pink) ticket. This system lessened the conductors work since the machine could be set to 'X' and the large number of popular short journey 1d, 2d and 3d tickets readily issued. For subsequent issues of tickets the designations 'INWARD' (to Southend) and 'OUTWARD' (from Southend) were added to indicate the direction of travel *(see ticket 9)*. All WMS fares were in whole pence units only, child fares being half of the adult fares rounded up to the nearest penny, thus 5d (adult) was 3d (child). There was only one exception a single fare of 1½d from Socketts Heath to

Grays on services 2/2B for which an additional 1½d surcharge ticket was made available. Following the loss of the London (Wood Green) service only services 2/2B (Grays) and 2A (Romford) had any fares that exceeded 2/- (10p) in value.

In the late 1920's an early 'Trambus' roll ticket machine had been tested but this did not meet with operator approval. Many years later Setright introduced their SM.A short range roll ticket machine. Although this was a much improved model the printing range was still rather limited. WMS only purchased a small number of these machines *(see ticket 21)* which were appropriate for their shorter services.

In 1948 WMS decided to adopt the newly introduced Setright Roll Ticket Register usually known as the Setright Speed, and WMS received the first production examples. This machine had much improved printing functions and could issue both high and low value tickets including all halfpenny combinations *(see tickets 22 – 24)*.

Following its acquisition by the British Transport Commission WMS was required to carry out an inventory of their ticket machines. As at 7 June 1948 the stock was quoted as follows:

New type Setright Speed	30
Old type Setright Speed	31
Insert types (1d & 3d)	99
(many not functional)	
Total number required for service:	
Southend	97
Hadleigh	10
Spare	11

In the immediate post-war period there was a shortage of suitable tinted card for the Insert Setright machines, hence plain white tickets with coloured bands were introduced *(see ticket 10)*. Further development of the Insert Setright machines continued since many operators still preferred them. The latest machines featured additional printing options such that two spindles were used for ticket values these being printed as words, with shillings in capital letters and pence in lower case, thus high value fares could now be issued, though not half-pennies which still required the use of overprinted tickets *(see ticket 20)*. Thundersley Hadleigh & District, Rayleigh Motor Services and Shoeburyness Motor Service all used the narrow Insert Setright machines and these later passed with the acquisition of these companies to WMS. An illustration from Borough Services has also been included *(see ticket 11)*.

Benfleet & District and Canvey & District also used the narrow Insert Setright machines which generally recorded fares in either 1d increments (Benfleet, *see tickets 12 to 14*) or ½d increments (Canvey, *see tickets 15 to 17*). Following their takeover by WMS a separate series of ticket blanks was introduced for use with these acquired machines, which included ½d surcharge issues *(see tickets 18 & 19)*.

After the takeover of the City Coach Company WMS continued to use the City Insert Setright machines, which were of the later LR.D model which printed on wide 30 mm ticket cards. Interim WMS style tickets *(see ticket 20)* were introduced until sufficient new Setright Speed machines were received to replace them.

At this stage WMS had a great variety of Setright machines in use obtained from a variety of sources over an extended period. Many of the machines were old and worn but at this time deliveries of new Setright Speed machines were slow due to heavy demand from other operators and shortages of suitable metal for production. Following the takeovers of Benfleet, Canvey and City the acquired ticket machines were put to a variety of uses. This, coupled with the replacement WMS tickets that had been introduced, resulted in many combinations of tickets and machines appearing. It was not until about 1953 that WMS was able to convert completely to the Setright Speed.

Following the complete introduction of the Setright Speed ticket machines emergency tickets needed to be carried by the conductor for use in the event of a machine failure. These took the form of Bell Punch duplex-style tickets which comprised two multi-value halves, folded and punched together, with one part given to the passenger and the other retained by the conductor. Belgraphic style pads were also used, the fare being written on a carbonised counterfoil and the card ticket underneath detached and given to the passenger *(see tickets 25 & 26)*.

For further details and examples of early WSMC and WMS tickets the reader is referred to the excellent article published by R. J. Durrant in *Buses Illustrated*, no. 7 (July 1950)

Fig.8.3 *HJ1759 is now at work. It featured in Fig.6.1 pristine, in a pre-delivery photograph. Just a few years later, around 1924 this WMS Daimler CK with Strachan & Brown bodywork is on service to Benfleet. The crew are proud to pose in front of their steed providing us with details of WMS uniform in those early days. Note the conductor's Bell Punch ticket machine and large rack of tickets poking out of his cash bag.   PJSA*

Bell Punch Tickets

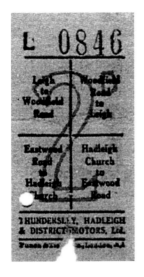

1   L 0846   Thundersley, Hadleigh & District

As no original THD ticket is available in the author's collection, this example has been reproduced from an auction catalogue. It is a geographic ticket in which fare stages were described by name. The ticket was cancelled by punching a hole at the point boarded. Only four stages were used since the THD routes were quite short.

2   B 7042   WMS

As new longer bus routes were inaugurated geographic tickets relating to each service number, or group of numbers were introduced. Group examples are known to exist for services 6 and 17 and for services 9, 9A and 13. The ticket shown covers routes 9, 9A and 13, is a 4d and is valid to Eastwoodbury as shown by the punched hole. Later tickets reverted to being punched at the stage boarded.

3   Kd 8707   Southend on Sea C'pn Tramways

This SCT geographic ticket shows more detail. It has IN and OUT sections for trams running in either direction. It is validated for a 1d journey from The Cricketers to High Street via Prittlewell. Note the facility to use as a luggage ticket.

4   A 2767   WMS

In certain cases the highest fare value would be valid between terminal points only. In this case the ticket would bear only these points and the fare. An example for route 10 to Paglesham is shown, single fare 1/- (5p).

5   Jh 7423   WMS

From 1926 WMS geographic tickets were replaced by more general tickets with fare stages shown in numerical order. These could be used on all services but required the conductor to memorise the fare stage points. A 2d ticket is shown cancelled at fare stage 12. The ticket was supplied by Punch & Ticket Co. of London. The reverse side carries advertisement for Day, Half-Day and Extended Tours.

6   Tx 5027   Edwards Hall Motors

Shown here is a 2d ticket entitled 'E. H. M. LTD.' It is cancelled at fare stage 1. The ticket was supplied by Punch & Ticket Co. of London. It can be seen that the fare stages are grouped into odd and even and that there is also a luggage category.

Insert Setright

7   Oc 6280   WMS

When the Insert Setright system was first adopted the class of ticket (single, return, exchange) could be printed. The machine recorded fares in 3d increments. This is a plain white ticket which was later replaced by a 3d surcharge. The ticket is therefore for a 3d ordinary (single) fare, issued by machine number W10.

8   I 4147   WMS

This is a 1d surcharge ticket. Other such tickets were issued overprinted with 1½d, 2d and 3d values.   If a passenger required a ticket with the overprinted value it was cancelled by an 'X' (nil). Thus ticket I 4147 is for a 1d fare. If the fare was higher the machine would be set to make up the summation value.

9   Xj 5448   WMS

This is a later design of ticket with Inward and Outward features. It is a 1/4d return (1/3d + 1d) inward to Southend fare stage 10 and cancelled (exchange) for the outward return at fare stage 01. A punched hole has also been made for good measure.

10   PH 5995   WMS

In the post war period there was a shortage of suitable tinted card, hence a coloured printed card was used instead. This is a 9d single made by a 6d print on a pre-printed 3d ticket travelling inwards towards Southend.

11   I 6288   Borough Services Ltd.

This 1½d single ticket has been overprinted, the ticket fare designated by X as seen previously with ticket 8. The machine number was B7.

12   Ui 6603   Benfleet & District

This is a 1d single ticket issued on 1 July. The class was not printed by the machine, instead a blank block was shown.

13   Fd 2611   Benfleet & District

A return ticket with 6d fare shown at base and the return trip has been cancelled at the top of the ticket using X designation

14   EK 4495   Benfleet & District

This is the reverse side of a single ticket showing timetable of buses to Benfleet and Southend. All Benfleet & District tickets featured this useful information

15   Ik 6870   **Canvey & District**

Shown is a 1½d single ticket, machine number X05. Single tickets were also produced on buff card as well as green. No class designation was shown on the ticket.

16   Yd 7485   **Canvey & District**

This is a 7d return ticket issued by machine number X23 on 7 September and cancelled by machine number X08 the following day. Incidentally 7d was the highest value ticket issued by Canvey & District. It covered a return journey over their full route from Leigh Beck to Benfleet.

17   Ba 0719   **Canvey & District**

Shown is a 1d ticket for conveyance of goods or parcels, machine number C2.

18   B 0549   **WMS**

This is an example of the replacement blank ticket used by WMS. It is a 2½d single for an inward journey.

19   Yb 6242   **WMS**

This is a WMS replacement ticket used with former Canvey & District machine C33. The ticket is a 3½d single fare (3d + ½d) from stage 01 on 16 August.

20   Fd 9327   **WMS**

This is another example of a WMS replacement ticket but used with an acquired City Coach Company machine (the later Setright LR.D model) which used the wide 30 mm card. The machine used could issue ticket values in both shillings and whole pence and was useful for longer distance services. It has 'SINGLE' overprinted so this is a 2d single issued by machine number CY19 acquired from City.

Setright SM.A

21   187   **WMS**

Shown is a 4d single ticket on buff paper. Since this machine had a reduced fare range WMS purchased only a limited number (E01 – E29) which were used only on their shorter services. The printed ticket extended only to 38 mm compared to the later Setright Speed tickets which extended to 42 mm.

Setright Speed Tickets

22   958   WMS

This is a 2½d single ticket issued on 12 September for an inward journey towards Southend from stage 12. The machine number is WMS112 indicating a machine which could issue all values of tickets from zero (required for returns cancellation, shown as two stars) to 19/11½d in ½d steps.

23   241   WMS

This is a 5½d Workmans return ticket cancelled by hole punched through word 'Motor' and by zero ticket printed on reverse side using the insert slot of another Setright. This ticket was issued by machine WMS104. After control of WMS passed to ENOC a buff roll with both company titles was introduced.

24   MA 8669 / 901   WMS

Shown is a five-day weekly ticket as used by WMS after ENOC had assumed control and also used by Hicks Bros of Braintree. The value of ticket was 10/- and cancellations for each journey are shown by punched holes in the appropriate day slots. These tickets were also issued by Southend Corporation Transport as evidenced by the machine number SO92.

Emergency Tickets

25   A 21783   WMS

This is a simple Belgraphic style ticket in which the fare and stage boarded were written by hand and a carbon copy given to the passenger.

26   P 0507   WMS

This emergency single Bell Punch multi-value ticket shows black printing on buff card. It has been validated by hand punch (available on Setright machine) for a 1½d fare.

Fig.8.4 (opposite) Selected fare tables.

Every conductor would at the very least have to become familiar with, and more likely to actually learn by heart, his fare tables as well as the Company rule book, illustrated opposite.

The fare tables are taken from timetable booklets dated as shown below:

1st June 1938	6B	12	18/19	E
24th May 1939	5B/6/6A			
27th September 1939	1	7	17	

Service 7.—Southend to Rayleigh
via Rochford, Ashingdon and Hockley.

Stage No.

FARE TABLE.

1	Southend, Victoria Circus
2	2d Priory Park
3	2d 1d Feeches Road
4	3d 2d 1d Anne Boleyn
5	4d 3d 2d 1d Rochford (Square or Railway Approach)
6	5d 4d 3d 2d 1d Rectory Road Corner
7	5d 5d 4d 3d 2d 1d New Victory Inn
8	6d 5d 4d 3d 2d 1d 1d Ashingdon (Hill Tops)
9	7d 6d 4d 3d 2d 2d 1d Ashingdon Schools
10	7d 6d 5d 4d 3d 2d 2d 1d 1d Blacksmith's Shop
11	8d 7d 6d 5d 4d 3d 3d 2d 2d 1d Hockley Station
12	9d 8d 7d 6d 5d 4d 4d 3d 2d 2d 1d Hockley Spa Hotel
13	9d 8d 7d 6d 5d 4d 4d 3d 3d 2d 1d 1d Bull Inn
14	9d 9d 8d 7d 6d 5d 5d 4d 3d 3d 2d 2d 1d Fountain Lane
15	9d 9d 8d 7d 6d 5d 5d 4d 4d 3d 2d 2d 1d Hambro' Hill Corner
16	9d 9d 9d 8d 7d 6d 6d 5d 4d 3d 3d 2d 2d 1d Rayleigh (Square)

Child's Fare—Between Warners Bridge and Rochford Schools, 1d. Single.

Workmen's Tickets—Issued up to 8 a.m. Weekdays only, Single Fare for
Return Journey with a minimum of 5d. (except in area of Rayleigh
U.D.C. when Workmen's Tickets will be issued up to 8.30 a.m.)

RETURN FARES.

Southend, Victoria Circus to—		
Anne Boleyn	... ...	5d.
Rochford	... ...	6d.
Rectory Road Corner	... ...	7d.
Ashingdon	... ...	8d.
Blacksmith's Shop	... ...	9d.
Hockley Station	... ...	10d.
Bull Inn	... ...	11d.
Hambro' Hill Corner	... ...	1/0
Rayleigh	... ...	1/1
Rayleigh to Rochford	... ...	10d.

Service 5b.—Cambridge Hotel to Shoebury Beach.

Stage No.

FARE TABLE.

1	Cambridge Hotel
2	1d Shoebury Beach

Service 6.—Pier Hill (Southend) to Plough Hotel (Westcliff)

Stage No.

FARE TABLE.

1	Pier Hill
2	1d Railway Hotel
3	1d 1d Wilson Road
4	1d 1d 1d Welcome Club
5	2d 1d 1d 1d Holland Road (for Westcliff Station up line)
6	2d 1d 1d 1d 1d Queen's Hotel (for Westcliff Sta. down line
7	2d 2d 2d 1d 1d 1d London Road
8	3d 3d 2d 2d 1d 1d Plough Hotel

Service 6a.—Southend (Kursaal) to Elms Leigh.

Stage No.

FARE TABLE.

1	Southend, Kursaal
2	1d Pier
3	2d 1d Swimming Baths
4	2d 1d 1d Nore Yacht Club
5	3d 2d 1d 1d Palmeira Towers
6	4d 3d 2d 2d 1d Chalkwell Avenue (Shelter)
7	5d 4d 3d 3d 2d 1d Chalkwell Park
8	6d 5d 4d 4d 3d 2d 1d Chalkwell Schools
9	6d 6d 5d 5d 4d 3d 2d 1d Elms, Leigh

RETURN FARES.

Kursaal to Ridgeway	... ...	6d.
Kursaal to Elms, Leigh	... ...	9d.

Service 6b.—Westcliff Station to Rayleigh Station.
via Prince Avenue and Arterial Road.

Stage No.

FARE TABLE.

1	Westcliff Station
2	1d London Road
3	1d 1d Plough
4	2d 1d 1d Fairfax Drive
5	2d 1d 1d 1d New General Hospital
6	3d 2d 1d 1d 1d Southbourne Grove (Prince Avenue)
7	3d 3d 2d 2d 2d 1d Kent Elms Corner
8	4d 4d 3d 3d 2d 2d 1d Bellhouse Lane
9	5d 5d 4d 4d 3d 2d 1d Glenwood Avenue
10	6d 5d 5d 4d 4d 3d 2d 1d Weir Hotel
11	7d 7d 6d 6d 5d 4d 3d 2d 1d Rayleigh High Street or Station

Workmen's Tickets—Issued up to 8.0 a.m. Weekdays only, Single Fare for
the return journey with a minimum of 5d. (except in the area of the
Rayleigh Urban District Council, when Workmen's Tickets will be
issued up to 8.30 a.m.)

RETURN FARES.

Westcliff Station to—		
Bellhouse Lane	... ...	7d.
Glenwood Avenue	... ...	8d.
Weir Hotel	... ...	10d.
Rayleigh High Street or Station	... ...	11d.

Service 17.—Pier Hill to Woodcutters Arms and Eastwood (The Chase) via Cliff Town Road and Southbourne Grove.

Stage No.

FARE TABLE.

1	Pier Hill
2	1d Railway Hotel
3	1d 1d Wilson Road
4	1d 1d 1d Welcome Club
5	2d 2d 1d 1d Westcliff Station
6	2d 2d 1d 1d 1d Crowstone Road
7	3d 3d 2d 2d 2d 1d First Avenue (Corner of Chalkwell Ave.)
8	3d 3d 3d 2d 2d 1d 1d London Road (Chalkwell Park)
9	4d 4d 3d 3d 2d 2d 1d Prittlewell Chase (High School)
10	5d 5d 4d 4d 3d 2d 2d 1d Woodcutters Arms
11	5d 5d 5d 4d 4d 3d 2d 2d 1d Jones Corner
12	6d 6d 6d 5d 4d 4d 3d 3d 2d 1d Eastwood Rise
13	7d 7d 6d 6d 5d 5d 4d 3d 3d 2d 1d Eastwood Road (The Chase)

Workmen's Tickets—Issued up to 8 a.m., Weekdays only, Single Fare for
Return Journey, with a minimum of 5d.

RETURN FARES.

Southend, Pier Hill to—		
Woodcutters Arms	... ...	8d.
Jones Corner	... ...	8d.
Eastwood Rise	... ...	9d.
Eastwood Road (The Chase)	... ...	11d.

Service 18.—Southend to Foulness (Court End).

Stage No.

FARE TABLE.

1	Southend, Victoria Circus
2	2d White Horse
3	2d Bournes Green
4	3d 2d Rose Inn
5	4d 3d 2d 1d Little Wakering Corner
6	4d 4d 3d 2d 1d Great Wakering Church
7	5d 5d 4d 3d 2d 1d Land Wick
8	7d 6d 5d 4d 3d 2d 1d Havengore Bridge
9	8d 7d 6d 5d 4d 3d 2d 1d New England Creek
10	10d 9d 8d 7d 6d 5d 4d 3d 2d Brick House Farm
11	11d 10d 9d 8d 7d 6d 5d 4d 3d 1d Foulness (Church End)
12	1/0 11d 10d 9d 8d 7d 6d 5d 4d 3d 1d Foulness (Court End)

RETURN FARES.

Southend, Victoria Circus to—		
Little Wakering Corner	... ...	7d.
Land Wick	... ...	9d.
Brick House Farm	... ...	1/5
Foulness (Court's End)	... ...	1/7
Gt. Wakering Crn. to Foulness (Court End)	...	1/0

Service 19.—Southend Pier to Ridgeway and Leigh (Elm Hotel)

Stage No.

FARE TABLE.

1	Southend, Pier
2	1d Swimming Baths
3	1d 1d Nore Yacht Club
4	2d 1d 1d Palmeira Towers
5	3d 2d 1d 1d Chalkwell Avenue Shelter
6	3d 3d 2d 2d 1d Chalkwell Station
7	4d 3d 3d 2d 1d 1d Grand Hotel
8	5d 4d 3d 3d 2d 1d 1d Leigh Pall Mall (Cnr. Station Rd.)
9	6d 5d 5d 4d 3d 3d 2d 1d Leigh, Elm Hotel (or Church

RETURN FARES.

Pier to Chalkwell Station	... ...	5d.
Pier to Grand Drive (bottom)	... ...	6d.
Pier to Grand Hotel	... ...	8d.
Pier to Leigh Church or Elm Hotel	...	9d.

Westcliff-on-Sea Motor Services Limited
and
Edwards Hall Motors, Limited.

General Rules & Regulations
For DRIVERS and
: CONDUCTORS :

The Company reserve full power to alter or
amend these Rules from time to time.

This Book is the property of the Westcliff-on-Sea Motor
Services Ltd. and must be produced at the request of any
Inspector or Official of the Company.

Service E.—Leigh Station to Hullbridge via Hadleigh, Daws Heath and Rayleigh.

Stage No.

FARE TABLE.

1	Leigh Station
2	1d Leigh Church
3	1d 1d Station Road
4	2d 1d 1d West Leigh Schools
5	2d 2d 1d 1d Sutherland Boulevard
6	3d 2d 2d 1d 1d Woodfield Road
7	3d 3d 2d 2d 1d 1d Hadleigh Church
8	4d 3d 3d 2d 2d 1d 1d Poors Corner
9	4d 4d 3d 3d 2d 2d 1d 1d Rivers Corner
10	5d 4d 4d 3d 3d 2d 2d 1d Woodmans Arms
11	5d 5d 4d 4d 3d 3d 2d 1d 1d Wheatleys Road
12	6d 5d 5d 4d 4d 3d 3d 2d 2d 1d Rayleigh High Street
13	7d 6d 6d 5d 4d 4d 3d 2d 2d 1d Rayleigh Station
14	7d 7d 6d 6d 5d 4d 4d 3d 2d 2d 1d Hambro Hill Corner
15	8d 7d 7d 6d 5d 5d 4d 4d 3d 2d 1d 1d Goldsmith Drive
16	9d 8d 8d 7d 6d 6d 5d 4d 4d 3d 2d 2d 1d Coventry Corner
17	10d 10d 9d 8d 8d 7d 6d 5d 5d 4d 3d 2d 2d 1d Hullbridge
18	11d 11d 10d 9d 9d 8d 7d 6d 6d 5d 4d 3d 3d 2d 1d Hullbridge

Workmen's Tickets—Issued up to 8 a.m., Weekdays only, Single Fare for
Return Journey with a minimum of 5d. (except in area of Rayleigh
U.D.C. when Workmen's Tickets will be issued up to 8.30 a.m.)

RETURN FARES.

Leigh Station to—		
Hadleigh Church	... ...	5d.
Rayleigh High Street	... ...	10d.
Hambro Hill Corner	... ...	1/0
Goldsmith Drive	... ...	1/2
Coventry Corner	... ...	1/2
Hullbridge	... ...	1/5
Station Road (Leigh) to Rayleigh High Street		7d.
Hadleigh Church to Rayleigh High Street		7d.
Rayleigh High Street to Hullbridge	...	7d

SPECIAL WORKMEN'S FARES.

Rayleigh to Coventry Corner	... ...	3d.
Rayleigh to Hullbridge	... ...	4d.

Service 12.—Southend to Creeksea via Rochford and Canewdon

Stage No.

FARE TABLE.

1	Southend, Victoria Circus
2	2d Priory Park
3	2d 1d Feeches Road or Manners Way (cnr. Oaken Grange Dr.)
4	3d 2d 1d Anne Boleyn
5	4d 3d 2d 1d Rochford
6	5d 4d 3d 2d 1d Mill Lane
7	6d 5d 4d 3d 2d 1d Stambridge Church
8	7d 6d 5d 4d 3d 2d 1d Stambridge Village
9	8d 7d 6d 5d 4d 3d 2d 1d Gore Corner
10	9d 8d 7d 6d 5d 4d 3d 2d 1d Scotts Hall Cottages
11	10d 9d 8d 7d 6d 5d 4d 3d 2d 1d Canewdon
12	11d 10d 9d 8d 7d 6d 5d 4d 3d 2d 1d Loftmans Corner
13	1/0 11d 10d 9d 8d 7d 6d 5d 4d 3d 2d 1d Creeksea

Workmen's Tickets—Issued up to 8 a.m. Weekdays only, Single Fare for
Return Journey, with a minimum of 5d.

RETURN FARES.

Southend, Victoria Circus to—		
Anne Boleyn	... ...	5d.
Rochford	... ...	6d.
Mill Lane	... ...	8d.
Stambridge Church	... ...	9d.
Stambridge Village	... ...	10d.
Gore Corner	... ...	1/0
Scotts Hall Cottages	... ...	1/2
Canewdon	... ...	1/4
Loftmans Corner	... ...	1/6
Creeksea	... ...	1/7
Rochford to Stambridge	... ...	5d.
Rochford to Canewdon	... ...	10d.
Rochford to Creeksea	... ...	1/2

Service 1.—Southend to Rayleigh
via Elms, Hadleigh and Thundersley

Stage No.

FARE TABLE.

1	Southend, Victoria Circus
2	3d Chalkwell Schools
3	3d 1d Elms (Leigh)
4	4d 2d 1d Sutherland Boulevard
5	5d 3d 2d 1d Hadleigh Ch. or Victoria House
6	6d 4d 3d 2d 1d Kenneth Road or Bread & Cheese Hill
7	7d 5d 4d 3d 2d 1d White Hart
8	7d 5d 4d 3d 2d 1d Woodman's Arms
9	8d 6d 5d 4d 3d 2d 2d 1d Gt. Wheatley's Road or Kingsley Lane
10	9d 7d 6d 5d 4d 3d 2d 2d 1d Rayleigh (Square)

Workmen's Tickets—Issued up to 8 a.m., Weekdays only, Single Fare for
Return Journey with a minimum of 5d. (except in area of Rayleigh
U.D.C. when Workmen's Tickets will be issued up to 8.30 a.m.)

RETURN FARES.

Southend, Victoria Circus to—		
Sutherland Boulevard	... ...	7d.
Hadleigh Church or Victoria House	...	8d.
Kenneth Road or Bread & Cheese Hill	...	10d.
Woodman's Arms	... ...	10d.
Gt. Wheatley's Road or Kingsley Lane	...	1/0
Rayleigh	... ...	1/1
Hadleigh Church to Rayleigh	... ...	7d.
Elms to Rayleigh	... ...	9d.

Fig.9.1 *This superb official WMS photograph of their Fairfax Drive premises dates from the early 1930s. Planning permission for an extension was refused for the unbuilt land behind the SCT trolleybus stop. This was later sold for housing. The shed nearest the camera was destroyed by fire in 1936 the area being converted to hard standing.* ERO

Chapter Nine
Premises Past and Present

In any outline bus company history it is first the buses and coaches, then the services and then the tickets that tend to attract most enthusiast interest. As far as the operation of the company is concerned it is the financial and company structure that is crucial, and we have dealt with the publicly accessible aspects of this as far as is practicable. Operational structures, scheduling, vehicle buying and maintenance policy, employment practices etc are also all vital but more appropriately dealt with in a business history, which this is not. We are left with publicity and marketing which we have illustrated throughout the text with brochures and timetables. Finally no organisation can function without the physical bases from which to operate. Offices, garages and bus stations usually get short shrift in bus books yet they are always there, in the background – often literally in the case of bus photos. Apart from being functional the buildings that the public sees and uses can also be used to promote the image of the company. London Transport is a prime example of a company that through Frank Pick's guidance achieved world-wide recognition for the excellence of its design in all aspects of its huge operations.

So what of WMS and its constituent companies? Clearly we should not make comparisons with LT but in the period of greatest growth, the thirties, design as a reaction away from Victorian 'fussiness' was influencing the go-ahead company managements.

The Bridge family with their Benfleet & District and Canvey & District operations and WMS each clearly saw the importance of image, especially in their competition with the smaller operators.

We have been fortunate to have both photographic records of the key buildings and even more so the complete survival of an almost unaltered piece of 1930s bus garage architecture. It is perhaps not surprising that the last is both on an island and at the most remote end of it, though even here development pressures would have led to its demolition but for a determined group of enthusiasts. The full story is given below. At the other end of the accessibility scale was the WMS HQ at Victoria Arcade, almost literally the hub of operations and indeed Southend itself. This light and modern glass fronted HQ was WMS for most people until London Road garage was opened yet today nothing survives, not even the road layout such has been the pressure on this central location.

This leads to that ever popular pastime comparing 'then and now'. For the WMS-o-phile visiting the Southend area we have provided contemporary views of the sites or surviving buildings together with their locations and photos of the buildings in their heyday. Not surprisingly all the sites but one are on bus routes and reference to the First Southend Metro map *Fig.2.40* should assist both in locating the sites and getting to them.

Victoria Arcade, Victoria Circus, Southend

WMS transferred its Headquarters to their impressive premises around 1932 to benefit from the dominant location at the busy focal hub in Southend where trains, trams and buses all came together. Offices and a social club and canteen were located on the upper level above the shop frontage either side of the arcade of shops that ran through to Broadway Market. WMS re-located their Headquarters to the extended and expanded London Road premises in September 1937. The area continued to be the central departure point for WMS services for several years afterward. At some stage the upper level was taken over by Taylors Furnishing Store *(see Fig.9.5)*. The whole vicinity of Victoria Arcade, Broadway Market, Bradley Street and Victoria Circus itself was comprehensively re-developed in the late sixties with the building of the inner ring road that separates High Street from Victoria Station. The Victoria Shopping Centre now stands on this site. It also necessitated a re-location of bus terminals in the area to 17-21, London Road *(see below)*. The direct pedestrian

route from the station to the High Street was blocked by this development resulting in either having to cross a busy dual-carriageway or divert through the Victoria Centre using two escalators. In 2009 the folly of this was at last recognised and an expensive programme of works started to reinstate level access.

Location: Walk south from Victoria Station, or north from Southend Central or north-west from the bus station

O.S. 1:25,000 plan TQ8885 1952, revised 9.1949

Fig.9.2 This shows the view in Figs.9.4 & 9.6 in August 2010. The enormity of the redevelopment of the heart of Southend can be judged by just how difficult it is the relate the two photos together in 'then and now' fashion. Victoria Arcade was where the 'Next' sign is on the Victoria Centre frontage, just behind and to the right of the non-functional clock. To get a photo empty of people the photographer rose at 0600 on a Sunday morning.   JRY

Fig.9.3 Although this reproduction is of poor quality it has the merits of showing the entire Victoria Arcade frontage and its immediate surroundings. The sign on the lamp-post in the foreground says 'Victoria Circus'; judging by the size of the small island it was yet to grow. The buses appear to have been specially assembled outside the WMS HQ for this official photo as evidenced by both the number of buses and the crews standing by their steeds for the photographer.   PJSA

Fig.9.4 In this view the complete frontage of the WMS HQ is visible, showing no less than two large signs for WMS, one on the roof and one as a 'decency-board' along the glass frontage of the upper floor social club. WMS AEC Regent/Park Royal JN2796 of 1933 with roof number box displaying 2B and one of SCT's long lasting AEC Regals complete this vintage scene.   JFP

194

Fig.9.5   *Some thirty years later I took this photograph of SCT bus 295(LHJ397) on route 7 at the same bus stop as the AEC Regent in Fig.9.4. The upper level of Victoria Arcade was not much altered (apart from the windows) and was occupied by Taylors Furnishing Store. The bus is a Leyland PD2/12 with Massey L27/28R bodywork new to SCT in 1955.   AGO*

Fig.9.6   *This commercial postcard photograph just pre-dates Alan Osborne's photo above. Quite how the elevated viewpoint was achieved we are left to surmise, perhaps by the use of a Corporation tower wagon? Victoria Avenue, the final approach for all us Londoners to the delights of the Southend seaside when arriving by City Coach or later 251, is seen at its best, comfortably full of Corporation buses going about their business. In this case they are mostly rebodied Daimlers and not one ENOC Bristol is in sight. The Victoria Arcade building remains as shops and an arcade, though not as WMS headquarters. In 2010 only some trees and the former Carnegie Library building (with bell tower) remain. Victoria Avenue is now a dual carriageway lined by early seventies office towers together with civic buildings, a new library, court and civic centre. All are in the then fashionable sixties concrete and glass style. And there are far fewer buses!   JRYC*

195

Fairfax Drive, Prittlewell

Fig.9.7 (above) *This 2010 photo looks west along Fairfax Drive and is taken from approximately the same point as the official WMS photo reproduced in Fig.9.1. The college building is behind the bus stop and the site of the WMS garage buildings was just to the left of and behind the Arriva Southend bus on service 29. The floodlights are those of the Southend United F.C. ground Roots Hall which adjoins the former WMS site. JRY*

Fig.9.7a (right) *This early post-war view shows the third shed from right in Fig.9.1, which after the fire became the easternmost building, with the yard now incorporating the extra area on which the destroyed structure had stood. Ex-Benfleet & District. HF7435 is an ex-Wallasey C.M. 1931 AEC Regent with 1944 NCB body. PJSA*

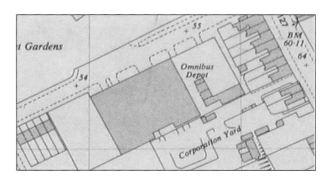

O.S. 1:25,000 plan TQ8786 1951, revised 10.1949.

Location: *Fairfax Drive/Victoria Avenue bus stop (in photo) on services 7,8,29.*

In 1924, WMS purchased a plot of land on the south side of Fairfax Drive, Prittlewell as the site for a proposed bus garage. Fairfax Drive was still an un-adopted road indicating the very rural nature of the area at this time. At the Southend Town Planning Committee meeting on 9 January 1925 approval was given for the purchase by the Corporation of a strip of land (200' x 6') from WMS which was required for thoroughfare improvement to construct a pavement. The Buildings Committee on 14 September duly approved plan number 15043 for the construction of a bus garage. This opened the following year. A view of the completed garage is shown in *Fig.9.1*.

WMS submitted a further plan (number 16999) for a motor bus garage but the Buildings Committee meeting of 5 September 1927 did not grant approval. Had this plan been granted then the enlarged WMS garage would have fronted North Street (now Victoria Avenue) over a length of 130 feet. This unused land at the corner of Fairfax Drive, Prittlewell was finally sold for housing in 1933 for the sum of £666. The terraced houses and small shops built on the site remain to this day.

There was a disastrous fire at Prittlewell garage on 5 March 1936 when ten vehicles were destroyed. The westernmost shed nearest to Victoria Avenue was damaged and the remains later dismantled and replaced by an area of hard standing. The easternmost shed furthest away from Victoria Avenue was later converted into a dedicated workshop.

In ENOC days, the Fairfax Drive garage (coded PL for Prittlewell) housed the coach and contract bus fleets that were used in the Southend area, the London Road garage (SD) being the base for the bus fleet. National Travel (South East) took over the ENOC and Tillings coach fleets from 19 May 1974 and rented the two remaining large garage bays at PL which they continued to use until October 1978 when ENOC again assumed control. The bays were then used for vehicle storage and coach operations. Prittlewell garage and works closed on 8 August 1981. Though non-operational it continued to be used for vehicle storage for a few more years. Demolition work commenced in 1986, to make way for a new £1.2 million purpose built sixty vehicle garage on a 1.4 acre site. This became operational on 28 June 1987, the day after the main London Road garage closed. This new base, which was then referred to as Southend, was officially opened by Paul Channon, Secretary of State for Transport, on 30 October. However, this new base was not to last for very long. ENOC became part of the Badgerline Holdings Group on 12 April 1990, following which the Company was restructured into two operating companies from 29 July. The South Essex area then became the preserve of Thamesway Ltd. The re-located Southend garage closed on Saturday 7 September 1991, when all operations were transferred to Hadleigh.

The premises were sold towards the end of 1992 to a Training Association and completely rebuilt once again, although it would appear that some components of the original side and rear wall may have survived. The site is now occupied by the Prospect College, a Regional Centre for Vocational Training. Their car park is on the site of the former WMS workshops, whilst the college building occupies what was previously the bus parking area and adjacent garage. The area is bounded to the rear by Roots Hall, the home of Southend United Football Club.

17-21, London Road, Southend-on-Sea

WMS opened their new purpose built garage at 33, London Road, Southend-on-Sea in 1922, the date being incorporated into the impressive entrance facade. In 1936 it was agreed that the London Road garage should be expanded and would also incorporate the Head Office. The adjacent premises at 35, London Road were soon acquired, these were purchased from Browns garage and had previously housed the fleet of Multiways Ltd. Further purchases of more properties including 17/21, London Road then followed which subsequently became the Head Office. A new garage building was then constructed along the rear of the intermediate properties which fronted London Road (including Jackamans at number 29) which thus connected 17/21 (the new exit) with 33/5 (the new entrance). The building was completed in 1937, the Head Office being transferred from 18/20, Victoria Avenue to 17/21, London Road from 2 September.

Under ENOC control, the London Road garage was coded SD and had the largest allocation of vehicles in the Company which often exceeded 160 during the summer months. The allocation also included Tylers Avenue (TA) and Pier Hill (PH), the codes in parentheses being paper codes only which merely indicated a location; the vehicles carried SD allocation plates. All coaches and contract vehicles were operated from Prittlewell, Fairfax Drive. Although these carried PL garage plates, they were all included in the SD allocation. After the WMS Head Office was transferred to New Writtle Street, Chelmsford, 17/21, London Road was retained as an enquiry and tours booking office.

Consequent upon the development of central Southend in the nineteen-sixties a new terminal for bus services was needed to replace Victoria Circus. During the construction of the new inner relief road, a rear entrance to the garage from Queensway (along the line of Dowsett Avenue) was created with parking for vehicles alongside the back wall. This made available sufficient space to allow the provision of a drive through Bus Station within the garage, adjacent to the 1937 exit, with a pedestrian entrance from London Road. The new Bus Station opened in July 1968, and was subsequently re-named Victoria Bus Station when the Central Bus Station opened in 1974.

The garage closed on 27 June 1987, all operations being transferred to the new garage at Fairfax Drive, Prittlewell. Along with other properties along London Road the buildings were later sold to Sainsburys, demolished and a new supermarket and car park built on the site, such that none of the original buildings (including the former Borough Services garage) now remains.

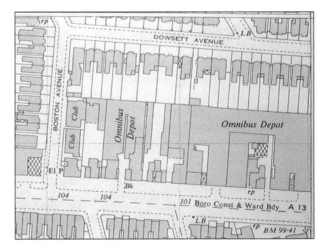

O.S. 1:25,000 plan TQ8785 1951, revised 10.1949

49, London Road, Southend-on-Sea

This small garage (which actually occupied nos. 49/51) was opened by Borough Services Ltd. After acquisition by ENOC on 5 May 1933, the garage continued to be used as a base for the Borough Services fleet which was retained as an operating subsidiary. This arrangement ceased on 30 October 1940, Borough Services Ltd. being placed into voluntary liquidation shortly afterward. At this time ENOC vehicles were still numbered in the original 'National' series, a continuous numerical sequence from 2001. The vehicles carried large (8″ x 5″) cast metal fleet-number plates, the background of which was painted in a specific colour to denote the garage allocation. Vehicles allocated to Southend carried a dark green code, a colour they shared with Grays (Argent Street) garage at the other end of service 70. When the nearby WMS garage at 17/21, London Road passed to ENOC in January 1955 there was no need to retain this small garage. It was later sold and found a new use as a commercial outlet for W. H. Houldershaw, printers and bookbinders. As mentioned above the London Road premises were all later demolished to make way for the new Sainsbury's supermarket and adjacent car park.

Location of both sites: *Walking distance from Victoria Station or Queensway/Victoria Avenue bus stop*

Fig.9.8a (top) and 9.8b (above) *The WMS premises on London Road were taken over by ENOC as their main Southend garage and offices. The original WMS facade in the distance next to Jackamans (see Fig.2.22) was by the time of this 1966 photo the entrance for buses with the wash-bay immediately inside. Behind the SCT Leyland Worldmaster 214 (FYS672) was the wide exit. The staff canteen was on the first floor immediately above the rear of the bus.   JRY*

Fig.9.9 *The scene in August 2010, again at 0600 hrs is virtually unrecognisable. Only London Road itself, the shops in the middle distance (left) and Nazareth House in the far distance (behind inverted triangle road sign and trees and adjacent to former SCT garage site) remain from the 1960s. The Sainsbury's car park is where the white block protrudes behind the glass store frontage. JRY*

Essex House, 459-61, London Road, Westcliff-on-Sea & Seaforth Road, Westcliff-on-Sea

Essex House was the former Holmes & Smith garage and WMS booking office opposite the Palace Theatre, Westcliff-on-Sea. The building was used to garage the H&S fleet of hire-cars as an overflow to their premises at Pier Hill. Essex House was later the base for their Humber limousines referred to as 'Supercars'. This location also featured as a pick up point and booking office in many early items of WMS publicity *(see page 57 and Fig.5.77)*. Holmes & Smith also owned a garage in Seaforth Road, Westcliff which had been used for horses, char-a-bancs and later hire cars *(see Fig.9.12)*. The Holmes family residence was adjacent at 24, Seaforth Road, the scene is essentially unchanged.

H&S finished with hire-cars around 1960 and then became distributors for the Rootes dealership for many years. H&S advertisements promoting both their Essex House and Pier Hill locations regularly featured in the Southend Standard local timetable guides *(see Fig 9.11 below)*.

The premises were later used by Toomey's as a Peugeot car dealership. At the time of writing (2010) the building was still in use as a showroom for 'Cars4all' and was painted in a vivid yellow and blue colour scheme. The Essex House name was still displayed and a Peugeot logo still in place on a side wall.

Fig.9.10 (top)   *Essex House in 2010.   JRY*

Fig.9.11 (left)   *Holmes & Smith publicity – 1960s and 1920s.*

Fig.9.12 (above)   *Seaforth Road just showing the corner of the original Holmes premises with advertising board, inset.   BA*

Location: Westcliff 'Plough' bus stop, services 1,2,3,5,26,27

Pier Hill, Southend-on-Sea

Because their mews premises at the Royal Yard, near the Royal Hotel in Southend were very cramped Holmes & Smith signed a 16 year lease on a motor garage in Pier Hill, Southend on 29 September 1913. The premises were used to house many types of motor vehicles including taxis, hire cars, hearses and char-a-bancs. Some of their fleet was also based at Essex House in Westcliff-on-Sea *(see above)*.

Pier Hill was shared with WMS (H&S being Directors thereof) where their Head Office and coach booking and departure station were located. In the summer of 1928, WMS received notice to vacate the Pier Hill premises as H&S required more space. H&S continued to trade here until they finished with their car hire business around 1960. Next door to the Coach Station stood the

Temperance Billiards Hall. This had originally opened as a cinema in 1909, lasting as such only until 1920. H. R. Bridge then purchased the building on 15 September, ownership being transferred to WMS on 2 February 1929. The premises were then converted into a Coach Station, though the date of opening appears not to have been recorded. The WMS Head Office was transferred from Pier Hill to 18/20, Victoria Avenue by September 1934, Pier Hill continuing as a boarding and departure point for WMS express services, tours and excursions.

After transfer to ENOC, Pier Hill (paper code PH, but coaches always carried PL) continued to be the base for 'Westcliff' coach tours. During the winter period, when operations were much reduced, it was used for surplus vehicle storage. The 'Westcliff' name was discontinued after 1962 when the Eastern National name was then displayed above the coach station entrance *(see Fig.9.17)*. The premises ceased to be used after the 1966 summer season, the building being sold the following year.

The two Pier Hill Coach Stations were actually located in Grove Terrace and not on Pier Hill. The whole area has since been comprehensively redeveloped as part of the Royals Shopping Centre. The former site of the Coach Station is now occupied in part by the Debenhams store and in part by the Pier Hill pedestrian walkway adjacent to the store which occupies the area towards Church Hill.

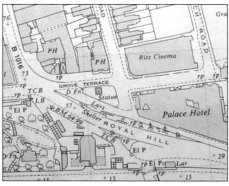

Location: *Walk through the Royals Shopping Centre from the Bus Station.*

O.S. 1:25,000 plan TQ8885 1952, revised 2.1950

Fig.9.13 *(left)*   *This commercial postcard dates from around 1910 and was probably taken from the Palace Hotel. The unbuilt plot to the right of Queen Victoria will shortly be built on to provide the first Holmes & Smith garage.   JRYC*

Fig.9.14   *The original WMS coach station at Pier Hill is shown in this early view. It was shared with the car hire business of Holmes & Smith Ltd. On the original photograph 'Holmes & Smith Garage' can be discerned on the dark board set in front of the apex windows above the full width WMS sign board. This WMS sign modestly advertises 'The finest fleet of coaches in the country, experienced and careful chauffeurs' To the right can just be seen the edge of Temperance Billiards Hall which was later purchased and converted into the new coach station. Daimlers HJ1309 and HJ3717 await custom.   JRYC*

Fig.9.15 This an enlargement from another commercial post-card. It shows the later WMS coach station referred to above and built on the site of the billiard's hall on the right. To the left, under the 'Senior Service Satisfy' sign is the original former Holmes & Smith garage. In the foreground steps lead down to Pier Hill and the delights of the sea front. JRYC

Fig.9.16 This is a later view of the WMS coach station that was built on the site of the Billiard Hall. DJN 552 a Duple Vista bodied Bedford OB is parked ready for a local tour. Note the line of posters advertising a range of excursions. To the left can just be seen the garage signboard for the Holmes & Smith Ltd Supercars business. EBEG

Fig.9.17 (below left) By 1966 ENOC had put the 'Pier Hill' premises up for sale though as can be seen they were continuing to trade from the kiosk during the summer months. By now Queen Victoria was no longer bothered by noisy coaches reversing into the coach station as she had been moved a quarter of a mile west along to the serenity of the cliff top gardens. JRY

Fig.9.18 (above) This 2010 view from the new walkway that leads to the new pier lift shows the dramatic change to the area resulting from the landscaping in the foreground and Royals Centre development. The site of the coach station is immediately to the left of the glass arcade. JRY

Tylers Avenue, Southend-on-Sea

The small garage at Tylers Avenue was the base of Service Saloons Ltd. a concern that commenced operations in February 1928. However, the Company soon ran into financial difficulties and operations ceased about eighteen months later. At this time the New Empress City Saloons terminal was at the Borough Garage opposite the Kursaal. Their coaches entered Southend by way of Southchurch Avenue and Sutton Road. City saw the opportunity for a more central station and duly purchased the Service Saloons premises. From 1 June 1930 they started from Tylers Avenue with a new route via the High Street to Victoria Circus and Victoria Avenue. Coaches terminating at Southend would enter Tylers Avenue, set down and then proceed along and turn right into Baltic Avenue and then turn right again up the slight slope into the rear of the two road garage and then make a third right turn into the terminal area which fronted Tylers Avenue. Through vehicles for Wood Green loaded alongside the Variety Theatre whilst short workings to places like Wickford received their passengers on the other side. The site remained essentially unchanged in WMS days. Under ENOC control, the garage was given the paper allocation code of TA, although Southend vehicles allocated to the main road 251 service always carried SD garage plates.

As a preliminary to the central Southend area re-development, Tylers Avenue garage was closed with the London services being extended the short distance to Seaway, E.N. terminal from 31 July 1964. The whole area was then re-developed and converted into a large car park. The Central Bus Station was opened nearby which became operational from 19 May 1974.

At the present time the whole site is now occupied by a large car park. The slight slope from Baltic Avenue, near Portland Avenue into the rear entrance to the garage can still be seen. Inspection of *Fig.6.48* shows a City Coach Co. Leyland PD2 turning right into the rear of the Tylers Avenue garage. The gabled houses in the background along Baltic Avenue are still extant enabling us to relate the 1950s site to the present.

Fig.9.19 *The great days of City are superbly illustrated in this view of the Tylers Avenue frontage. Nearest the camera is a twin-steer Leyland Gnu bound for Wood Green. A Leyland Tiger is on a short working to Wickford. The corner to the right was a cinema, the wall to the left the side of the enquiry office and the garage was behind the buses where a Commer saloon can be seen. To complete the passengers every needs a cafe was located in the white house at the back.* JRYC

O.S. 1:25,000 plan TQ8785 1951, revised 10.1949.

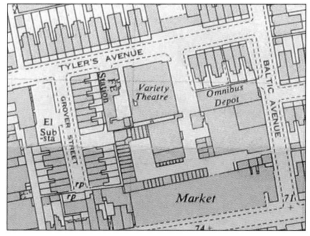

Location: *Short walk north from bus station, Tylers Avenue still exists on right before railway bridge. The site is towards end of Tylers Avenue at the Baltic Avenue end. Rear entrance was almost opposite Portland Avenue.*

Fig.9.20 *This is the view depicted in Fig.9.19 above as it appeared in August 2010. It was taken in Tylers Avenue looking at what was the City Coach terminus, immediately behind the modern car park sign (centre of photo). JRY*

Fig.9.21 *This view taken in Baltic Avenue on the corner of Portland Avenue shows the entry into the bus terminal, through the corrugated garage shed. The house behind fronted onto Tylers Avenue. All the buildings shown (and of course the bus) have gone though the street layout remains the same. The bus is City LT16, a Leyland TS7T new in 1936 with Heaver B43C bodywork.   JRYC*

Fig.9.22 *This shows the scene depicted in Fig.9.21 as it looked in August 2010. The car park exit behind author Alan Osborne is approximately where LT16 was parked. The office block in the distance is on the north side of Tylers Avenue behind the car park which stands on the City Coach terminal site.   JRY*

Oak Road, Hadleigh

These premises were used by the Thundersley, Hadleigh & District Motors Ltd. from September 1915 to operate their bus service to Leigh. The garage was at 296, London Road on the corner of Oak Road South, hence the name chosen. WMS obtained control of the THD business on 28 December 1933, the Company being wound up on 31 July 1935. In the interim a Company of the same name was registered to administer the premises which WMS continued to use as its Hadleigh base.

As part of the Benfleet & District / Canvey & District takeover by WMS on 2 March 1951, the Oak Garage passed to H. A. Bridge and was used to house the Superior Coaches fleet. The building was later managed by Benfleet Garages Ltd., and in 1963 was altered to become a car showroom. In April 1976 application was made for a change of use of the rear portion of the premises from car sales to car servicing. The front portion continued to be used as a car show-room, in later years by the Benfleet Motor Company. The area was again put up for sale and an application was lodged to convert it into a Bistro style restaurant, which did not take place.

At the present time (2010) the front part of the premises on London Road is in use as a car showroom for Jordach, although the facia is much altered. The rear portion on Oak Road South (designated as 296A, London Road) is used by the Castle Motor Company as an MOT Test Centre. Thus nearly a century later the premises are still extant and still in use in connection with motor vehicles.

Fig.9.23   *This view was taken in August 2010 from just east of Hadleigh Church looking along London Road towards Southend. The two garage premises previously occupied by TH&D can be seen in the background fronting to London Road and 'siding' to Oak Road. The large Lidl sign marks the eastern boundary of the plot of land.   JRY*

Broadway, Hadleigh

In October 1939 WMS considered the possibility of building a new garage at Hadleigh to take the place of their existing Oak Road garage which had an output of around 10 vehicles at the time. Whether this was a war-time contingency plan to disperse the fleet to reduce losses because of potential bomb damage in central Southend is not known. In April 1940 the necessary land (approx. 22,600 square feet) situated 150 yards east of Hadleigh Church on the south side of the Broadway was purchased. Although two 5000 gallon underground fuel storage tanks were installed the new garage was never built. Despite extensive researches it has not been possible to determine whether the site was ever used as a bus parking area.

Following the formation of the British Transport Commission the land was valued at £4500 and was then considered as surplus to requirements. A sustained attempt to sell the site was made but this was all to no avail. In order to achieve some revenue from the location a number of advertising hoardings was erected on the site in 1952. The plot of land was eventually sold in 1955 to Benfleet Garages Ltd. (a Bridge family subsidiary) with a condition that the location was not to be used for the operation or maintenance of public service vehicles. At the present time (2010) the 160′ depth site is occupied by the Lidl supermarket. The large Lidl sign marks the eastern boundary of the plot of land.

Location of both sites: *Hadleigh Church bus stop service 1,2,5,26,27 and walk back 200 yards towards Southend.*

London Road, Hadleigh

In 1932 the Bridge family chose to have their new bus garage at Hadleigh designed in the 'moderne' style fashionable in the 1930s and a quite striking building resulted. The original rectangular facia incorporated a central set of ten wide and two narrow vertical recessed flutings and two outside sets of four flutings giving a 1930's version of a castellated roof line which hid the usual shed roof apex shapes of the garage behind. The Hadleigh premises have seen many changes over the years. The garage passed to WMS on 2 March 1951 with the takeover of Benfleet & District, the small WMS allocation at Oak Road, Hadleigh was transferred to London Road at the same time. The garage passed to ENOC and was allocated garage code HH. Following the closure of Canvey (CY) garage in April 1978, their allocation of 11 vehicles was absorbed.

The garage passed into Thamesway ownership on 29 July 1990 and then underwent considerable expansion following the closure of their Southend base at Fairfax Drive, Prittlewell, the operations being transferred in from 8 September 1991. This required the demolition of several properties along London Road to allow the construction of an enlarged bus parking area.

Ownership then passed to FirstBus plc on 16 June 1995. Thamesway became a trading division of Essex Buses Ltd. on 1 March 1996, and then in November 1997 owners FirstBus plc changed their name to FirstGroup plc who subsequently announced

on 6 November 2001 that local names would no longer be carried and that geographical names would be applied to each operating unit. The Chelmsford unit would become First in Essex with only the First name being displayed on the vehicles. There was another name change on 2 January 2003 to First Essex Buses Ltd., the present owners of Hadleigh. It is interesting to note that all of the original WMS premises in the Southend area have now closed and that only the Bridge family base at Hadleigh remains as the present focus of operations in the vicinity.

Looking at the garage in 2010, it can be seen that the roof has since been simplified to an apex shape which has resulted in the two outer sets of flutings being truncated. The central set remains unchanged. The original garage entrance has now been sealed and a staff entrance door constructed in it. The original ground floor has been subdivided by the addition of a mezzanine floor. An enquiry office has been built on the eastern side. The greater part of the original garage has now been converted into offices whilst the rear portion is still used for bus parking. The original A13 London Road has been widened and converted into a dual-carriageway and its level raised such that there is now a slight downwards slope into the premises. A large roundabout has been constructed at Victoria House Corner with entry to the garage site from the roundabout.

Location: Hadleigh, Victoria House/bus garage bus stop (shown) on services 1,2,5,26,27.

Fig.9.24 *This view shows the garage as built with Benfleet & District lettering across the fascia, apparently in thin neon tube lettering so characteristic of thirties shop and cafe signs. The vertical recessed fluting and squared off and tile-edged upper frontage which so enhances the facade was also a thirties architectural fashion called the 'moderne' style. DSG*

Fig.9.25 *This fine view of Hadleigh garage in WMS days is enhanced by a bus, though not one owned by the Bridges. Proceeding along London Road towards Hadleigh is a Campbells of Pitsea utility re-bodied pre-war AEC Regent on their service 6. It is just passing 'The Duchy' and the hairdressing salon which were adjacent to the garage, all of which have now gone. The Benfleet & District lettering has been replaced with that of WMS though in a similar style.   FC*

Fig. 9.26 *This 2010 view was taken from the same point as Fig.9.25 above, allowing for road dualling etc. The original garage block is level with the First Dennis Dart though now far less stylish due to modifications, as indeed is the bus compared with the Campbells AEC Regent above. Between the building and the roundabout in the background is the bus parking and wash area.   JRY*

Leigh Beck, Point Road, Canvey Island

When built in 1934 (for the Bridge family to house the Canvey & District fleet) this building, like the other Bridge premises at Hadleigh, was also constructed in the 'moderne' style. The rectangular frontage in this case was embellished by truncated vertical brick courses covered in plasterwork.

The garage passed to WMS on 2 March 1951 with the takeover of Canvey & District and then to ENOC in January 1955 when it was allocated garage code CY. The building then remained essentially unchanged until closure after service on 29 April 1978 when the allocation of 11 vehicles was transferred to nearby Hadleigh. The building was subsequently purchased by the Eastern National Preservation Group and now houses the Castle Point Transport Museum.

At the present time (2010) the building is remarkably unaltered. The lower windows have since been blocked up whilst the upper right side windows have been altered. A number of aerials have been installed on the roof. A Canvey & District Motor Transport name once again adorns the entrance. The museum is open on the 1st and 3rd Sundays from April to October and also during the Annual Transport Show in October.

Location: *Canvey Leigh Beck, two stops before end of services 22,27,28.*

Fig.9.27 This view of Canvey & District JN2682 was taken towards the end of both its life and that of the company. It is a TSM (Tilling-Stevens) of 1933 with Park Royal body, one of three bought new by H. R. Bridge for Benfleet & District route 3 (see Fig.2.19). The 'Leigh Beck Farm' terminal displayed was just along the road from the Leigh Beck garage. Both bus and garage have a run-down appearance the former with dents and the latter flaking stucco. The company's name above the entrance provides evidence of better days.   PJSA

Fig.9.28   This views shows Leigh Beck garage on Point Road in WMS days, another building in the fashionable 'moderne' style of the thirties. Clearly the Bridge family employed the same architect here as for the Benfleet garage.   FC

Fig.9.29 Canvey garage was closed by ENOC in April 1978. By great good fortune, and a lot of hard work, it was purchased by the ENPG and thus avoided the usual fate of such premises, demolition for housing. It now houses the Castle Point Transport Museum and remains largely unchanged externally, as shown in this August 2010 view. Note that the Canvey & District M. T. Co. Ltd. sign has been re-instated above the entrance. Most appropriately a former WMS Bristol KSW/ECW is parked in the garage entrance.   JRY

Fig.10.1 *Preserved Bristol K5G/ECW AJN825 is seen arriving at the North Weald bus rally in 1988. By then it was nearly fifty years old. This nearside view shows the restored brushed aluminium bonnet cover, a WMS feature in the late thirties.   AGO*

Chapter Ten
Bus and Coach Survivors

Despite the 'Westcliff-on-Sea' fleet-name finally disappearing from the streets almost half a century ago there are a surprising number of WMS vehicles that survive, some of which can still be seen today at bus rallies and running days whilst others are securely stored and are rarely available to be viewed. However, some of them are disguised with different liveries and fleet-names. In this chapter the stories of a selected few of these vehicles are told. The survivors selected are presented in chronological order of age. They are as follows (with their current livery):-

JN5783	chassis only		AJN825	Westcliff-on-Sea	red & cream
FOP429	Southend Corporation	cream & blue	LEV917	Eastern National	cream & green
EJN638	Westcliff-on-Sea	cream & red	WNO478	Eastern National	cream & green

For the histories of these vehicles and their roads to preservation, read on!

JN5783	**AEC Q**	**762158**	**Harrington C35C**	**new 1935**

JN 5783 was one of the very last petrol-engined AEC Q's to be built. Requisitioned by the War Department in July 1940 it was later acquired by Smith of Pylle, Somerset and then lay disused from 1958-60. AEC purchased JN5783 and transferred it to the Thornycroft works at Basingstoke with the intention that it should be restored and repainted in original WMS livery of cream and red. However, investigation revealed the body to be beyond economical repair. The chassis was restored by AEC apprentices and was presented to the Science Museum in 1964. It was moved to the Large Exhibits storage facility at the National Museum of Science and Technology at Wroughton, near Swindon and placed in hangar D2 for long term storage. On 18 October 2009 the *Buses* 60th Anniversary Event was held at the site. A number of vehicles from the Science Museum Collection were moved to Hangar L4 for viewing by selected parties and fortunately JN5783 was one of these exhibits. Public access to view the vehicle is possible only by appointment from the Museum Conservator.

Fig.10.2 (above) Photographs of the AEC Q coaches are somewhat rare. This posed view on a private hire shows all three Qs together with JN5782 nearest the camera. Note the white wall tyres, an indication of the prestige of these coaches. PJSA

Fig.10.3 A colour photograph of the oldest WMS vehicle in existence! The AEC Q chassis of JN5783 is seen at Wroughton in 2009. AGO

AHJ404   **AEC Regal**   **6623042**   **Duple C32F**   **new 1938**

After sale by WMS AHJ404 was exported to Malta. There the chassis was fitted with a locally-built Schembri body and registered 571. Over the years the Maltese registration system has changed several times and hence the vehicle has carried index marks A-1548, Y-1500, Y-0799 and finally FBY799. In its time on the island the vehicle has also carried a number of liveries, latterly orange with many embellishments including the legend 'Westcliff On Sea' to indicate its pedigree. It was still at work in 2003, but was out of service the following year. It is now presumably scrapped since its former registration FBY799 has now been allocated to a replacement King Long vehicle.

Fig.10.4 *This is the final guise of AHJ404, an AEC Regal delivered in 1938. It is seen leaving the Bus Station at Valetta. It now carries a Schembri body and registration FBY 799. Probably not much more than the chassis frame remains of AHJ404, maybe also the axles and gearbox but not the AEC engine. A photo of this coach in its original state is shown in Fig.3.19.*   *JB*

Fig.10.5 *These two AEC Regal/Duples, BHJ132 on the left and BJN119 the right, date from 1939 but were similar in specification and body style to AHJ404. They were caught here at the end of their lives in bus livery behind ENOC's Maldon depot.*   *FC*

AJN825   **Bristol K5G**   **47.87**   **ECW L27/26R**   **new 1939**

AJN was new to WMS then loaned to Bristol Tramways during the war. It was originally fitted with a sliding canvas roof on the upper-deck, later removed and panelled over. It passed to ENOC and was numbered 1269. When withdrawn in 1959 it became part of the British Transport Commission Museum at Clapham for preservation though still under ENOC ownership. Custody later lodged with the Tilling Association in 1967 and then AJN returned to Central Works, Chelmsford in 1969. It was then loaned to the Eastern National Preservation Group, Basildon where it was restored to pre-war WMS livery. It was later housed at the Castle Point Transport Museum, Canvey Island. In 1988 it returned to ENOC at their request and was retained as a publicity/heritage vehicle, later passing to Thamesway and then Essex Buses Ltd. On 14 December 1996 whilst in winter storage at Walton-on-the-Naze garage, the bus was severely damaged in an arson attack on the building. It was then removed to Chelmsford. After painstaking repair work by a group of company employees the bus was repainted and made roadworthy for 2001. Under First Group ownership AJN825 was re-numbered 90231, having been 9001 in the ancillary fleet since 1995. Ownership of the vehicle passed to The 825 Preservation Group, North Essex in February 2007. After its thorough restoration the vehicle continues to be a participant at many bus rallies. To many people AJN825 represents their sole experience of WMS it being the only active vehicle to currently wear the traditional red & cream livery.

Fig.10.6 This view shows AJN 825 in service outside Southend Victoria station. Although still proudly displaying a 'Westcliff-on-Sea' fleet-name it was then owned by ENOC carrying fleet-number plate 1269 between the Westcliff name and the headlight. Comparison may be made with Fig.10.1 and the cover photo of this remarkable survivor in all its colourful glory. *RFM*

FOP429   **Daimler CWA6   11994**   **Duple H30/26R**   **new 1945**

This vehicle was new to Birmingham City Transport as their number 1429. It was acquired by Canvey & District in 1949, passed to WMS in 1951 and then to ENOC being numbered 1199 in 1954. The vehicle did not stay in the ENOC fleet for very long since it passed to Southend Corporation as their 244 in 1955. The Corporation rebuilt the vehicle to O30/26R in 1956, modified it to O33/26R in 1963, with wooden slatted seats on the upper deck. FOP was

Fig.10.7 FOP429 is another 'living link' in the history of bus services in south-east Essex and of WMS. It was purchased, with others, by the Bridge family to modernise their acquired Canvey & Benfleet services. It passed to WMS, survived the disastrous floods of 1953 which caused so much loss of life and damage on Canvey, and finally was acquired by SCT ending its days on Southend seafront. *PJSA*

Fig.10.8 FOP429 restored to its last PSV guise as SCT 244 is seen at the 15/16 August 2009 event. It is back running on the sea-front with a background both modernistic, the new pier lift, and historic, the restored Palace Hotel. *JRY*

withdrawn in 1970 having spent many years operating on the Southend sea-front service. In 1971 it was then bought by the Northern Counties Bus Preservation Group, Newcastle-upon-Tyne but returned south to the Eastern National Preservation Group in 1982 being housed at the Castle Point Transport Museum, Canvey Island. When the ENPG was disbanded in late 2007 the vehicle was donated to the CPTM. The vehicle is preserved in its final PSV state as an open-topper in Southend Corporation livery and is still very active.

LEV917	**Leyland PD1/1 461011**	**Alexander H30/26R**	**new 1946**

This bus was new to the City Coach Company of Brentwood as LD1, and remarkably it was their first double-decker. It was one of only two highbridge vehicles ever operated by City. LEV passed with the Company to WMS in 1952 retaining its City fleet-number. When later re-painted into the WMS red livery it lost its City number. LEV then passed to ENOC being numbered 1112 in 1954 before becoming fully owned in 1955. Along with many other Leylands LEV ran from Canvey garage on service 26 (Canvey – Benfleet). It was then retired from regular service and converted to open-top (O33/26R) for use on the Southend sea-front services. 1112 was re-numbered 2102 in 1964 before being withdrawn the following year. Fortunately it was acquired by the Springhill Vehicle Preservation Group. LEV has undergone extensive renovation and has toured several countries including France, Germany, Greece, Bulgaria, Czechoslovakia, Portugal, Hungary, Yugoslavia, Italy and Switzerland. It is kept in the ENOC open-top cream and green livery and retains its final fleet-number 2102. It is still active (2010).

Fig.10.9 Former City Coach LEV917 loads at Canvey sea front (Casino) on a return working to South Benfleet on service 26A. It has been repainted into WMS red livery and was one of only two former City Coach vehicles to be so treated. It carries ENOC fleet-number plate 1112 and the white circle garage allocation code for Canvey just below the windscreen. WRL

Fig.10.10 LEV917 is pictured at Wroughton airfield on 7 August 1988 after completion of restoration work. JS

EJN 638   Bristol LS6G   89.032   ECW C39F   new 1952

This coach was new to WMS. After acquisition by ENOC it became fleet-number 362. It was re-numbered 302 in 1964 and withdrawn the following year being sold to Western National where it became 3809 lasting until 1967. EJN then entered the fleet of Sherrin, Carhampton, Somerset where it stayed until 1973 before moving to Bristol initially joining the fleet of Evans, Kingswood and then spending time with Sparkes, Warmley. It ended its working days with Hughes, Peterchurch, Herefordshire close to the Welsh border. The vehicle was secured for preservation in 1977 by a Hereford based member of the Eastern National Preservation Group. By 1989 it was in the hands of an unidentified Braintree owner before passing to Wilcock of Great Dunmow. The current owner, from April 2005, is Ian Mahoney of Brentwood and restoration is still (2010) in progress. It carries cream and red livery but retains the beading below the windows that was added during ENOC days.

Fig.10.11 EJN638 'lays over' at Euston Square Coach Station in London, awaiting a return working on express service D. PJSA

The WNO batch of Bristol KSW5Gs

Some readers might not consider these as true WMS vehicles since they did not carry Southend CBC registration numbers. The KSWs were the major batch of vehicles delivered to WMS whilst the company was under ENOC control and thus received Essex registration marks. They included the UEV, UVX and WNO buses from 1952 and 1953. It is the last batch that has proved remarkably resilient and a number are in preservation. This is due to their selection by ENOC for conversion to open-top in the mid-sixties to replace the various PD1s then operating at Southend and Clacton. This new lease of life ensured a longer than average service life and even then on withdrawal by ENOC some found further PSV use. They are the largest group of WMS survivors. Although they entered service in 1953 in ENOC green livery they proudly carried 'Westcliff-on-Sea' fleet-names.

Fig.10.12 WNO478 (ENOC 2380) in ENOC cream and green open-top livery, rounds the corner at Chalkwell Shelter on 16 August 2009 with a full upper-deck load enjoying the ride. JRY

WNO478 *(see Fig.10.12)* entered service in 1953 in green and cream livery but with 'Westcliff-on-Sea' fleet-names. Following the 1954 re-numbering scheme WNO478 became 1423 being re-numbered again in 1964 to 2380. It was converted to O33/28R in 1966 and was withdrawn in 1971 when it passed to Palmer, Basildon and subsequently to the Eastern National Preservation Group, being kept at the Castle Point Transport Museum. When the ENPG was disbanded at the end of 2007 the vehicle was donated to the CPTM. WNO is preserved in its open-top form in ENOC cream and green livery as 2380. It is a regular performer at bus rallies and the CPTM open days where it is always a very popular attraction.

Other WNO Open-Toppers

Several other WNOs have survived. Three of these can be seen in the Essex area. WNO479 was in the ownership of First (Essex Buses Ltd) until late 2010, smartly restored to ENOC cream and green. It was then sold to a private preservationist. WNO480 is in the two tone blue livery of the defunct Town and Country of Grays and now owned by Ken Larkin. The final survivor is WNO484 which is now in the SWT Collection and is disguised in South Wales Transport cream and red colours with whom it operated for some time as fleet number 500.

On 15/16 August 2009 a special Southend running day event was held which operated free vintage buses covering much of the seafront route originally introduced by WMS as their 6A. The route used included the extension through to Shoeburyness East Beach as per the revised SCT/ENOC 67/8 operation introduced in 1955. Three WMS survivors attended and worked along their old stomping ground. Two were KSWs WNO478/480 and the other the ex-BCT, C&D, WMS and SCT Daimler CWA6 FOP429 preserved as SCT 244. This gathering was a most fitting tribute to WMS, and a pictorial record of the event is an appropriate point at which to end our vehicle discussion in this book.

Fig.10.13 WNO480 takes a break at Shoeburyness East Beach terminus on 16 August 2009 in wonderful summer sunshine. The two-tone blue livery certainly makes this WNO stand out! JRY

Fig.10.14 WNO479 is seen in company with Richard Payne's unusual Jersey Motor Transport Morris-Commercial CVF/Wadham of 1948 at the Clacton rally on 6 June 2010. Note that the waist-rail double beading and fleet-name box and flash have been removed on WNO479 and WNO480 compared with WNO478 shown in Fig.10.12. JRY

Chapter Eleven
'Extra!' – The photos we just could not leave out

Having researched, re-researched, written, re-written, edited, re-edited, selected photos, re-selected photos it became clear that there were some photos that would not easily fit into the structure of the book, yet in different ways encapsulated the story of WMS. Here they are. Only brief captions are included for identification as by now you will realise the significance of the selection. *All photos in this chapter are PJSA unless otherwise credited.*

Fig.11.1 (above) A line up of 1930 Dennis F coaches in a publicity photo which uses the WMS name painted on the western end wall of the Fairfax Drive premises as an advertising backdrop.

Fig.11.2 (top right) Also normal control coaches, these Tilling-Stevens were bought second-hand from Southdown in 1936 as replacements for losses sustained in the Fairfax Drive fire of that year, but were not the stuff of which publicity photos were made. They are seen on 15 May 1949. The last of them was withdrawn in May 1950. VCJ

City Coach changed from being 'one of the players' to being part of WMS. This brought classic Leylands to a fleet almost entirely composed of AECs and Bristols. However, all buses were welcome in those days of high passenger demand and delays in the supply of new vehicles. The two shown here, now owned by WMS but still operating on their traditional route, were in any case younger than many WMS veterans.

Fig.11.3 (upper) NVX311, a PD1A/Beadle of 1948, has brought a full load of trippers from north and east London many of whom are alighting here at Victoria Station. JRYC

Fig.11.4 (right) The ENOC Bristol LS showing 251 and the ENOC fleet-number plate (1134) on the Leyland tell us that despite the WMS fleet-names on former City PD2/12 FJN203, WMS was by the time of the photo a part of ENOC. The LS has worked via Shotgate (two journeys per hour) whilst the double-decker, by way of its height, has had to travel via Battlesbridge (four journeys per hour). JRYC

Fig.11.5 (bottom right) The unique Gilford 163DOT of Borough Services races (Gilfords were notoriously fast) along London Road, passing Leigh Cemetery heading for Southend. A remarkable photo in several ways. Few enthusiasts took photos of moving buses because of slow film speeds. No one knew that this unique bus would last just a year in service before its fatal crash. Finally, the photograph has managed to survive eighty years to find its way into our book. Yes, remarkable!

Dennis Lances

In 1931 WMS bought three new Dennis Lances with Park Royal bodywork JN960-2. A pre-delivery view of JN962 is shown in Fig.6.16. JN960 was withdrawn quite early but JN961/2 survived until 1950 (see p.157) but much altered and with AEC engines and radiators. Indeed, WMS referred to them as 'Dennis (AEC conversion)'.

Figs.11.6 and 11.7 (above) *The body on JN961 was extensively rebuilt.*

Fig.11.8 *The body of JN962 was scrapped. It was replaced with the Weymann body removed from JN4745 before it was rebodied by ECW (see Figs.5.10 and 5.13).*

Fig.11.9 *The sixth Lance NJ5976, was converted to open-top and initially gained a home-made AEC style radiator.*

WMS must have quite liked their own Lances as in 1950 they bought BH&D's entire Lance fleet (NJ5974-9). Five were for contract use, two of which are shown in Figs.5.70 & 5.71.

Fig.11.10 *Later NJ5976 was treated to the real thing.*

Fig.11.11 *NJ5976 finally become the star of a commercial post-card as it loaded passengers outside Peter Pan's Playground.*

Brand New

Figs.11.12 & 11.13 (left and above) At the beginning of the thirties a new generation of double-deckers appeared. This 48 seat highbridge Brush bodied Daimler CH6, was shown at the November 1931 Commercial Motor Show in fleet livery before visiting operators as a demonstrator. WMS tried it but clearly were unimpressed, despite their previous Daimler purchases and did not take it into stock. Their next double-deck purchases were AEC Regents which became the preferred choice.

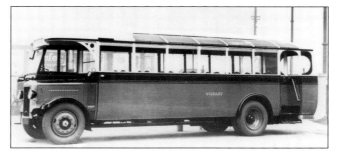

Figs.11.15 (above) & 11.16 (below) These bodybuilder photographs (Strachan & Brown on the ADC, Strachan the AEC Reliance) of unregistered saloons from the mid-1920s, a Daimler and AEC Reliance show very similar bodies but with detail differences,.

Fig.11.14 (above) HJ1387 a small Daimler saloon from the early 1920s was bought and operated by WMSC.

Pot Pourri

Fig.11.17 *HX2980 began our book (see Fig.0.3), and almost ends it. After this ex-AEC demonstrator's Short body wore out the bus was sent to ECW at Irthlingborough in 1942. The result was a new body of pre-war quality and design with not a trace of utility as is clear in this view of it by Leigh Station on the elusive 23 service.*

Fig.11.18 *HX2980's third life, was as a Gardner 5LW powered open-topper, in which guise it lasted into ENOC days as 1150 not being finally retired until 1956.   ENEG*

Fig.11.19 *This most interesting rear view shows a bus on the sea-front service at Chalkwell Shelter. It is YW2548 a Hickman (?) bodied Dennis E. The bus was new to A. H. Young the founder of New Empress Saloons, a key name in our WMS story. YW2548 passed to City as DH3 in July 1928 and was sold to WMS four years later, thus our photo can be dated to the post-1932 period.*

Fig.11.20 *This is an enlargement from a commercial postcard of the Western Esplanade opposite the open-air swimming baths (now Casino). It shows competition at work for the profitable sea-front business with an EHM bus passing a WMS Daimler toastrack.   JRYC*

Fig.11.21 *WMS certainly took advantage of the demonstrators that major manufacturers offered in the late twenties and early thirties. HJ7670 was an ADC 802 or 'London Six' which could be powered by either a Daimler petrol engine of just 5.76 litres or an AEC 7.6 litre unit. It was new in 1928 with a Short body. It could not be considered one of ADC.s successes – just twenty were sold. However, WMS bought this demonstrator and it may be seen repainted and at work in Figs.0.2 and 6.11. Here it is seen at Victoria Circus in 1928 whilst on demonstration. It makes a striking contrast with the open staircase bus in front.*

AEC Regents

One may, perhaps, be forgiven for thinking that in the post-war years, every pre-war WMS double-decker was different, both Bristols and AECs. Stresses and strains of the war years had led to rebuilding and rebodying as noted in Chapter Five. This is the opportunity to portray a few more of these 'uniquely WMS' buses.

Fig.11.22 *(top)* *Weymann bodied JN3230 is seen brand new in 1934.*

Fig.11.23 *(centre)* *Identical bus JN3229 about twenty years later now shows the effects of a rebuild by Beadle. On the station forecourt is an ENOC Bristol K on service 11 to Chelmsford.*

Fig.11.24 *(left)* *JN2799, one of the five with Park Royal bodies delivered in 1933 also shows the effects of a rebuild, in this case by ECW in 1942.   ENEG*

And finally.....

Now, almost at the end, we pay tribute to what must have been extremely reliable, popular and hardy machines NPU170, and MVW970/1 if the number of times they were photographed is any guide to their use. They were three Weymann bodied diesel-engined AEC Regents new in 1935 to Sheffield C.T. bought and re-registered by Benfleet & District. In the course of time they passed to WMS and ultimately ENOC.

Fig.11.25 *NPU170 in WMS ownership but still on its home route is caught in this wonderfully atmospheric 'contre-jour' photograph.*

Fig.11.26 *NPU170 in B&D ownership sits in the mud at Benfleet creek terminus.* LTPS

Fig.11.27 *MVW970 also now with WMS waits to run to Benfleet.* VCJ

Fig. 11.28 *MVW971 is now ENOC 1172, seen at Prittlewell yard in company with JN6885 now ENOC 227.*

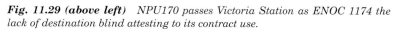

Fig. 11.29 (above left) *NPU170 passes Victoria Station as ENOC 1174 the lack of destination blind attesting to its contract use.*

Fig. 11.30 (above right) *(MVW970)* **and 11.31 (left)** *(NPU170) Finally, we must face reality. It really is that final moment both for our coverage of 'Westcliff Motor Services: An Outline History' and the former Sheffield AEC Regents. They sit, unloved in a scrapyard, and soon will be no more, just a memory, like WMS itself.*

Appendix: WMS Summary of Revenue & Expenditure for August 1936

STATISTICS.

NAME OF COMPANY. WESTCLIFF-ON-SEA MOTOR SERVICES LIMITED.

For the Month of ....AUGUST............19.36.

VEHICLE POSITION	OWNED on last day of Month						LICENSED on last day of Month						MAXIMUM IN SERVICE on any day during Month				
	Last Year		This Year				Last Year		This Year				Last Year		This Year		
	Motor Spirit	Fuel Oil	Motor Spirit	Fuel Oil			Motor Spirit	Fuel Oil	Motor Spirit	Fuel Oil			Motor Spirit	Fuel Oil	Motor Spirit	Fuel Oil	
S.D. Omnibuses ...	79		29				79		29				79		27	7	
D/D			31						31						31	14	
Coaches	23		15				23		15				23		15	6	
TOTAL Passenger Vehicles	102		75				102		73	27			102		73	27	
Depot Vans and Lorries...			3						3						3		
Parcel Vehicles ...			4						1						3		
Staff Cars			-						-						1		
Motor Cycles ...			7						6						6		

		Last Year		This Year
Car Miles (Service and dead miles) :				
Run on Motor Spirit (A) ...				297176.4
Run on Fuel Oil (B) ...				151073.7
Total ...				448250.1
Per Car owned per week				999
Per Car Licensed per week				1016
Lost on Schedule ...				427
Run to each mile lost				1054
Run by Depot Vans and Lorries				3802
„ Parcel Vehicles				-
„ Staff Cars ...				2857
„ Motor Cycles				-
Accidents (Number) ...				84
Omnibus Breakdowns :				
Number				55
Miles run per breakdown				8181
Fuel :				
Motor Spirit :				
Used on Service and dead miles (C) ...Galls.				48989
Used for other purposes... ...Galls.				331
Total ...Galls.				49320
Average price per Gall. including tax				12.28d.
Amount of tax per Gall....				8.d.
Miles per Gall. (item A ÷ item C)				6.06
Fuel Oil :				
Used on Service and dead miles (D) ...Galls.				111442
Used for other purposes ... ...Galls.				25
Total ... ...Galls.				111108
Average price per Gall. including tax				12.60d.
Amount of tax per Gall....				8.d.
Miles per Gall. (item B ÷ item D)				13.55
Lubricating (Engine) Oil :				
Average price per Gallon				14.4
Miles per Gallon...				286
Passengers :				
For Month ...			2094264	2124679
To Date ...			11,369,938	12,883,280
Receipts per Car owned per week ...			255. 8. 5.	255. 17. 6.
Expenses per Car owned per week ...			234.19. 1.	234. 8. 7.
Balance per Car owned per week ...			210. 9. 4.	222. 8.11.
Ratio of Expenses to Receipts to Date			92.55	86.52
Weather :				
Days Fine			23	20
„ Fair			3	5
„ Foul			4	6

THE WESTCLIFF-ON-SEA MOTOR SERVICES LTD.

2.

SUMMARY OF REVENUE AND EXPENDITURE for the Month of August 1936

SUMMARY.

	LAST YEAR			THIS YEAR			INCREASE DECREASE	
	£	Per Car Mile d.		£	Per Car Mile d.		+ £	- £
Receipts for Month ...	24132	13.94		25240	13.46		1108 +	
Expenses for Month ...	15790	9.14		15102	8.05			688 -
Balance for Month ...	8342	4.80		10138	5.41		1796 +	
Receipts to Date ...	128023	9.87		137585	9.78		9562 +	
Expenses to Date ...	118493	9.14		119048	9.46		555 +	
Balance to Date ...	9530	.73		18537	1.32		9007 +	

EXPENDITURE.

	LAST YEAR			THIS YEAR				TO DATE		
	TOTAL £	Per Car Mile d.		TOTAL £	Per Car Mile d.		Increase Decrease £	TOTAL £	Per Car Mile d.	Increase Decrease £
1. Fuel ...	3099	1.79		3136	1.67 +		37	24968	1.77 +	1752
2. Tyres ...	390	.23		356	.19 -		34	2666	.19 -	303
3. Lubricants ...	156	.09		154	.08 +		2	1205	.09 +	59
4. Cleaning ...	537	.31		384	.21 -		153	2992	.21 +	1120
5. Drivers ...	2723	1.58		2991	1.60 +		268	21834	1.55 +	1343
6. Conductors ...	1974	1.14		2020	1.08 +		46	15982	1.14 +	1195
7. Traffic Charges ...	346	.20		400	.21 +		54	3342	.24 +	750
8. Sundry Running ...	98	.06		191	.10 +		93	876	.06 +	110
9. Licences ...	603	.35		639	.34 +		36	4946	.36 +	414
10. Rolling Stk.—Chassis	2234	1.29		823	.44) -		1068	10915	.78 +	5817
„ „ Body				220	.12)					
„ „ Lighting				123	.06)					
11. Buildings, etc. ...	468	.27		387	.21 +		81	3551	.25 +	91
12. Staff Cars & Lorries	•	•		100	.05 +		100	631	.05 +	681
13. Publicity ...	64	.04		163	.09 +		99	1083	.07 +	573
14. Insurance ...	389	.23		449	.24 +		60	3213	.23 -	246
15. Clerical Staff and Office Charges	762	.44		437	.23 +		325	3878	.27 +	1828
16. Administration ...	475	.27		243	.13 -		232	3128	.22 -	383
TOTAL 1 to 16.	14318	8.29		13216	7.05 -		1102	105210	7.48 +	2257
17. Depreciation ...	1472	.85		1886	1.00 +		414	13838	.98 +	2812
TOTAL 1 to 17.	15790	9.14		15102	8.05 +		688	119048	8.46 +	555
18. Parcels ...										
TOTAL 1 to 18.	15790	9.14		15102	8.05 +		688	119048	8.46 +	555

CAR MILEAGE.

	LAST YEAR TOTAL	THIS YEAR TOTAL	Increase Decrease +	TO DATE TOTAL	Increase Decrease +
Service Miles ...	412584	428953	16369 +	3277182	173676 +
Dead Miles ...	2982	21034	13052 +	100092	93539 +
TOTAL ...	415566	449987	34421 +	3377274	265215 +

Form WM 97. H.C.&Co. 39651. 100 5/36

THE WESTCLIFF-ON-SEA MOTOR SERVICES LTD.

REVENUE — Month of August 1936

Form 97.

LAST YEAR TOTAL £	LAST YEAR Per Car Mile d.	ROUTE	THIS YEAR TOTAL £	THIS YEAR Per Car Mile d.	+/−	INCREASE/DECREASE £	Car Miles	+/−	INCREASE/DECREASE
		SOUTHEND:-							
1284	13.2	1. Rayleigh	1283	14.20	−	1	21683	−	1664
2330	12.2	2 & 2B. Grays	2557	13.55	+	227	45304	+	328
1712	12.9	2A Romford	1800	13.59	+	88	31789	+	66
1374	16.6	3. Benfleet	1463	17.73	+	89	19805	+	41
280	15.4	4. Wakering	296	12.79	+	16	5555	+	1186
814	16.9	4A. Shoebury via Wakering	351	11.83	−	463	7120	−	4473
240	8.6	4B. Barling	248	8.99	+	8	6620	−	45
1335	20.6	5. Shoebury	1719	18.43	+	384	22384	+	6807
1550	23.	6. Royal Hotel & Plough.	1434	22.26	−	116	15463	+	721
1174	19.5	6A. Elms & Kursaal	1062	18.74	−	112	13901	+	532
1379	10.8	7&8.Hockley and Rayleigh.	2348	10.68	+	969	52788	+	22072
261	9.4	9. Hullbridge	229	5.91	−	32	9304	−	2647
181	9.9	10. Paglesham	168	10.09	−	13	3998	−	366
10	7.8	11. Fambridge	12	8.50	+	2	339	−	73
676	9.7	12. Creeksea	530	9.77	−	46	15470	+	1218
1419	17.4	17. Woodcutters	1456	17.75	+	37	19690	+	111
60	16.	18. Foulness	58	12.83	−	2	1085	−	183
2164	19.5	19. Pier & Leigh	1826	19.17	−	338	22863	+	3800
.		Steamer Emergency	2	13.33	+	2	36	+	36
		LEIGH:-							
290	10.7	E. Hullbridge	532	11.92	+	242	10715	+	4202
408	9.2	F. Rayleigh	416	9.54	+	8	10470	+	145
256	10.2	G. Jones Corner	258	10.31	+	2	6006	+	25
132	7.3	B. Somerset Cres.	134	7.72	+	2	4164	+	161
44	6.9	C. Hadleigh via Thames Drive	60	9.25	+	16	1557	+	28
857	10.1	D&A.Highlands B'vard & Hadleigh	753	10.66	−	104	16959	−	3363
		SHOEBURY:-							
82	6.3	5B.Cambridge Hotel & Beach	46	13.27	−	36	832	−	2269
20312	14.	*Carried forward*	21141	13.87	+	829	365900	+	18220

THE WESTCLIFF-ON-SEA MOTOR SERVICES LTD.

REVENUE SUMMARY — Month of August 1936

Form 97.

LAST YEAR TOTAL £	LAST YEAR Per Car Mile d.	ROUTE	THIS YEAR TOTAL £	THIS YEAR Per Car Mile d.	+/−	INCREASE/DECREASE £	Car Miles	+/−	INCREASE/DECREASE
20312	14.	*Brought forward*	21141	13.87	+	829	365900	+	18052
1307	13.7	Express Services	1168	12.81	−	139	21881	−	933
1581	13.7	Tours & Tour-sions.	2013	17.58	+	432	27474	−	294
748	12.5	Contract Carriages	729	12.77	−	19	13698	−	624
		Parcels—Omnibuses	15		+	10			
		,, Vans, etc.							
179		Other Receipts	174		−	5			
		Dead Mileage					21034	+	18052
24132	13.94	TOTAL FOR MONTH	25240	13.45	+	1108	449987	+	34421
103891	9.24	Brought forward	112345	9.21	+	8454	2927287	+	230794
128023	9.87	TOTAL TO DATE	137585	9.78	+	9562	3377274	+	265215

STRICTLY CONFIDENTIAL   FORM 1.

THE WESTCLIFF-ON-SEA MOTOR SERVICES LIMITED

REGISTERED OFFICE: 18/20, Victoria Avenue, Victoria Circus, Southend-on-Sea.

RETURN OF OMNIBUS REVENUE AND EXPENDITURE

for the MONTH of AUGUST 1936

and TEN MONTHS to date.

Remarks on special circumstances affecting this return:—

Contractive cost figures for August, 1935 are not actual figures for that month, but have been calculated on the average cost for the year ended 31st October, 1935.

Select Bibliography

Books

R. C. Anderson and G. G. A. Frankis, *A History of Western National*, David & Charles, Newton Abbot, 1979.
K. Blacker, R. Lunn and R. Westgate, *Londons Buses, Vol. 1, The Independent Era – 1922 – 34, pt. 1*, H.J. Publications, St. Albans, 1977.
K. Blacker, R. Lunn and R. Westgate, *Londons Buses, vol. 2, Country Independents 1919 – 39, pt. 1*, H.J. Publications, St. Albans, 1983.
S. J. Brown, *Daimler Buses in Camera*, Ian Allan, Shepperton, 1978.
J. W. Burrows, *Southend-on-Sea and District Historical Notes*, Southend-on-Sea, 1909.
V. E. Burrows, *The Tramways of Southend-on-Sea*, Advertiser Press, Huddersfield, 1965.
B. Coker and P. Skinner, *Birch Bros. Ltd., On the Move*, Rotary Club of Rushden, Rushden, 2003.
R. J. Crawley, D. R. MacGregor and F. D. Simpson, *The Years Between 1909 1969, vol. 1, The National Story to 1929*, MacGregor, Hedingham, 1979.
R. J. Crawley, D. R. MacGregor and F. D. Simpson, *The Years Between 1909 1969, vol. 2, The Eastern National Story from 1930*, O.P.C., Oxford, 1984.
J. Cummings, *Railway Motor Buses and Bus Services in the British Isles, Vol 1, 1902 – 1933*, O.P.C., Oxford, 1978.
M. S. Curtis, *Bristol Lodekka*, Ian Allan, Hersham, 2009.
R. Delahoy, *30 Years of Co-ordination*, Tour Notes, E.B.E.G., 1985.
R. Delahoy, *Southend Corporation Transport, Trams, Trackless and Buses*, Yarnacott Publications, Thorpe Bay, 1986.
G. W. H. Dodson, *75 Years of Service in Essex, 1930 – 2005*, First Essex, Chelmsford, 2005.
M.Doggett, *Eastern Coach Works Vol.1*, T.P.C., Glossop.1987.
B. Everitt, *The Story of Moore Brothers, Kelvedon, Essex*, Everitt, Chelmsford, 1998.
P. H. Gardner, *Eastern National Allocation History*, Gardner, Wolverhampton, n.d.
R. N. Hannay, *Dennis Buses in Camera*, Ian Allan, Shepperton, 1980.
R. J. Harley, *Southend-on-Sea Tramways*, Middleton Press, Midhurst, 1994.
J. Hibbs, *The History of British Bus Services*, David & Charles, Newton Abbot, 1968.
K. A. Jenkinson, *Preserved Buses*, Ian Allan, Shepperton, 1976.
K. A. Jenkinson, *West Yorkshire*, T.P.C., Glossop, 1977.
D. Kaye, *The Pocket Encyclopaedia of Buses and Trolleybuses 1919-1945*, Blandford, London, 1970.
Kellys *Directory of Southend-on-Sea and Neighbourhood*, various editions.
P. Lacey, *A History of the Thames Valley Traction Company Limited, 1931 – 1945*, Lacey, Wokingham, 2003.
A. M. Lambert, *Southdown Fleet History, pt. 5, 1928 and 1929, A New Dynasty – The Titan*, Southdown Enthusiasts Club, 1999.
S. Lockwood, *Kaleidoscope of Char-a-bancs and Coaches*, Marshall Harris & Baldwin, London, 1980.
D. MacGregor, *The National Way, Silver Jubilee of the Eastern National Omnibus Co. Ltd.*, Cotterell, Brentwood, 1955.
T. MacLachlan, *Grey Green and Contemporaries, Book 1 (to 1960)*, Arthur Southern, Ratho, 2007.
C. Morris, *Western National Omnibus Company*, Ian Allan, Hersham, 2008.
O. J. Morris, *Fares Please, The Story of London's Road Transport*, Ian Allan, London, 1953.
National Association of Road Transport Museums, *Buses Restored 2000*, Ian Allan, Shepperton, 2000.
L. H. Newall, *A History of Motor Vehicle Registration in the United Kingdom*, Newall, Sidmouth, 1999.
A. G. Osborne and P. Snell, *The City Coach Company, an Illustrated History*, South Anglia Productions, Frinton-on-Sea, 1988.
A. G. Osborne, *Transfer of Eastern National Grays Area Services to London Transport, 1933 – 1951*, E.N.E.G., 1980.
A. G. Osborne, *City Coach Company Ltd., Fact File 1*, E.B.E.G., 2002.
A. G. Osborne, *J. W. Campbell & Sons Ltd. of Pitsea, Essex, Fact File 3*, E.B.E.G., 2002.
A. G. Osborne, *Eastern National A.E.C. Regents & Renowns, Fact File 6*, E.B.E.G., 2004.
R. Palmer, *Eastern National Omnibus Co. Ltd., Fleet Record, 1964 -1990*, E.N.E.G., 1994.
G. J. Robbins and J. B. Atkinson, *The London B-type Motor Omnibus*, World of Transport, Twickenham, 1991.
D. Roberts and J. Senior, *Eastern Coach Works of Lowestoft – a Retrospect*, Venture Publications, 1995.
J. Shearman and J. Martin, *A History and Details of Preserved Leyland Bus Registration No. LEV 917*, Springhill Vehicle Preservation Group, Tunbridge Wells, 2005.
F. D. Simpson, *Westcliff Route and Details*, handwritten notes, Simpson, Exmouth, n.d.
F. D. Simpson and P. F. Clark, *The Bridge Family and its Buses*, Omnibus Society, 1983.
P. J. Snell, *Westcliff-on-Sea Motor Services Ltd., in Focus, vol. 1*, South Anglia Productions, Frinton-on-Sea, 1987.
P. J. Snell and A. G. Osborne, *Westcliff-on-Sea Motor Services Ltd., in Focus, vol. 2*, South Anglia Productions, Frinton-on-Sea, 1991.
L. A. G. Strong, *The Rolling Road*, Hutchinson, London, 1956.
T. Tilling Ltd., *The War that Went on Wheels, Tilling, London, 1945*; republished edition., Autobus Review Publications, Bradford, 1978.
A. Townsin, *Blue Triangle*, T.P.C., Glossop, 1980.
A. Townsin, *The Best of British Buses, no. 2, The A.E.C. Q Family*, T.P.C., Glossop, 1981.
A. Townsin, *The Best of British Buses, no. 7, A.E.C. Regents 1929-42*, T.P.C., Glossop, 1982.
O. Woodliffe, *Grey Green from Ewer to Arriva*, Woodliffe, London, 2001.
F. Woodworth, *East Kent*, Capital Transport, Harrow Weald, 1991.
I. Yearsley, *Hadleigh Past*, Phillimore, Chichester, 1998.
I. Yearsley, *A History of Southend*, Phillimore, Chichester, 2001.

P.S.V. Circle Publications (listed in chronological order, with publication reference numbers)

Westcliff-on-Sea Motor Services Ltd., Fleet supplement, P14, 1951.
Thomas Tilling and Brighton, Hove and District Omnibus Co. Ltd., Fleet History, PK2, 1958 ; 2nd supplement, *PK2A/1*, 1961.
Eastern National Omnibus Co. Ltd., Fleet History, pt. 1, 1930 – 1954, PF4, 1965; *pt. 2 1954 – 1965, PF5*, 1966 and supplements (*PF4A, PF5A, PF5B*).
Vehicles Acquired by London Transport 1933 – 1939, LT6, n.d.
City Motor Omnibus Co. Ltd., New Empress Saloons Ltd., City Coach Company Ltd., Fleet History, PN6, 1981.
Eastern Counties Omnibus Co. Ltd., Fleet History, 2PF2, 1981.
A.E.C. Regent Chassis List, 001 – 2071, CXB81, n.d.; *2071-3800, CXB84*, 1983.
The Bristol Tramways and Carriage Company Limited, Fleet History, part 2, 1937 to 1949, 2PH5, 1983.
Colchester Borough Transport and Southend Borough Transport, Fleet History, 2PF7, 1986.
Current Fleet Lists of Bus and Coach Operators, Malta, OG99, 1998.
Eastern National Omnibus Co. Ltd. 1930 – 1945, Fleet History, revised edn., 2PF4, 2003.
History of London Passenger Transport Board & London Transport Executive, Hired Vehicles 1940-1, 1948-50 & 1951 Grays Area, LT14, 2007.

Periodicals

Buses Illustrated / Buses	Bus Fayre / Fare Stage	Eastern National Enthusiasts Group magazines/news sheets
Essex Bus News	P.S.V. Circle news sheets	London Bus Magazine
		Omnibus Magazine

Cross Reference Guide to Registration Numbers/Figure Numbers

Registration	Fig.	Fig.	Fig.
P14A1	2.1		
F1808	2.4		
F5619	6.2		
F5654	2.2		
EV587	2.9		
EV1925	2.17	5.25	
GJ2005	5.52		
GN184	2.31		
GW6273	5.54		
GX131	5.16	5.63	
HF5341	2.29		
HF7435	2.30	9.7a	
HJ1310	6.8		
HJ1313	2.7		
HJ1385	6.2a		
HJ1387	11.14		
HJ1389	6.4		
HJ1759	6.1	8.3	
HJ1879	2.5		
HJ2055	6.3		
HJ2313	6.6		
HJ3319	5.15		
HJ3717	0.1	3.12	9.14
HJ3812	2.8		
HJ4643	5.51		
HJ4920	5.2		
HJ6882	2.11		
HJ7078	6.10		
HJ7334	2.12		
HJ7363	4.2		
HJ7616	5.40		
HJ7670	0.2	6.11	11.21
HJ8034	2.13		
HJ8038	3.13		
HJ8588	3.2		
HJ8592	6.12		
HJ8677	0.2		
HJ8934	5.42		
HJ9119	6.13		
HJ9189	6.14		
HJ9578	2.16	11.5	
HJ9875	3.23		
HJ9876	3.23		
HX2980	0.3	11.17	11.18
JN823	4.3	5.24	
JN841	3.3		
JN953	6.15		
JN955	0.4		
JN961	11.6	11.7	
JN962	6.16	11.8	
JN2310	4.4		
JN2681	2.19	2.27	
JN2682	2.19	9.27	
JN2683	2.19	2.32	
JN2767	2.20		
JN2796	2.25	9.4	
JN2798	5.3		
JN2799	5.60	11.24	
JN2800	5.32		
JN2818	4.7		
JN3228	6.39		
JN3229	11.23		
JN3230	11.22		
JN3457	5.33	6.18/9	6.55
JN3715	2.26	4.6	6.19
JN3717	5.8		
JN3718	5.38		
JN4294	5.57		
JN4295	5.34		
JN4612	6.21	6.22	6.55
JN4744	6.38		
JN4745	2.38a	5.10	5.13
JN4746	6.39		
JN4747	5.43	5.73	
JN4748	5.73	6.37	
JN5457	2.21		
JN5461	5.21	6.23	
JN5782	10.2		
JN5783	10.3		
JN6880	6.24		
JN6882	5.49		
JN6885	1.6	5.8	11.28
JN6886	5.74		
JN6889	5.45	6.25	
JN6895	5.9		
JN6896	5.7	6.28	
JN6897	5.37		
JN7499	2.23	5.39	
JN7501	3.6		
JN7986	6.34		
JN8564	5.44		
JN8566	5.53		
JN8567	6.26		
JN8570	6.30	6.31	
JN8572	6.29		
JN8584	3.17		
JN9529	1.12		
JN9532	6.27		
JN9541	5.58	6.32	6.35
JN9542	0.5	6.40	
JN9543	5.12	5.29	
KJ2449	6.17		
KV1396	11.12	11.13	
ML1582	5.50		
MV3394	5.68		
MY2542	5.5		
NJ5974	5.70		
NJ5976	11.9	11.10	11.11
NJ5978	5.71		
PU3365	2.10		
UF4509	11.2		
UF4510	5.32		
UG1033	4.9		
VX4108	5.62		
VX7189	6.20		
WH1552	5.69		
WN4761	2.32		
XV7551	1.9		
YW2548	11.19		
AAP829	1.7		
AHJ402	5.26	6.33	
AHJ404	3.19	10.4	
AHJ405	3.24		
AHJ835	4.5		
AJN823	5.20		
AJN824	6.36		
AJN825	Cover	10.1	10.6
AJN826	5.36	5.55	
AVF354	5.72		
BDA366	4.10		
BHJ132	10.5		
BHJ532	5.58		
BHJ533	2.22		
BHJ808	5.59		
BJN114	5.4		
BJN119	10.5		
BRX915	5.69		
CHJ254	5.34		
CHJ255	2.38b		
CJN321	5.31		
CJN323	5.22	5.47	
CJN324	2.34	6.42	
CJN325	6.43		
CJN326	6.41		
CXW441	9.21		
DEV475	5.6		
DHJ21	5.30		
DHJ22	3.18		
DHJ428	4.13		
DHJ607	6.44		
DHJ609	2.36		
DHJ610	6.54		
DJN552	9.16		
DJN553	6.49		
DJN554	4.12		
DJN556	5.35	5.56	
EHJ29	5.76		
EHJ442	4.14		
EHJ445	5.48		
EJN633	5.41	5.46	
EJN638	10.11		
FBY799	10.4		
FJN158	5.14		
FJN161	5.27		
FJN163	6.52		
FJN165	5.75		
FJN202	6.48		
FJN203	11.4		
FJN211	6.47		
FOP417	6.46		
FOP429	10.7	10.8	
FOP459	2.34		
FOP461	5.72		
FOP462	5.18		
FYS672	9.8		
HVW213	9.19		
HVW214	2.33		
JVW561	1.11		
KEV534	2.28		
KEV535	2.34	5.17	
KHK863	2.34		
KHK864	5.66		
LEV917	10.9	10.10	
LHJ397	9.5		
LHY949	6.45		
MVW970	5.67	11.27	11.30
MVW971	11.28		
NPU170	11.25/6	11.29	11.31
NVX302	1.10	5.64	
NVX311	5.65	11.3	
NVX312	4.8		
UEV842	5.23		
UVX666	6.50		
WNO478	10.12		
WNO479	10.14		
WNO480	10.13		
XVX26	6.51		
XVX30	6.53		
280NHK	3.20		
206YVX	1.8		